D1094478

CLASSICS IN EDUCATION
Lawrence A. Cremin, General Editor

☆   ☆   ☆

THE REPUBLIC AND THE SCHOOL
Horace Mann on the Education of Free Men
Edited by Lawrence A. Cremin

AMERICAN IDEAS ABOUT ADULT EDUCATION
1710–1951
Edited by C. Hartley Grattan

DEWEY ON EDUCATION
Introduction and Notes by Martin S. Dworkin

THE SUPREME COURT AND EDUCATION
Edited by David Fellman

INTERNATIONAL EDUCATION
A Documentary History
Edited by David G. Scanlon

CRUSADE AGAINST IGNORANCE
Thomas Jefferson on Education
Edited by Gordon C. Lee

CHINESE EDUCATION UNDER COMMUNISM
Edited by Chang-tu Hu

CHARLES W. ELIOT AND POPULAR EDUCATION
Edited by Edward A. Krug

WILLIAM T. HARRIS ON EDUCATION
(in preparation)
Edited by Martin S. Dworkin

THE *EMILE* OF JEAN JACQUES ROUSSEAU
Selections
Translated and Edited by William Boyd

THE MINOR EDUCATIONAL WRITINGS OF
JEAN JACQUES ROUSSEAU
Selected and Translated by William Boyd

PSYCHOLOGY AND THE SCIENCE OF EDUCATION
Selected Writings of Edward L. Thorndike
Edited by Geraldine M. Joncich

THE NEW-ENGLAND PRIMER
Introduction by Paul Leicester Ford

BENJAMIN FRANKLIN ON EDUCATION
Edited by John Hardin Best

THE COLLEGES AND THE PUBLIC
1787–1862
Edited by Theodore Rawson Crane

TRADITIONS OF AFRICAN EDUCATION
Edited by David G. Scanlon

NOAH WEBSTER'S AMERICAN SPELLING BOOK
Introductory Essay by Henry Steele Commager

VITTORINO DA FELTRE
AND OTHER HUMANIST EDUCATORS
By William Harrison Woodward
Foreword by Eugene F. Rice, Jr.

DESIDERIUS ERASMUS
CONCERNING THE AIM AND METHOD
OF EDUCATION
By William Harrison Woodward
Foreword by Craig R. Thompson

JOHN LOCKE ON EDUCATION
Edited by Peter Gay

CATHOLIC EDUCATION IN AMERICA
A Documentary History
Edited by Neil G. McCluskey, S.J.

THE AGE OF THE ACADEMIES
Edited by Theodore R. Sizer

HEALTH, GROWTH, AND HEREDITY
G. Stanley Hall on Natural Education
Edited by Charles E. Strickland and Charles Burgess

TEACHER EDUCATION IN AMERICA
A Documentary History
Edited by Merle L. Borrowman

THE EDUCATED WOMAN IN AMERICA
Selected Writings of Catharine Beecher,
Margaret Fuller, and M. Carey Thomas
Edited by Barbara M. Cross

EMERSON ON EDUCATION
Selections
Edited by Howard Mumford Jones

ECONOMIC INFLUENCES UPON EDUCATIONAL
PROGRESS IN THE UNITED STATES, 1820–1850
By Frank Tracy Carlton
Foreword by Lawrence A. Cremin

QUINTILIAN ON EDUCATION
Selected and Translated by William M. Smail

ROMAN EDUCATION FROM CICERO
TO QUINTILIAN
By Aubrey Gwynn, S.J.

HERBERT SPENCER ON EDUCATION
Edited by Andreas M. Kazamias

JOHN LOCKE'S *OF THE CONDUCT
OF THE UNDERSTANDING*
Edited by Francis W. Garforth

STUDIES IN EDUCATION DURING THE
AGE OF THE RENAISSANCE, 1400–1600
By William Harrison Woodward
Foreword by Lawrence Stone

JOHN AMOS COMENIUS ON EDUCATION
Introduction by Jean Piaget

Studies in Education
during the
Age of the Renaissance,
1400–1600

By WILLIAM HARRISON WOODWARD

With a Foreword by
LAWRENCE STONE

☆

CLASSICS IN

No. 32

EDUCATION

☆

TEACHERS COLLEGE PRESS
TEACHERS COLLEGE, COLUMBIA UNIVERSITY
NEW YORK

Manufactured in the United States of America

Contents

Foreword

By LAWRENCE STONE

Of all the institutions of civilized society, none is more resistant to change than education. Even constitutions are altered more frequently and with less fuss. The reason for this extraordinary inertia in matters educational seems to be threefold. The first and most important cause is the resistance of the teaching profession itself. Set in its ways, trained and accustomed to using certain forms of instruction to impart certain bodies of information and doctrine, this powerful professional group always, at all times, and in all places, resists and obstructs with all the power at its command the calls for change that arise from the inexorable transformations of the society around it. Secondly, the innovators are usually men who are either outside the professional educational establishment altogether, like the Italian humanists who were mostly secretaries to political leaders rather than university professors, or who are forced upon it by state intervention, like the humanists infiltrated into Oxford and Cambridge in the reign of Henry VIII, or the scientists given posts in Oxford by the Parliamentary Commissioners in the 1650's. Thirdly, it is extremely hard for the reformers to offer conclusive proof that their novel proposals are self-evidently superior to current practice. Educational theory is peculiarly subject to bold hypotheses that are not capable of empirical verification or refutation.

As a result, there have been only two major educational upheavals in the whole history of the West over the past thousand years, the first occurring during the Renaissance, and the second in our own time. Today a whole series of forces has converged to bring about revolutionary changes in scale, in social patterns and purposes, and in curriculum. The demand of an increasingly complex civilization for very large numbers of skilled administrators has led to an expansion of higher education which is everywhere shattering the Renaissance ideal of the training of a restricted elite. From the sixteenth century to the early twentieth, education was a privilege conferred on a hereditary, wealthy landlord class, the purpose of which was to give them a distinctive culture and to equip them for the wielding of political power; now it is a wide-open avenue of social mobility which gives the children of the lower and middle classes access to the levers of political and economic power, and itself confers the social prestige which was formerly a by-product of birth. For the first time in several hundred years Latin is no longer a common language for the educated of all European nations, and knowledge of classical literature is no longer a common experience. Insofar as a common European culture still exists, it is based on the English language and the Second Law of Thermodynamics.

If the scale and class-pattern of education have been changed in our time, so also has the curriculum, as the demands of science have made vast inroads into what was for centuries a training exclusively in the liberal arts. Finally, an insatiable demand for specialists has led firstly to the rapid growth of graduate study, which is replacing the old undergraduate liberal arts training as the final stage in the education of the future leaders of the nation, and secondly to the emergence of a whole host of new institutions which offer specialized instruction in business, public administration, law, medicine, education, and so on. A new managerial, professional, technological, and scientific society has demanded a new educational program, and in large measure it has got it, at any rate in the United States, although only after a prolonged and bitter struggle for more than a hundred years.

What was overthrown in this recent battle was a set of educational ideals, an educational system, and a curriculum which were established as the result of another upheaval some 450 years ago, at the time of the Renaissance, and it is with the careers and ideas of some of the leading figures in that earlier revolution that this book is concerned.

As today, it seems to have been profound changes in the character of the society which forced change upon reluctant schoolteachers and university professors. Basically what happened was a change in the function of the old feudal elite, as warfare became more professional and as first the city-states of Italy, and later the nation-states of Western Europe, demanded a larger and better trained bureaucracy to manage their expanding range of business. In the middle ages, the kings and nobles had ruled largely with the aid of men in religious orders and lawyers, who drafted and wrote the necessary documents. These men, who were often from fairly humble origins, had a near monopoly of the higher educational facilities, and therefore of the literary and cultural products of the day. The spread of literacy among the laity, enormously stimulated as it was by the output of the printing press, began to shatter this monopoly just at the time when the military role of the lay aristocracy was declining. In the middle ages, aristocratic education had consequently been only secondarily concerned with scholarship and letters, the most important element being training in social deportment and professional military expertise. But now the eldest sons of the ruling class found themselves obliged to acquire a familiarity with the reading and writing of documents if they wished to retain their hold on political power at the center. Younger sons found it hard to obtain an estate on which to live, and fairly hard to get a commission in the army. They were forced to turn to professional careers in the bureaucracy, the law, the church, or medicine, all of which demanded literary skills.

What made the Renaissance so unique a period in educational history was the fortuitous coincidence of these new social demands with a major shift in curricular ideas as a result of the discovery by a group of Italian intellectuals and secretaries of the literature first of Rome and then of Greece. These men led a major intellectual revolution, which overthrew the scholastic philosophy and logic of the middle ages and substituted for it a new set of educational objectives and methods. The aim was not, as in the medieval university, to turn out low-born professionals at the service of a semiliterate warrior aristocracy, but to civilize and refine that aristocracy itself, to turn this tiny social elite into an association of men of high birth and superior morals who had been given a literary and rhetorical training in the classics. This new man, the creation of the Renaissance humanists, was to be active in the service of the state, familiar with the major texts of classical literature, and expert in the rhetorical arts of persuasion. His training was primarily in pure classical literature and grammar, the two being closely associated; history, mostly of the ancient world; and moral philosophy, much of it culled from classical authorities. To this was added, in proportions which varied from educator to educator, instruction in Christianity, mostly patristic theology; physical exercise, to fulfill the adage *mens sana in corpore sano;* and training in deportment on medieval lines. To implement the new ideals there was created a new set of educational institutions, both schools catering to an exclusive, secular elite, and private tutors living in the great households and instructing the children. These institutions could be squeezed in without much difficulty between the medieval elementary schools, which taught basic literacy, and the medieval universities, which specialized in training for the professions of the church, law, and medicine.

As can be observed from a close study of Woodward's succinct and elegant survey of the ideas of the leading theorists of the day, the radicals were far from united in their interpretation of just how they should go about achieving the ideals they had in mind. All were seeking to turn out the cultivated amateur with a taste for public service and a background of classical literature, but there are noticeable differences in approach. Some, like Alberti, Vives, and Elyot, were thinking about a rural gentry class, and were concerned with the activities of the private tutor living and working in the big house in the country. Others, like Vittorino da Feltre, were more urban in their outlook and experience, and favored the boarding school. Some, like Palmieri and Melanchthon, stressed service to the state as the principal end of education; others, like Gilbert and Cleland, were more concerned with instruction in the practical arts; others again, like Castiglione, were trying to develop the manners and tastes of the sophisticated courtier. Most stressed the amateur quality of the finished product, the superiority of virtue over knowledge; but some, like Guarino, were emphatic about the need for serious classical scholarship.

Some were deeply Christian in their outlook and were careful to reconcile pagan and Christian ideals and authorities; others were less worried by this problem. Some, like Alberti or Cleland, laid emphasis on careful training in self-expression in the vernacular; others, like Erasmus, were less enthusiastic or were even hostile to the attempt. Almost all, except perhaps Gilbert, were contemptuous of science, either as a body of useful knowledge or as a means of instruction. Some regarded Greek as essential for a comprehension of Latin civilization; others thought it could be relegated to a secondary role. Some wanted to reduce the teaching of grammar to a minimum, and use it only to give support to a study of the ancient texts themselves; others, in their enthusiasm to recover the purity of the ancient language, and in their hostility to the "speculative" grammar of the scholastics, gave a prime role to their own "historical grammar." Most of these early humanist educators were opposed to physical punishment as a method of securing the attention of children, and advocated winning their enthusiasm by devising a curriculum to suit their capacities and interests. Many were in favor of a surprisingly intellectual training for women, although all thought mothers were unsuited to be left in charge of boys after the age of seven.

An important and still unsolved question is how far the high ideals of these early Renaissance reformers were achieved in practice. What actually happened in the

schoolrooms and lecture halls? Certain aspects of their
advice were clearly put fully into practice, and molded
the education of Europe down to the twentieth century.
The idea that education is a matter of training a tiny
elite to rule was one; that it is secular in outlook,
orientation, personnel, and direction, is another; that it
is based on classical literature and grammar rather than
the vernacular is a third; that its products are quintes-
sentially amateurs rather than professionals is a fourth.
In these respects the triumphs of the Renaissance educators are beyond dispute.

Beyond that point, however, doubts and uncertainty
begin to creep in. Studies in the sixteenth century too
often reveal a state of affairs which would have horrified
these gentle, scholarly, and high-minded reformers. All
too often we find a narrow-minded pedant drilling the
most desiccated aspects of grammatical lore into the
heads of uncomprehending children by dint of routine
physical punishments, often of considerable brutality. As
the nation-state grew, so grew the court, and the "courtesy" element in education grew with it. By the seventeenth century Castiglione's courtier was everywhere replacing Guarino's scholar; the dilettante, the state
servant; the sophisticated man about town, the man of
virtue. Furthermore, the attitude of suspicion and contempt towards natural science, which has been so marked
a feature of upper-class educated opinion in so many
parts of Europe for so many centuries, is due in large
measure to the antiscientific attitude of the Renaissance
educators. Reasonable enough when first formulated in
the fourteenth and fifteenth centuries, it became a positive hindrance when modern science at last began to get
under way in the seventeenth century. The revolt against
the barbarity of late medieval Latin in practice merely

killed a language which, whatever its deficiencies by Ciceronian standards, was at least alive and developing. In its place was put a resurrected corpse, a language which, for all its admitted purity, was dead, and indeed meant to be dead so that the purity would never be contaminated by the living processes of growth. The hostility of many educators to the vernacular, the insistence that boys speak nothing but Latin all their waking hours, even at meals and on the playing field, did not have altogether happy consequences, and it seems likely that Shakespeare owed much of the amazing range and flexibility of his style to the fact that his Latin was little and his Greek less.

On the other hand more unquestionably valuable suggestions, like the need to give women a serious education, or the need to guide children by inspiration rather than fear, have had to wait till the twentieth century to be implemented.

When all is said and done, however, there can be no doubt that the humanists whose views are set out in this book had a profound effect on Western civilization as we know it. It was their vision of an elite of aristocrats brought up on the poetry, history, and philosophy of the ancient world, and imbued with a desire for public service, which created the culture of Europe and North America from the sixteenth to the nineteenth century. Few landed aristocracies in history have been educated up to the level of their cultural and political responsibilities, and insofar as this was achieved in the West during these centuries, it was the work of the educational reformers of the Renaissance. Their work is therefore of immediate practical relevance to the history of the modern world.

BIBLIOGRAPHICAL NOTE

Since Woodward wrote these essays, there has been a good deal of work done on Renaissance education. The best general introduction is E. Garin, *L'educazione in Europa, 1400–1600* (Bari, 1957). R. R. Bolgar, *The Classical Heritage and Its Beneficiaries* (Cambridge, England, 1954) explores with a wealth of erudition the evolution of classical studies in Europe, while P. O. Kristeller, *The Classics and Renaissance Thought* (Cambridge, Mass., 1955) tackles the same theme on a narrower front.

E. Garin has published two very useful collections of Italian educational texts, with commentaries: *L'educazione umanistica in Italia* (Bari, 1949) and *Il pensiero pedagogico della Umanesimo* (Florence, 1958).

For Vittorino da Feltre there is a modern biography by A. Gambara, *Vittorino da Feltre* (Turin, 1964); there is Woodward's own study in *Vittorino da Feltre and Other Humanist Educators* (Cambridge, England, 1897); and there are lengthy extracts from his work in Garin's *Il pensiero pedagogico . . .* , pp. 504–718. The writings of Guarino da Verona may be studied in Garin, *op. cit.*, pp. 305–503, and aspects of his career, in R. Sabbadini, *Guariniana* (Turin, 1964). There are extracts from Alberti's educational writings in Garin's other collection, *L'educazione umanistica . . .* , pp. 121–155, and from those of Palmieri on pp. 107–120. Erasmus' *The Education of a Christian Prince* has been edited by L. K. Born (New York, 1936), and *The Praise of Folly,* edited and translated by H. H. Hudson (Princeton, 1941). A very interesting study of the background of Guillaume Budé's work is A. Renaudet, *Préréforme et humanisme à Paris pendant les premières guerres d'Italie* (Paris,

1953). There is a modern biography of *Jacopo Sadoleto* by R. M. Douglas (Cambridge, Mass., 1959). Little has been done on Vives as an educator since Foster Watson edited and translated *Tudor Schoolboy Life: The Dialogues of Juan Luis Vives* (London, 1908) and wrote a pioneering study on *Vives and the Renascence Education of Women* (New York, 1912). The most recent biography of Melanchthon is C. L. Manschreck, *Melanchthon, the Quiet Reformer* (New York, 1958).

Courtesy literature has been intensively studied in recent years, almost entirely by American scholars. James Cleland's *The Institution of a Young Nobleman* has been edited by M. Molyneux (New York, 1948), while Castiglione's *The Book of the Courtier*, in the Hoby translation of 1561, is available in the Everyman Library (London, 1928), edited by W. D. Henderson. The standard works for the sixteenth century are R. K. Kelso, *The Doctrine of the English Gentleman in the Sixteenth Century* (Urbana, 1929) and J. E. Mason, *Gentlefolk in the Making* (Philadelphia, 1935). On women there is R. K. Kelso, *Doctrine for the Lady of the Renaissance* (Urbana, 1956). In the seventeenth century, the ideal underwent some important modifications, which may be studied in W. E. Houghton, Jr., "The English Virtuoso in the Seventeenth Century," *Journal of the History of Ideas*, III (1942), and in George C. Brauer, *The Education of a Gentleman, Theories of Gentlemanly Education in England, 1660–1775* (New York, 1959). The social and political consequences of the educational changes are brilliantly sketched by J. H. Hexter in "The Education of the Aristocracy in the Renaissance," *Reappraisals in History* (London, 1961), pp. 45–70.

Even more striking is the scale and quality of work on Renaissance education in England. There are two recent scholarly surveys of the period: J. Simon, *Education and Society in Tudor England* (Cambridge, England, 1966) and K. Charlton, *Education in Renaissance England* (London, 1965). It should be noted that they differ somewhat in their conclusions. The late medieval background has been described in C. McMahon, *Education in Fifteenth Century England* (Baltimore, 1947) and R. Weiss, *Humanism in England in the Fifteenth Century* (2nd ed.; Oxford, 1957). Developments in the early sixteenth century can be followed in two excellent books: D. Bush, *The Renaissance and English Humanism* (Toronto, 1939) and F. Caspari, *Humanism and the Social Order in Tudor England* (Chicago, 1954); and there is a careful study of a leading educational reformer by S. E. Lehmberg, *Sir Thomas Elyot, Tudor Humanist* (Austin, 1960). Changes in the curriculum have been traced in M. H. Curtis, *Oxford and Cambridge in Transition, 1558–1642* (Oxford, 1959) and W. I. Costello, *The Scholastic Curriculum at Early Seventeenth Century Cambridge* (Cambridge, Mass., 1958), and the fascinating story of the post-humanist education of a great writer can be followed in detail in H. F. Fletcher, *The Intellectual Development of John Milton* (2 vols.; Urbana, 1956, 1961).

Studies in Education

during

the Age of the Renaissance

1400—1600

by

WILLIAM HARRISON WOODWARD
Professor of Education in the University of Liverpool

CAMBRIDGE:
at the University Press

PREFATORY NOTE.

THE present volume, it is hoped, may serve a double purpose. Its subject appeals to all those who are concerned in classical education and desire to make acquaintance with the achievements of the great scholars and teachers who laid the foundation of higher education for the modern world. To many such readers it will come as a surprise to find how problems thought peculiarly modern and solutions propounded as original and profound were commonplaces with their predecessors three centuries ago. The book may prove useful, also, to students of another type, to those, namely, who are taking up systematic enquiry into the history of education as a subject of post-graduate reading. To them these *Studies* point the way to wider enquiry, and, in particular, to examination of sources.

The author has, intentionally, made choice of certain writers on the ground that, although of high educational interest, they have not hitherto been treated, in English at least, from this special standpoint. The theme of the book viewed as a whole will be seen to be the origin and development of the idea of a liberal education—embracing character, manners and instruction—during the two important formative centuries of modern Europe. The history of classical scholarship, in the strict sense, lies outside the scope of these *Studies*. Most opportunely, the Cambridge University Press is on the point of issuing the second volume of Dr J. S. Sandys' *History of Classical Scholarship*, which as covering the period treated in the present work may with much advantage be read along with it.

Particular recognition is due of the kindness of Mr P. S. Allen of C.C.C. Oxford in rendering valuable help in determining difficult points in connection with the chronology of events in the lives of Agricola, Erasmus and Vives. The appearance of the first volume of his edition of the correspondence of Erasmus is an important land-mark in the history of humanism. To Dr Sandys, also, who has kindly read the proofs of a large part of the book, I gratefully acknowledge my indebtedness for valuable criticisms.

LIVERPOOL,
 October, 1906.

CHAPTER I.

THE QUATTROCENTO AND THE BEGINNINGS OF HUMANIST EDUCATION[1].

IT is scarcely necessary to affirm the need of approaching the study of Education upon the method of historical enquiry. Like any other complex body of facts—whether in the form of an institution or of organised knowledge or beliefs—it may be attacked by way of direct analysis or by following down the lines of historical development and expansion. It may reasonably be argued that where circumstances admit of it, the historical method will always prove illuminating; that we shall understand chemistry the better for tracing the growth of the science from alchemy; or astronomy, by working down from Greek theories of the universe through mediaeval astrology to Copernicus and Kepler. But there can be no hesitation in agreeing that a complex phenomenon which is essentially concerned with the adaptation of conviction and knowledge to varying social states must be studied upon such method to be rightly apprehended. For "education" is an evolution; its principles, its organisations, and its practice are the products of a long series of experience; and of this experience certain historical areas at any rate can be closely studied, and in particular within the limits of modern Europe—Europe since Petrarch—can be very faithfully studied.

[1] In the notes throughout this book authorities are quoted under brief titles. The *full title* of each work referred to in the text or notes is given in the bibliographical appendix.

Such examination quickly reveals one obvious law. The aim and the curriculum of education are dependent upon and vary with the ideals and interests of successive ages. The school and the school-master only express the dominant intellectual and social aim of their time : they follow and obey ; they do not lead or control. Nor is this truth inconsistent with the conservatism which so often marks educational progress. For the necessary adjustments in social order are never in automatic correspondence to the ideas which give rise to them. Strong personalities, an overmastering wave of religious or intellectual conviction may, and sometimes do, hasten the process. In education, as we well know, continuity of tradition is of the nature of a virtue ; methods and instruments acquire intrinsic merit without regard to changing aims ; the pressure of the outer world in normal times is but slowly felt. But in creative epochs the barriers no longer serve. The old fabric must adjust itself to the new need. If, entrenched behind traditional repute, or vested interests, it resist for a time (often enough with a sense of right), new organisation and reformed curriculum, expressing changed ideals, ultimately take rise. In whatever ways, the social demand is met and instruction corresponds to the dominant thought of the time. Trojan yields to Greek.

It is obvious that such a method of enquiry as is here suggested involves a wide connotation of the term education. For if education be treated as belief, thought, and social ideal in their application to the up-bringing of youth, the study of its history implies of necessity acquaintance with the ethical and religious concepts, the literature, the politico-social environment of the period whose schools and teachers are under review. Hence the claim is reasonably made that the history of education is primarily a liberal rather than a professional subject. It provides, indeed, a standpoint—and a particularly instructive one—from which to regard the culture of a given epoch. And, conversely, it is no less true that the edu-

cational ideas of such an era as the Italian Renaissance
can be rightly apprehended only in the light of a sound
perception of the related aspects of that most complex phenomenon. Nor would any one doubt that the attempt to grasp
the significance of the education of an Athenian youth or of a
well-born Roman boy, without a parallel knowledge of ancient
Society, must end in producing a distorted impression of the
facts. At the same time, the student of educational history
may fairly contend that he is concerned, not with the genesis of
the culture of a given age, nor even with the question of its
abstract worth. It is enough that he takes the environment of
a given epoch—spiritual, aesthetic, social—as he finds it set
out for him by authorities, and examines its effects upon the
educational end as then conceived, and the curricula, instruments, and methods by which the age attempted to realise it.

The Revival of Learning is but one factor in the Renaissance, although it is impossible to isolate it from the rest. For
example, it was rendered possible by the general social progress
of north Italian communities, and itself reacted upon their
aesthetic development, each of these being further elements in
the Renaissance. But the origins of that marvellous forward
movement in northern Italy are outside the scope of this
enquiry. It is enough to say that the soil was prepared,
politically and socially, for a new spiritual advance, and that
its form was determined by the simultaneous outburst of
interest in the ancient history, language and literature of
Rome.

The characteristics of the Revival will appear in the following chapters. They have been the subject of a vast literature,
in which England has taken a not unworthy share. But it is
perhaps right to admit that we have no historian or critic of
this great age to be placed on equal rank with Burckhardt or
Voigt, Reumont or Pastor. The work of the first named
writer, which is worthily translated into English under the title
of *The Civilisation of Italy in the time of the Renaissance,* is

the finest critical presentation of a complex culture-epoch in literature.

Two motives stand prominently forth as the sources from which was born the enthusiasm for antiquity which is the characteristic of the Quattrocento. The first is that of patriotic sentiment, the second aesthetic attraction. Both were united in Francis Petrarch in whom the nascent revolution found both its impulse and its first expression. It is of importance to recall the significance of the fact that the Italian of the Renaissance regarded himself as the direct heir of the glories of Rome. To restore the magnificence of Roman culture, and therewith the virtue of the Roman citizen and the Roman polity, was his inspiring aim. Patriotic feeling was not content with claiming past glories; it preached the duty of their renewal, and idealised the Augustan period as the Golden Age of mankind which could be brought back again by laborious study of the thoughts and deeds of its great exemplar. It was beyond doubt a sincere enthusiasm which inspired Petrarch, Salutati, Niccoli, Ambrogio, and the notable group of Florentines who stand on the confines of the old culture and the new. The difference between the humanism which they represent and the mediaeval instinct of reverence for Rome is partly that which divides a conscious and critical apprehension of historic continuity from a traditional dependence upon a mysterious, quasi-magical past. The distinction is that between Vergil as Bruni or Vittorino expounded the poet, and the myths of the later middle age of Vergil the necromancer. Partly, moreover, the new patriotism owed its characteristic to the objective standpoint which scholarship began to make possible, whereby the great past was seen in a certain detachment from accepted ideas of conduct and belief. The men of the early Renaissance were ready to initiate a new age, to take up the chain of historical unity where the barbarian had snapped it, to claim the entire antique culture as the due possession of modern Italy. Hence a vivid realisation of classical tradition, which rendered overt imitation and reproduction of the past inevitable to that age and intelligible to ourselves. The outward form of life notably in building, in public speech, or in names must be made the symbol of the antique spirit by which humanity might again aspire to perfection. And no truer expression of the new ideal could be found than the forms and methods of the education of imperial Rome.

Yet the instinct of the eagerly advancing spirit of the north Italian people for grace and harmony, for rhythm, for the fullness of grave and dignified emotion, in which they were to find the deepest satisfaction of their aesthetic sense—this responded not less readily than the patriotic sentiment to the treasures, artistic and literary, of ancient Rome, as they were now for the first time rightly known. Like Petrarch, the educated Italian revelled in "eloquence," fell straightway under the dominion of the majestic Vergilian hexameter, yielded himself as to a caress to the flowing periods of the rhetorical moralist. The Augustan literature appealed to him like the early imperial sculpture and the proportioned spaciousness of Roman buildings. All was reasonable, comprehensible, charming the senses by virtue of line and form or of impressive rhythm. Thus the Revival revealed to him, with all the charm of the unexpected, both a new field of aesthetic enjoyment and an unconscious capacity for it. The finer minds of Florence had, before the fourteenth century was out, exhausted the culture of their time; they were, not knowing, groping for a fuller world. When, almost by accident, it opened out before them in the form of their historic past they leapt forward to make it their own. For the age was ripe: intelligence, artistic potentiality, many-sided human vitality, sheer vigour of personality, the social and material environment, were all ready, and could be satisfied with nothing less than the absorption of a whole civilisation. The genius of the time which might, under other circumstances, have pushed forward scientific enquiry, or religious reform, or national unity, or foreign exploration, was irresistibly drawn to antiquity and to the great arts of speech, of building, of painting, in which this enthusiasm found constructive expression.   Progress on other lines was suspended for a century ; and the social order as it advanced—in the home or the state, in language, in fine art, in leisure, in education—took a cast in which antique suggestion was the dominant motive.

That this reliance upon ancient standards involved a profound spiritual revolution was clearly seen by a few, doubtfully suspected by others, but for the most part cheerfully ignored. In truth, the Christian presumption of the supremacy of the passive virtues had, broadly speaking, never been more than formally accepted by the Italian spirit.   Hence the function of the Revival was primarily to reveal the Italian to himself, to exhibit the characteristics of his personality displayed on the most striking scale, viz., that of an entire culture, in process of rediscovery before him.   Hence the Revival of ancient learning appealed to every genuine child of Italy.   For in it he saw enforced his own innate self-assertion, his love of fame and distinction, his deep-seated sense of individuality.   The virtue of the mediaeval Church was submission, suppression of personality.   The Graeco-Roman ideal, as he interpreted it, was a diametrically opposite estimate of life.   Development of personal force, with its corresponding assertion in society, in politics, in letters, or art, was in reality the *virtù* of the Renaissance.   It illustrates its strength, and no less explains its foibles.   The artifices of expression, skilful imitation of things worthy as a substitute for becoming worthy, was the inevitable outcome of the ideal when it had passed its noon.

Patriotic sentiment, aesthetic attraction, and the instinct for individuality united, therefore, in creating a new standard of "the knowledge that is of most worth" in the Italy of the Quattrocento.   Progress meant a restoration of a past perfection, not the evolution of a new idea.   To attain it, moreover, the methods of antiquity were not less authoritative than its achievements.   The re-creation of ancient virtue, with

the prosperity, national pride, culture, and peace, which were
its outcome, was to be attained in no other way than by re-
storing the training of Greece and Rome.   There was, there
could be, no question as to the sanction of such a restoration.
'Where lay the secret of Alexander's wisdom, of Trajan's virtue,
but in the fact that Aristotle and Plutarch moulded their
youth?' Hence the passionate belief that the new age depended
first and foremost upon the adoption of a right education, of
that education, in other words, which had been handed down,
though now wholly forgotten, by the wise masters of antiquity.

The concept of a new education as the natural product
of humanist feeling took its rise in those centres which were
foremost in cultivating the study of antiquity.   Florence, above
all, with its associations of Dante and Boccaccio, its strenuous
civic life, its progressive and ambitious merchants ; Venice, the
centre of trade with Greek lands ; Padua, the meeting-place of
scholars from every country of Europe, proud of its intimate
associations with Petrarch, stand in nearer relation to the new
studies at the beginning of the century.   Chrysoloras was called
from Constantinople to lecture in the revived University of
Florence by invitation from the city in 1396, and stayed three
years there, until driven away by Niccoli's jealousy.   Vergerius
and Barzizza, who had Vittorino da Feltre for his pupil, laid
the foundation of the humanist tradition in the University of
Padua.   At Venice, patricians were ready to engage humanist
teachers for their sons and, when Padua came under the
dominion of the Republic, took a keen and intelligent interest
in their new-won University, which was thereafter attended
by a large proportion of the youth of the old Venetian
houses.

There were forces making for the spread of classical
enthusiasm which can be identified.   Vergerius had written
his most attractive treatise on the principles of the new education, *De Ingenuis Moribus* ; Guarino translated Plutarch's tract
on the bringing-up of children ; Bruni and Francesco Barbaro

were framing the humanist ideal of instruction suitable for a woman. But above all other influences, the Council of Constance had indirectly brought about the re-discovery of forgotten works of classical antiquity—amongst them, Quintilian's *Education of the Orator* (1417), destined to prove the most significant of them all. With this fruitful research in south Germany, and notably in St Gallen, the name of Poggio, humanist and Apostolic Secretary, is for ever associated.

The influence of the treatise of Quintilian, great as it was in imperial Rome, was still more fruitful of results in the Renaissance. It is not too much to say that it was left to the Quattrocento to render him full appreciation. The mediaeval writers, who knew Quintilian only imperfectly through mutilated MSS., regarded him sometimes as a moralist, sometimes as an orator, and only here and there as a school-master. But humanists from Petrarch downwards seized his importance as the prime authority upon the Roman educational ideal. It should be noted that neither Plato nor Aristotle contributed to any marked extent (in the case of Vittorino only does this statement need qualification) to form the education of the Italian Revival before 1470. Greek literature on the subject was mainly represented by Plutarch, who writes as a Roman in Greek dress. Hence it is to Quintilian that M. Vegius, Poggio, Guarino, Vergerius, Palmieri or Alberti consistently look for guidance; as does also the most distinguished of all the teachers of the early Renaissance, Vittorino da Feltre[1].

[1] Authorities for the statements given in the text relative to Vittorino da Feltre are to be found in Woodward's *Vittorino da Feltre*, to which recourse may also be had for versions of the tracts of Vergerius, Bruni and B. Guarino mentioned in this chapter. Students will gather much valuable information from Bassi (on Quintilian) and Luzio-Renier (on humanism at the court of the Gonzagas) in the *Giorn. Stor. d. Lett. Ital.*; Gerini, Rösler, Creighton, Sandys (*Harvard Lectures* and the *History of Scholarship*) may also be added to the authorities enumerated in the bibliographical list of writers quoted in *Vittorino da Feltre*.

"Quintilianum ut optimum vitae atque eruditionis auctorem miris laudibus extollebat," says Platina of Vittorino; whose favourite pupil, Ognibene da Lonigo, became under his guidance a renowned authority upon the *Institutio Oratoria.* Indeed in the Mantuan School is to be found an exposition of the precepts of Quintilian adapted to modern Italian life. Every educator of the Revival, whether man of theory or man of practice, whether on Italian or Teutonic soil, Aeneas Sylvius or Patrizi, Agricola, Erasmus, Melanchthon, or Elyot, steeped himself in the text and in the spirit of this treatise.

Quintilian describes indeed what may appear at first sight to be a somewhat restricted type of training, viz., that of an orator[1]. But his ideal orator falls in nothing short of the concept of the highly educated man, with the added qualification that he is expert in forensic or public speaking. It was an education adapted to all who were born, or aspired, to place in society, with its consequent duty of social service. In Italy at the Renaissance, with its multiform political units, republics, city-states, highly-organised despotisms, their diplomacies, and civil services, a large proportion of the upper and educated class was inevitably concerned in duties and careers in which a sound intellectual training, coupled with skill in expression, was essential to success. Oratory then, not less than in ancient Rome of the period of transition, was the practical exhibition of knowledge and personality in its application to affairs. Philosophy and "eruditio" generally were handmaids to the many-sided arts of government. Hence Cato defined an orator as a man of sincerity expert in speaking. Only a "good man" can be a perfect orator. The name of the Orator is sacred, and his ideal takes the place filled in Stoicism by the "perfectly wise man." Quintilian, therefore, appealed to the moralist from his insistence on truthfulness as the foundation of education; to the man of learning from his

[1] Upon Roman education, as it actually was, Wilkins' *Roman Education* should be read.

demand that the orator must be versed in the entire circle of available knowledge, to the man of affairs from the ultimate end which he set before his pupils, that they should become competent, as logical and persuasive speakers, to place both character and wisdom at the service of the community. Hence one characteristic note of early humanism, that knowledge is desirable in proportion to the use which can be publicly made of it, and that wisdom hoarded up and not expressed partakes of selfishness. From such an attitude to that of approval of display for display's sake the step is not a far one.

It is necessary thus to lay stress upon the position of the humanist school-masters in relation to Quintilian. The education of the Italian Revival has often appeared as a sudden growth, abnormal in its swift ascent to completeness. But we must bear in mind that early in the fifteenth century Quintilian was fully available: and that his judgment upon instruction was accepted as final and authoritative where circumstances admitted of its application. The secret of antique perfection—literary and political—was held to be embedded in the doctrines of Roman education. It is typical of the general feeling that Erasmus (1512) should apologise for touching upon methods or aims in teaching "seeing that Quintilian has said in effect the last word on the matter."

Vittorino was born in 1378 at Feltre, in the Venetian Alps, and was a student at Padua when the influence of P. P. Vergerius began to make itself felt in the University. Vittorino worked under, and afterwards with, Gasparino Barzizza, the pioneer scholar of the Renaissance, who from 1407 professed for several years Latin Letters at Padua. From Guarino da Verona, whose work is dealt with in a subsequent chapter, Vittorino learnt Greek, during intermittent residence at Venice between 1414 and 1418. Before 1420 he set up a boarding-house at Padua, for students to whom he acted as tutor in Latin and Mathematics, in which subject he was an exceptionally competent teacher. He was recognised as a notable moral influence in this cosmopolitan University, holding high the standard of conduct as well as of learned study. His Latin scholarship was of such quality that in 1422 he received the appointment to the chair of Rhetoric vacant on the departure of Barzizza.

The Marquis of Mantua, Gianfrancesco Gonzaga, was at this time seeking a tutor for his children. He was a "new man" amongst neighbouring ruling families, and he desired a scholar who should add repute to his Court by his recognised distinction, and should at the same time equip his sons for success in that struggle of wits which meant life or death to the minor Houses of Italy in that day. He turned first to Guarino, by whose advice he approached Vittorino. After much hesitation his offer was accepted, Vittorino holding that the career of a master, with these so special responsibilities, was no less a life of service than the life in religion to which he felt himself drawn. At the end of 1423 he was at work in Mantua, making ready for his new duties. The school was set up in the casino, a sumptuous garden-house in the park of the Castello. It had borne the name of La Zoyosa, or the Pleasure House, but was re-named by Vittorino "La casa Giocosa," the Joyful House, and it was by his order decorated with frescoes of children at play, in keeping with his sentiment. Here Vittorino and the children of the Marquis lived and worked. There were by degrees added to the group pupils of other standing, sons of parents of position. Later on, a varying number of poor scholars, chosen by the master himself, who of his own stipend, and of the charity of the Marquis and the lady Paola his wife were boarded, and taught, and in some cases clothed, free of all payment. We hear of forty and even of seventy such pupils. This was an essential principle of Vittorino's doctrine : equality of opportunity for real ability. A successor, himself one of this group, Ognibene, upheld the same practice both at Mantua

(1449–1453) and afterwards at Vicenza where he carried into practice the humanist instruction of Vittorino as head-master of the renowned communal school[1].

The general aims of the Mantuan school, as they were developed during the two and twenty years in which Vittorino stamped upon it the impress of his remarkable personality, was to effect a reconciliation of the moral and religious teaching of the Church with classical instruction on lines approved by Quintilian and with the knightly disciplines of the Italian Castello, all being suffused with something of the Greek feeling for grace and harmony. The breadth and dignity of Vittorino's conception of a humanist course of training thus regarded stands out ever more impressively the further our enquiry penetrates. It was no platitude that he purposed to train mind, body and spirit in one relation. With not a few humanist professors of this doctrine it is merest pretence. His education moreover was held by him to be a thoroughly practical discipline, preparing youth for a life of action, and training both mind and character for the due exercise of judgment in affairs. His was a school for statesmen, for administrators, for high ecclesiastics, for captains of distinction, for school-masters like-minded with himself. But the pedant, the ostentatious rhetorician, the narrower type of grammarian were never characteristic products of his school. As regards the particular function of instruction, he did not view a sound knowledge of literature or language as the decoration of a leisured life. Instruction be held to be a factor of profound importance in the moulding of the moral element in personality. The function of man as citizen was that which Vittorino always kept in view. "Not everyone," he used to say, "is called to

---

[1] Prendilacqua, who knew him intimately both at Mantua and afterwards, says of him: "there is no greater Master in Italy, none so highly respected, none so successful in attracting to learning our Italian youth," p. 44. Like Vittorino he was deeply interested in Greek patristic literature, and was the first authority in Italy upon the *De Oratore*.

be a lawyer, a physician, a philosopher, to live in the public eye, nor has everyone outstanding gifts of natural capacity, but all of us are created for the life of social duty, all are responsible for the personal influence which goes forth from us." Nor did Vittorino share that contempt for life "in religion" which marked the general mass of humanists.

Vittorino had solved the problem of the relation of Christian conviction to pre-Christian culture by his confident acceptance of their compatibility under the supremacy of the Christian motive. He frankly disowned the fears of the sectarian and the obscurantist who conjured up visions of neo-pagan belief and morals. Classical history, letters, and ethics were to him a historic past which had fallen into its due place under the higher law of Christianity. Hence, if the Christian life were rightly inculcated as part and parcel of humanist training the proper subordination of antique ideals would be secured. On the other hand, Vittorino in no way sympathised with the dreams of a restoration of the ancient culture, in language, for example, or in political order, or, still less, in standards of conduct, professed by certain humanists. But he was able to select from ancient literature and moral teaching all that seemed to him ennobling, as appealing to a boy's sense of right and feeling for self-sacrifice; and he knew how much there was in classical history and in the poets and prose-writers of antiquity which enforced Christian lessons of conduct and life. And more, there is in the records which we have of him left by pupils and contemporaries that which indicates that he felt the Christian desire for inner harmony to be in accord with a feeling after that aesthetic satisfaction which results from the consciousness of things beautiful, of outward grace and proportion, in the human figure and its trained activity, in nature, and in musical tone. He had much of that sense of rhythmic order which marks his great contemporary L. B. Alberti. The touchstone of good or evil was not supplied by the catch-word of Christian or pagan, but by the response of his own spiritual temper, alert to recognise all that made for wholesomeness and strength.

Vittorino offered no technical or professional disciplines. His aim was to lay foundations in liberal culture to serve as the necessary preliminaries to specific training for careers. Judgment, wisdom and integrity said his master Vergerius, are cultivated by liberal learning. From the Casa Giocosa young men no doubt passed to Padua or Bologna for Medicine or Law; but a complete education in Classical letters, and in mathematics could be better acquired at Mantua than in any University, until, at least, the foundation of Ferrara (1442) in the latter years of the life of Vittorino. The Court schools, in fact, were the chief centres of higher humanist teaching in the early Renaissance. The hard and fast line between school and University did not exist so far as these studies were concerned. A hundred years later in France and in Germany work was done in schools of the same rank, and on the same methods, as that done at the same time in the Faculty of Arts of the Universities. Certainly during the life of Vittorino no University (Ferrara again excepted) seriously regarded Letters otherwise than as a step towards the professional degrees of Theology, Law and Medicine, and held them, therefore, in modest esteem.

The instruments of training were drawn exclusively from classical and patristic sources. This applies not less to mathematics, natural science, ethics, history and geography. Vittorino accepted from Quintilian the ideal of the educated man as one who can express himself with sincerity, with readiness, and persuasiveness upon the entire circle of knowledge. The mere aptitude of the rhetorician he despised. He himself left no elegant epistles, or ornate declamations. Nevertheless he placed the art of prose composition in Latin and Greek at the summit of the literary disciplines. Vergil, as a Mantuan, was, as always, upheld as the first of poets. Gianlucido Gonzaga, the third son of the Marquis, like

Alessandro, the fourth, a boy of studious bent, knew all Vergil by heart and wrote very passable verse. Lucan, as with most humanists, comes next: Ovid, Plautus, Juvenal and Horace he held to need cautious use in schools. Terence was regarded with favour as a guide to Latin conversation, which is the true justification for reading Plautus: "quod hi plurimum eloquentiae conferrent" says Platina of Vittorino's opinion. Seneca naturally appeals to him on score of lofty "sententiae." Livy was, on the historical side, the favourite author. The foundations of the critical study of the text were laid at Mantua, as we know from the preface to the *Editio Princeps* (1471) written by a distinguished pupil, the Bishop of Aleria, who prepared this and several other classics for the first Roman Press. Sallust and Quintus Curtius were taught to beginners. Pliny's *Historia Naturalis* was read for its vast range of interesting matter.

Quintilian naturally occupied a large place. Vittorino discusses the *Institutio* at some length with Ambrogio Traversari, on the occasion of his visit to Mantua. Upon the *De Oratore* of Cicero he was almost continuously engaged. The *Epistles* of Cicero were important for composition and nearly the entire range of his speeches was available for the rhetorical training of elder pupils. Platina has left certain interesting notes upon Vittorino's method of teaching composition. "He would perpetually remind his pupils that before putting pen to paper they must, as it were, attune their minds to the particular bit of writing required by reading and re-reading an appropriate model passage from a sound author. He himself was most particular in correcting exercises and propounding happier renderings. Sometimes in composing a declamation a boy would insert a sentence which gave a turn of personal compliment to the master, whereupon Vittorino would return it to the writer for prompt correction with unmistakeable disapproval." Elsewhere we are told that anything in the nature of fine writing, of prolix or over-laden description, or of empty commonplace decked out in verbiage was ruthlessly torn up.

Yet Vittorino attaches great weight to genuine power of expression. He was typically Italian in this respect; though he was averse to mere artificiality and to the preposterous displays of empty declamation which counted for so much with smaller men. But, as will be shown in later chapters of this book, the function of public speaking in its several aspects was highly prized in Italy, and could not be ignored by any Master in the position of Vittorino. Apart from such a motive, he held strongly that knowledge is best tested by reproducing it, by carefully prepared exposition and by imparting it to others. The place of disputation in the mediaeval school was taken in the humanist by the Declamation, and later on in German and English schools by the Essay. But the root idea is identical; the variation in form is but a matter of historical development. That Vittorino meant by expression composition in Greek or Latin and not in Italian is undoubtedly true.   But the reaction of sound practice in the elaborated languages of antiquity upon facility in the vernacular is an easy thesis to defend.

The study of History naturally appealed to that patriotic impulse from which, as has been said, the new education, like the humanist ideal itself, derived no small part of its sanction. For history meant for Vittorino the story of ancient Rome and only in a secondary degree that of Greece: both of them, also, as presented in authoritative literary dress. Hence to study history signified a reading, reverential in spirit rather than critical, of the narratives of Livy, Sallust, Caesar or Plutarch[1].   The history of contemporary Italy found no place in a humanist school.   For the heroic age of the Italian race

---

[1] It is worth noticing that Tacitus, though prized by Petrarch and a subject of study by Guarino, found no place in humanist instruction. It was probably in part a question of style, partly of subject-matter; but the main objection was the extreme scarcity of MSS.

fell within antiquity, and ancient literature alone afforded a narrative of events fittingly adorned to carry conviction of truth and suggest political instruction. It was of course far too early for a critical study of history, and the teaching of political and constitutional development was merely tentative. Hence the attraction of such historians as lend themselves to the biographical treatment of their subjects. Plutarch's popularity with all humanists turns upon the ease with which his biographies could be turned to didactic use for edification. But there was a sound instinct in this handling of historical material. The actual politics of the day fostered a belief— and no one can deny that it was well founded—in the overwhelming significance of the individual in affairs, and especially the immense potentiality for good or evil that resided in a strong personality. It was inevitable, therefore, that an Italian humanist should seize upon the notable figures of antiquity as illustrations of moral principle and political action. It was said by more than one scholar that history was mainly of use as furnishing concrete types of abstract ethical standards. Yet again, the literary aspect of history stands in intimate association with the passion for fame to which every humanist appeals, as a matter of course, as the strongest motive to exertion. Without the historian there is no history; the prince, the soldier, finds no praise unless an enduring monument of imperishable words be raised to him. And without fame life is meaningless. It is but one more expression of the individualist instinct of the race. The study of history, then, as a humanist school-master understood it, was the contemplation of notable deeds told by a master of words.

Upon the place of Greek in the Mantuan School it may be claimed that Vittorino attached more importance to it than did any other of the masters of the earlier Renaissance, hardly excepting Guarino. He was fortunate enough to possess as his colleague Theodore Gaza, the best of the native Greek scholars in Italy. Vittorino was well equipped as a teacher of the language. But he had, further, a definite touch of the Greek spirit, and more than any of his Italian contemporaries approached a sympathetic comprehension of Plato. We can conjecture that the *Erotemata* of Chrysoloras (probably in Guarino's Latin version) was used as a guide to the grammar. Xenophon, Isocrates, Demosthenes, and Homer are the authors more specially mentioned by pupils as read at the school. The author's text and the grammar were, as usual in the case of Greek, no doubt dictated as part of the class-lesson. Platina records that Vittorino made some use of Aristophanes both "for reason of the purity of his Attic diction" and also as "ad formandum bonum virum, quod vitia insectaretur, aptus." Most interesting is the same biographer's reference to the frequent reading of Aeschylus, since apart from the condition of the text the inherent difficulties of the poet must have involved immense effort in the then state of Greek scholarship.

It is extremely probable that Greek was studied on a method different from that followed in the case of Latin. For the humanist taught his pupils grammar and composition through the latter language, and used Greek primarily as a channel of instruction in poetry, science, or history. No doubt the Guarinos laid stress on pure scholarship. But it is generally true that the study of Greek in humanist schools was literary rather than linguistic, and in its later stages has for its chief end "eruditio," or subject-matter[1].

Under Vittorino's tuition Carlo dei Gonzaga, "whilst a mere boy," says Prendilacqua, translated Plutarch's *Life of Agesilaus* into Latin, a fitting exercise for one destined to be a soldier. Ognibene, when hardly in his teens, produced a version of the *Life of Camillus*, and of the fables of Aesop. So Beccaria,

---

[1] Hence the range of Greek reading was much wider and freer than in the classical schools or the Universities of the following centuries. The standard of Attic purism was not as yet accepted in the fifteenth century; and we find in schools Chrysostom, Basil, Polybius and Plutarch read alongside of Plato, Thucydides and Xenophon.

who found a patron in our own Duke Humphrey, was a translator of repute, and even attempted to render the *Ethics* in Latin dress. A remarkable statement is made by Prendilacqua concerning Alessandro: "he was as a boy carefully grounded in Greek, as he grew older, in Latin; as he drew to manhood his interest lay mainly in sacred studies." This particular pupil was notably studious, gentle and peace-loving, a favourite at home and with the people of Mantua, regarded by his master as the most promising of his immediate charges. So that it may not be inferred that this was a customary practice. It would not, in any case, follow that a grammatical method was pursued with a young beginner, although we do not definitely know the lines upon which rudiments were taught in the Giocosa.

It should be remembered that one obvious motive to the reading of classical, and particularly of Greek, authors lay in the fact that every student of antiquity, and of the ethical and scientific lore enshrined in ancient literature, was compelled to have recourse to original sources. There were not yet available historical, geographical, archaeological, or mathematical works based upon, and coordinating, the contents of the classic writers. To read Roman history involved of necessity a first-hand study of Livy. Greek history was only to be had from Thucydides, Xenophon, or Plutarch. Geography must be learnt from Strabo or Ptolemy, Mela or Dionysius. Aristotle, Theophrastus, and Pliny were the indispensable manuals of science. In other words, the antique civilisation had not yet been systematised, and the only avenue to genuine knowledge lay in the ancient books. "Sine Graecis literis caeca est omnis eruditio," said Erasmus, who declared, with Melanchthon, and many other of his contemporaries, that the low state of legal, medical, and mathematical knowledge was due to the ignorance of Greek writers in the original. And Vittorino would have endorsed *ex animo* this typical humanist judgment.

Something should be said upon the place of music in

Vittorino's educational scheme.   More completely than any other humanist master, Vittorino entered into the Greek feeling upon this subject.   He was himself undoubtedly susceptible to the effect of music.   He introduced it at meal times, finding that certain boys became so absorbed in it that they forgot to eat—to their advantage.   It was his doctrine—though it is nowhere explicitly stated it transpires obviously enough through the records left by his pupils—that education consists primarily in the influences, perceived or no, of environment, amongst which aesthetic elements had a significant place, if indeed these could be definitely separated from moral forces.   Thus he rejoiced in the dignified character of the school buildings, the playing fields, and their site.   Hence, also, the importance he attached to the voice, bearing, manners of a boy, as affecting his fellow pupils.   He wholly sympathised with Plato's judgment upon musical modes.   Trivial and worthless music, explicable only as the expression of a corresponding mental temper, was to be suppressed, lest it tend to engender in others the spiritual condition which it suggests.   Wholesome music, " Dorian," martial or solemn, the boys regularly cultivated in song, and in the case of individuals in instrumental practice.   Music, again, had its more rigorous aspect in that the theory of it was a part of mathematics, and as such appealed strongly to Vittorino. For he was celebrated in his Paduan days and later as a teacher of geometry and astronomy, and certain of his pupils were highly reputed for their knowledge.   But we have nothing which enables us to determine in what respects his methods call for notice.   It was, however, characteristic of higher education in the fifteenth century that the standard of algebraical and geometrical teaching was very low, and there was an avowed divorce of school mathematics from all commercial applications.

There is no reason to suppose that Vittorino had girl pupils other than those belonging to the Gonzaga house, who included Barbara von Hohenzollern, the Brandenburg princess, brought up for several years at Mantua and ultimately married to Ludovico, the heir to the Marquisate. It will be safe to assume that he took much the same view as Lionardo Bruni, whose tract, *De Studiis et Literis*, treats of a woman's instruction. Cecilia Gonzaga was carefully educated both in Latin and Greek. She grew up a young woman of devout temper, held in affectionate regard by her preceptor, who stood by her in the crisis of her life, when she rejected the marriage with the worthless Oddantonio di Montefeltro—he was assassinated at Urbino in 1444—proposed for her by her father. Cecilia had already for some time contemplated a conventual life, drawn to it by her studious instincts as well as by her religious feeling, and now she declared her purpose to the enraged Marquis. The Marchioness, supported by Vittorino, definitely took the side of her daughter. The marriage was broken off, and on the death of Gianfrancesco both Paola and Cecilia entered religion. It is clear that in Vittorino's case humanism stood in no conflict with Christianity in the man or in the teacher.

It was expressly remarked of him that he considered, almost with reverence, the tastes and bent of each of his pupils. So soon as they manifested any special gift he would adjust subject and method. As their capacity for responsible choice developed as they drew towards manhood, he allowed them to concentrate their interest upon classics, mathematics, or philosophy, or upon poetry or music. This respect for individuality and sincere effort to further it gained for him the confidence of men of very varied type who entrusted their sons to his charge. It was quickly seen that Vittorino was no mere " grammar master "; he was in the best sense of the phrase a well-balanced man of the world, surveying life from a standpoint wholly different from that of a professed scholar who had drifted into teaching, which fairly describes perhaps the majority of school-masters of that century and the following. He writes, for example, to the father of the boy Frederigo, the future

Duke of Urbino, " that his son's genius points to the career of a soldier and captain of men. In order that he may prove worthy of his talent, Vittorino will cultivate in him keenness of intellectual temper, which, united with a frank nature and a strong bent towards action, will render him the most highly equipped captain of his time." "If," he adds, "you will be advised by me, you will encourage and respect his ambition. It will in the event, as I confidently believe, redound both to his honour and your own ; and that, not in his life-time only, but in centuries yet to come."

That a true humanist education should lay the basis of training for any honourable career was the principle of the Mantuan school. Professional equipment must rest upon such foundation, and is wisely postponed until manhood approaches. Thus pupils stayed at Mantua until they had passed their twenty-first year. No University could add anything to the training in scholarship there acquired. Instruction in classical learning was the function of the civic or Court school, and a scholar or teacher claimed distinction on grounds of education at Mantua or Ferrara, at Cremona or Vicenza, rather than at Pavia or Bologna. The Universities never retained men of the stamp of Aurispa or Filelfo ; and not until the closing decade of the century did Padua and Bologna attain established repute as centres of higher classical learning. The staff of Greek teachers, the library, the copyists, at Mantua, the admittedly high place there given to the language and thought of Greece placed Vittorino's school at the head of all centres of humanist instruction, until the development of the new " studium" of Ferrara (1442–1445) which coincided with his own declining years.

Vittorino, as a genuine product of the Renaissance, required as a correlative to a fine intellectual humanism a standard of physical excellence and personal bearing to match. With all his severity Vittorino had none of that contempt for the body professed by the ascetic. He desired to discipline it in order to render it more perfect. Hence the importance attached to diet, clothing, and exercise : boys were inured to cold and prolonged exertion. Artificial heat was scarcely tolerated. Games were enforced, and lounging or solitary habits were repressed. Vittorino was always in the playing-fields. He carried with him certain of the pupils during the summer heats to Goito and the hill-country above Lake Garda. Provision was made for military exercises of various kinds. The purport of such training was to develop an easy, graceful bearing, suppleness, and dignity of figure. The social end was always present to his mind. Personality was compact of mind, of character, and of bodily presence, with all that pertains to it. Indeed the latter in a subtle manner must express the spiritual nature ; wherefore the individual will be known by his courtesy, his refinement of speech, by the things he avoids not less than by his unconscious preferences. Voice, intonation, gesture, says Platina, drew much attention from Vittorino : anything that betokened lack of control was promptly dealt with, such as grimaces, restlessness, uncouth attitudes. Occasion will arise later to show how this relation of personal culture to social gifts was developed in the high Renaissance in Italy. But the essence of it is already to be discerned in the Mantuan Court school.

The relations of Vittorino with the Gonzaga family illustrate in an attractive way the influence which a scholar-teacher might exert in the social and political life of the Court. From the day of his arrival he established his authority in all that concerned the training of the children of the ruling House. He spoke plainly to the Marquis himself upon the influence of home example. The bitter feud between Ludovico and his father, which others wholly failed to heal, yielded to the affectionate remonstrance of Vittorino, who pleaded for his pupil with the obdurate father. The Marchesa, an admirable wife and mother, was ever ready to help him in his plans for benefiting poor scholars, as he too was eager to share in her works of religion and charity in the city of Mantua. Both she and her husband called Vittorino into counsel on State affairs—for she acted often as Regent during the absence of the Marquis on military duty as Captain-General for the Venetian Council. Ludovico, the eldest son, who succeeded his father in 1444, was specially devoted to his old master, to whom by common consent he owed it in large part that he grew up to be a man of seriousness and integrity. He proved an admirable ruler. Alberti was his intimate friend, and was several times resident in Mantua. Thither he brought Mantegna. Pisanello came also and executed medals of Cecilia and of Vittorino, which are amongst the most attractive of that great artist's works. From Ludovico, indeed, dates the distinction which Mantua enjoyed for a century as the seat of a notable Court life, and the centre to which gravitated all that was finest in artistic production. The young Marquis did much to uphold the distinction of the school upon Vittorino's death. For the first year the loss was acutely felt, so truly had Vittorino been the life and heart of the school; half of the pupils were withdrawn, and the outlook was discouraging. But Ognibene was made Head in 1449; steeped through and through with the spirit of his old master he quickly restored the old level of efficiency. His repute was such that he was urgently (though vainly) demanded by the Duchess Bianca Maria Sforza as tutor to the heir of Milan. After a stay of four years at Mantua he yielded to repeated pressure from the city of Vicenza. He had meantime compiled a Latin Grammar on Vittorino's method, which is still amongst the most interesting of early humanist manuals.

The personal character of Vittorino can scarcely be hard to realise, even from this brief account of his activities. The essential note is a single-eyed devotion to the responsibilities which he had undertaken, combined with deep personal affection for his pupils. The individuality which characterised his teaching rested upon his intimate knowledge of the temper and ability of each pupil. He was an ardent humanist, yet the Christian faith and ideal were to him truths so self-evident that the danger of conflict between old belief and new learning had no meaning. His work it was, with Guarino da Verona, to establish, on a basis which still endures, an ideal of the training of youth worthy of the "spacious time" into which they had been born. It was an ideal which should conserve what was worth retaining from the mediaeval discipline, should unite with it instruments and modes of instruction drawn from the ancient world, and, viewing all in the light of a modern and Christian State, thus erect a comprehensive education fitted to the many-sided society of the Renaissance. It is true that the concept of education thus carried into practice by Vittorino has rarely been actually realised elsewhere. A system may fairly claim to be judged in the light of its most complete achievement. To perceive, then, the inner spirit of humanist education, to understand its aim, its method, and its results, the critic must turn to the Mantuan school. And whatever justification there may be for the charges of narrowness, of pedantry, of harshness, of obliviousness to the actualities of life, laid against classical teachers and instruction of a later day, certain it is that they do not remotely touch the ideal school of the humanities which is here reviewed.

CHAPTER II.

GUARINO DA VERONA.
1374–1460.

MENTION was made in the last chapter of the intercourse of Vittorino with Guarino Veronese. The two scholars, nearly contemporary in age, were intimate friends and for many years near neighbours; and Guarino left behind him a reputation as a humanist school-master hardly second to that of Vittorino.

Guarino dei Guarini[1], known from the place of his birth as

---

[1] The contemporary biographers of Guarino are a writer known as "L' Anonimo Veronese," Pannonius, Carbone, and Vespasiano da Bisticci. The first of these wrote an appreciation of his master Guarino in Oct. or Nov. 1424, when the latter was still at Verona. He is accurately informed of the main incidents of the first half of Guarino's career: his residence at Scio, his work at Florence and Venice, his invitation to Mantua. He had access to such knowledge as Guarino himself chose to impart about his early life. The text is contained in Cod. Ambros. O. 66. f. 21–27 at Milan. It was used by Querini and by Rosmini. The *Panegyric* of G. Pannonius is dated 1453. The author (an old pupil) is extraordinarily ignorant of the actual facts and dates of Guarino's career: but he is good on details of instruction as he knew them when pupil at Ferrara. Carbone and Vespasiano are not of much value.

The best modern work before Sabbadini is by N. Cittadella, *I Guarini*, Bologna, 1870; it is based upon the Ferrara archives. But the present-day knowledge of the life and work of Guarino is mainly the result of the research of R. Sabbadini, till lately Professor of Latin at Catania. The *Vita di Guarino* and the *Scuole e Studii di Guarino* are accessible to students. But the monumental collection of the Letters, with its appendices, is still in MS. It has been carefully examined by the present writer for purposes of this work. When this *Correspondence of*

Guarino da Verona or Guarino Veronese, was born in 1374, the son of a worker in metal, apparently artisan rather than artist. By his father's death the boy was left at the age of twelve to the care of a devoted mother, a pious and most capable woman, from whom he derived the profound religious feeling which always characterised him. His youth was passed in his native city, which ranked then as now amongst the most dignified towns of Italy, inhabited by a population alert, proud, and well-to-do. Receiving under the noted teacher Marzagaia a good grounding in Latin—obviously of the pre-humanist type—he passed on presently, after the ordinary method of the earnest student of the period, to Padua and Venice in search of further instruction. At what date he came under the in-fluence of Giovanni di Conversino[1] is not certain. But during the period 1390–1403 he made the acquaintance of Vergerius, Sicco Polentone, and other scholars of Padua, and came into relations, perhaps as tutor, or as fellow student, with members of certain Venetian families of position. It is too much to say that the Paduan school of classical study was humanist, except in so far as it was independent of mere professional ends. Its Latin lacked the marks of "elegantia, puritas, concinnitas"; its "eruditio" was meagre; Greek it did not know. But in Padua were found certain characteristics of a new atmosphere. For there were individual teachers, such as Vergerius, to whom Latin was not merely an instrument of Theology, Law, or Medicine. Conversino brought to his teaching the Petrarchian outlook and feeling for progress through the ancient ways; he had a sense of a mission for Letters as a force making for higher things. There is no doubt that, next to Florence, Padua offered the most encouraging *milieu* for an ardent student of antiquity, and when Barzizza moved thither from

Guarino Veronese appears it will prove the most considerable contribution to the early history of humanism produced in this generation.

[1] On Conversino see Woodward, *Vittorino*, p. 3, and authorities there quoted.

Milan in 1407 its importance in the development of the revival was established.

In these three centres Guarino, learning and teaching, spent the first thirty years of his life. Then came the great opportunity of his career. In 1403 there fell in his way the chance of a journey to Greece (i.e. Constantinople) in the service of a Venetian merchant and State official, Paolo Zane. It was an adventure by no means free from risk for a peaceful student, but Guarino eagerly embraced it, and in Greece he remained for nearly five years. Any scholar to whose happy lot it fell to visit the mystic home of Greek learning was the object of keen envy by his brethren. But Guarino had besides the supreme good fortune of admission to the household of Chrysoloras, who had just returned from Italy after teaching Greek at Florence and Pavia. Manuel Chrysoloras, renowned both as scholar and as diplomat throughout the West, was a relative of the reigning Emperor of the East, and occupied a beautiful house with gardens reaching to the Bosphorus. The famous city, with its marvellous site, its climate, vegetation, and above all the solemn associations of its vast antiquity, left, as he has recorded, a deep impression upon the Italian scholar. For two years he worked incessantly at Greek ; the son of Chrysoloras, the young Johannes, a teacher of litera- ture to the noble youth of Constantinople acted as Guarino's master. We may readily imagine how urgent a stimulus he found in the monuments of ancient art, in libraries filled with the masterpieces of Greek oratory and poetry, the very titles of which were lost to the Western world, above all in a people in whose mouths the living speech of Pericles or Demosthenes was the vernacular tongue. Nor could he fail to discern along the horizon the shadow of the Infidel inexorably advancing to the fulfilment of the doom which Guarino was to live to see. Very little, unfortunately, of his correspondence relating to this period has been preserved, though we know he kept up regular intercourse by letter with friends at Venice, amongst them a young scion of the family of Barbaro, Francesco, an ardent lover of letters, and all his life intimately attached to Guarino. During this period he tried his hand, as so many other beginners were destined to do, at translating Lucian and Plutarch, and no doubt saw something of Greek lands outside the limits of the straits. Of one opportunity of visiting the Aegean we have record. Perhaps in the capacity of secretary or commissioner on behalf of Paolo Zane, he made journeys to Rhodes and Chios, bringing away with him, as we should expect, useful finds in the way of codices. But in 1408 he was back in Venice.

Guarino was now thirty-four years of age. He had passed through the first and most important stage of his intellectual development, whereby his place in the progress of scholarship and of education was once for all determined. The first factor was the influence of the Paduan school of studies, the seat of those early awakenings of the humanist spirit within a small but notable group of earnest-minded scholars, such as we descry it in the correspondence of P. P. Vergerius. To this succeeded the momentous impulse contributed by his contact with the very centre of the Greek world. It is barely possible for us to-day to understand the significance of that plunge into the heart of antique culture to the ardent spirit of a humanist on the threshold of the Renaissance.

Guarino had hoped to find on his return to Italy a congenial post at Venice; but being disappointed he went to Bologna (February, 1410), where he made acquaintance with Poggio and L. Bruni, and probably with other scholars, sojourning there in the suite of the Pope, as secretaries to the Curia. At the instance of Bruni he was at once invited to Florence, where for the first time he found his true calling as a teacher of Graeco-Roman antiquity. To have been the familiar pupil of Chrysoloras, to have actually seen Greece, were an absolute title to respect in Florence. He at once opened school, the private venture of a small knot of citizens with Niccoli at their head, which speedily became of high repute.   Men of the distinction of Palla Strozzi and Ambrogio Traversari were his strong supporters ; so that it naturally came about that when the Studio of Florence was re-opened in 1412 Guarino was nominated by the municipality to the chair of Greek, which Chrysoloras alone had filled before him. Guarino's lot was thus cast in the stirring intellectual life of the true birth-place of the Revival.   The circle of Niccoli, Pandolfini, and Strozzi, of Bruni and Traversari, constituted *society* in the truest sense of the term.   For social intercourse was in Florence already a fine art.   The constant communications with other cities within and beyond the limits of Italy, the coming and going of notable diplomats, princes, and ecclesiastics, the high level of capacity which marked its merchant citizens, the absence of the heavy hand of feudalism, the dignified type of its people, their careful speech, their intelligence, their instinct for a wholesome yet comely life—such characteristics placed Florence in the very front rank of civilised Europe, and offered a promising soil for a great movement in art and thought.   From Florence, too, it was easy to maintain relations with men of like interests in Rimini, Ferrara, Verona, Padua, and Venice.   And it was in Florence especially that Guarino learnt from visible experience that the ancient world stood in no divorce from the ideals and activities of the world of the day.   The noble doctrine of "utilitas," so prominent in the teaching of every humanist, was exemplified there : for in Florence it was set forth in action as in precept that the end of humanist studies was the well-being of the community on its highest side : integrity of administration, purity of justice, patriotic pride, lofty self-respect, and a life which offered a wide-spread well-being to the commonalty.   Rarely has a nobler enthusiasm actuated a movement whose immediate interest lay in Letters.   And though we admit that it was but in part justified by its results, only the shallowest criticism will judge the activity of the great scholars and lovers of antiquity, amidst whom Guarino was henceforth a leading figure, as a narrow and trivial dilettantism, and the education which they built up as a thing of pedantry and artifice.

Now Niccoli, the most self-conscious of Florentines, was the notable patron of men of Letters in his native city, and was a difficult man to work with. Guarino had a full measure of the scholar's pride, and brooked ill the testy condescension of the wealthy collector and powerful citizen. Chrysoloras had—so we must conclude—quitted Florence to escape him. And perhaps there were jealousies amongst other scholars, and Guarino, a man of forty, was not patient over-much. He was a stranger too; and his affections lay in his own Verona and in Venice, where he had left intimate friends. Young Francesco Barbaro, one of these, happened to be on a visit to Florence at the moment (1414) when friction could no longer be hid, and carried off Guarino with him to Venice, where he found a flattering reception: "ut videretur imperatorem triumphantem adventasse," we are told by one who was there at the time. He at once opened school for young patricians, which was attended also by scholars ambitious of a knowledge of Greek, amongst them Vittorino, who was but three or four years his junior. His friendships amongst men of learning steadily increased. Some of the best work of his life was done at this period. His knowledge of Latin was strengthened by continuous study of Cicero and the principles of rhetoric. He devoted much time to Quintilian, from whom he derived an authoritative basis for his educational methods. At this time he began to give shape to the manuals of Greek and Latin Grammar which he put into circulation at Ferrara some years later. In 1418 he married, and, returning to Verona, was elected to the position of Civic Professor of Rhetoric in his native city. In 1420 he was invited to Vicenza; in 1421 or 1422 to Mantua; but he was unwilling to quit Verona. He advised the Marquis Gonzaga to turn to Vittorino. Interest in Greek

learning was growing apace.   Many promising scholars, of
varying ages, made their way to Verona.   Even the preaching
Friars were represented in his lecture-room.   Alberto da
Sarzana, ever afterwards a courageous friend of his master, was
his pupil ; although Guarino had but few associates—most humanists had none—amongst Franciscan and Dominican monks.
Like Vittorino, however, he held two distinguished "religious"
in deep regard, Traversari the Florentine, and Bernardino of
Siena.   At this time, nevertheless, Guarino laid himself open to
justifiable misconception by his encomium upon the notorious
Hermaphroditus of Beccadelli, whom he proclaimed "a second
Theocritus."   As a consequence, abuse of Guarino rang in all
pulpits.

Following the example of Barzizza, he took boarders into
his house at Verona, carrying them in the summer heats to his
villa in the neighbouring Valpolicella, of which he had become
possessed through his marriage.   We have many allusions to
his country home.   His children, of whom at least twelve
lived to grow up, did him credit, and were most of them of
like interests with himself.

In 1429 an offer was made to him, which, amidst the
circumstances of his advancing years and family responsibilities,
he did not feel able to refuse.   The Marquis Niccolo d'Este
invited him to Ferrara as preceptor to his son and heir
Leonello.   The stipend was a good one, 350 ducats : and this
was subsequently increased.   Indeed it was perhaps the best
paid post held by a humanist teacher.   In the first instance
he was engaged as instructor to Leonello ; but with liberty,
apparently, as in Vittorino's case, to undertake the education
of other youths of the city.   Later on, when Leonello married
(1435), he acquired a house of his own and took in many
boarders.   In 1436 the number of distinguished scholars drawn
to Ferrara by the opportunities afforded by the d'Este princes
had so far increased that the Municipio took the first step
towards the foundation of a "Studio pubblico," appointing

Guarino civic Professor of Rhetoric. Leonello, now Marquis, organised the school on broad lines[1], and in 1442 obtained for it from the Emperor full rights of a University. Thus the University of Ferrara, so brilliant a centre of humanism, of cultured society, and of fine art, and in particular so bound up with the beginnings of scholarship in our own country, was due directly to the influence and renown of Guarino. As Professor of Rhetoric he lived at Ferrara, working unremittingly until his death, at the age of 86, in the year 1460.

From 1408 until he died the life of Guarino was at once that of a scholar and of a teacher. His was that covetable fortune to experience no divorce, rather the most intimate union, between his strongest and finest interests and his professional occupations. The study of Antiquity, not as yet organised, mapped out, specialised, was his absorbing pursuit. From Homer to Basil, Plautus to Augustine; from the first textual criticism of a MS. to principles of rhetoric or to the geography of the ancient world; from "constructions of place" to the adjustment of pagan and Christian ethics—the entire field of classical civilisation presented itself to Guarino and his contemporaries as one consistent and undifferentiated phenomenon. At the same time his professional work was simply to expound, codify, and impart the results of this research. Hence the perpetual freshness which marked the teaching of one who was not only a student of other men's learning, but an explorer in unvisited fields. That Guarino should compile a tract on orthography, or *de arte Diphthongandi*, was natural. But when he was in the later seventies he plunged—the first modern to attempt it—into the vast problem of ancient geography; at the age of 79 he began to correct and translate the text of Strabo, and finished the work in three years.

The educational aim of Guarino is rightly judged to differ

[1] "Quel fiore di gentilezza e di sapere che fu Lionello d'Este," is the account given of him by authorities most competent to judge. Cp. Luzio-Renier, *Giorn. Stor. d. Lett. Ital.* xiii. 125.

from that of Vittorino in laying more stress upon the training of scholars for professional careers than was characteristic of the Mantuan school. We gain the impression that Guarino's own absorption in scholarship—in a wide sense of the term— determined his views and practice in education. From Ferrara proceeded the scholarly ecclesiastic, or University Professor, the well-equipped orator, the erudite school-master. It was partly, no doubt, a question of social circumstance. Boys of small prospects, relying for their future upon their cleverness and scholarship, were destined for the Church, for teaching, or for subordinate place in chancellery or Curia. Guarino's own sons, for example, became one a professor in succession to himself, another a canon, a third a civilian Secretary, a fourth a practising physician. If he gave smaller place to military or courtly training, it was probably because the school drew fewer boys from the highest social class than that at Mantua. We must notice also the close association of Guarino's teaching with the University organisation, as contrasted with the different and, no doubt, more varied scope which might characterise a Court school in which the Master had an entirely free hand. The environment of the "Giocosa" was more attractive; pre- paration for society more in evidence; and the presence of girls as fellow pupils—of which we hear nothing at Ferrara—is significant. It seems to have been accepted in their own century that with Guarino classical instruction tended to be conceived as the chief end of education, with Vittorino rather as one instrument of a complete training.

The characteristic of the rising humanist schools was their combination of public teaching with a system of boarding and tuition. It was borrowed, no doubt, from the practice of the University and now applied to boys, and as in other ages the privilege, when granted by a careful public body, was taken into account as a set-off against a certain thriftiness of stipend. The three masters of distinction who developed this type of school—Barzizza, Vittorino, and Guarino—were all associated

with Padua, and may be termed the representatives of a Paduan
method of training. Guarino carried the system with him to
Florence, Verona, and finally to Ferrara, just as Vittorino
and his successors practised it at Mantua. The analogy of
the College or hostel of an English University readily suggests
itself, but it must be remembered that the Italian " contuber-
nales," as boarders were called, resembled the resident pupils
of the head-master of a public day-school, or of a professor in
a Faculty, without the continuity or the control which a corporate body secures. The parallel rather is with a " private
Hall" under the statute of 1882 in modern Oxford, or in the
case of Mantua, with the School-house of a public school. In
the same way a large proportion of the students of the University of Paris lived in private halls of the regents or lecturers
in the fifteenth century. Guarino devoted the morning to his
public teaching as professor; but the rest of the day was given
to the tuition of his resident pupils and to research. It was
upon this side of his work that the stimulus of his personal
influence was most keenly felt. "How often," says one of the
boarders, "did we keep at work until midnight; and then,
fired with determination to excel, begin again long before day-
light." This personal force of Guarino, aided by the impulse
afforded by the high recognition of scholarship, eloquence,
and administrative capacity which marked the capital cities of
northern Italy tended to make youth keen. Guarino was
single-eyed in his devotion to work and teaching, and like
Vittorino stood on a different plane to that occupied by the
self-seeking, restless humanist, who was prone to bring learning
into disrepute. Hence the "contubernium" of Guarino included
men of mature years : now distinguished teachers and scholars
like Lamola, or brilliant patricians like Francesco Barbaro, now
youths of fourteen or sixteen years from Hungary or the Rhine.
There is no evidence to show whether William Gray or other
English pupils of Guarino were ever in his "house." No
doubt, with beginners, he followed Barzizza's plan of employing

assistant tutors; and we know that he was the object of the usual complaints that the day-boys received less attention than was due to them.

Barzizza records that he received "40 scudi veneziani" for a pupil's board and tuition for one year; his patrons were wealthy Venetian merchants, who paid readily a fee which we may take as practically equivalent in present value to the inclusive fees of a boarding-house in a great public school. But Barzizza had but a poor official stipend and never seemed able to save money. Guarino, on the contrary, was a careful man; he stipulated for a guaranteed income as Professor of Rhetoric (1436) of 400 "lire di Ferrara," with full right to take boarders, whom he presently accommodated in a house which he bought and adapted for the purpose.

It is impossible to study either the educational treatises or the practical activities of the school-masters of this first age of humanism without recognising the importance of P. P. Vergerius[1] as the true founder of the new education. His tract, *De Ingenuis Moribus et Studiis Liberalibus*, written in or about 1404, had far-reaching influence, notably upon scholars of the Paduan school and upon Florentine humanists, such as Palmieri and Traversari. It is more than probable that Guarino imbibed something of the zeal of Vittorino during their intercourse in Venice, strengthened later by the engagement of the pupil of the latter, Margherita Gonzaga, to Leonello d'Este. We cannot fail to regret the loss of the correspondence which must have passed between these two great teachers. It is not necessary to seek in Giovanni Conversino, Guarino's early master in Latin, any special influence in the moulding of his educational method; and hardly more in G. Barzizza, whose practical capacity lay exclusively in somewhat rudimentary teaching of Latin, and whose absorbing interest lay in textual criticism. He was, moreover, ignorant of Greek.

---

[1] On Vergerius, see p. 8 above, and *Vittorino*, pp. 14 and 93.

Guarino, like Vittorino, was, in a true sense, an original teacher. Together they were the first scholars and masters to conceive and to elaborate a complete scheme of literary education adapted to the modern age. They searched the entire range of antiquity for the finest elements which it offered for a method of training which should fit youth for the Italy of their day. Plato, Aristotle, Roman practice and theory, Patristic authority were all laid under contribution, and a broad concept of education set up in which faith and morals, art, letters, and gymnastics should each find their due place. It is needful to restate the dominant importance of Quintilian in that aspect of education which concerns instruction in Letters.

As regards the physical basis of training in the schools of Guarino it is to be noticed that our knowledge of his practice is confined to the short period (1429–1435) when he was tutor to Leonello. The education of a young prince obviously demanded much attention to out-door exercises; and humanism in its best days did not supersede, but was imposed upon, the courtly training of the noble class. Thus military exercises were essential, not less so riding and hunting—a species of practice for war, as Guarino calls it; swimming and ball-play. The motives, however, show traces of the new atmosphere. Swimming is indeed good for health, but it is, besides, an aesthetic enjoyment, for the swimmer rejoices in the gleam of light upon the blue water; the green banks of the stream, the brilliancy of the sky are grateful or stimulating; moreover, Horatius, who kept the bridge, was a bold swimmer; and Caesar's skill saved his life, just as, let not Leonello forget, Alexander nearly lost his, bathing in the ice-chilled Cydnus. Walking and ball-games have authority in the practice of Scipio or Laelius. Snow-balling, curiously, is commended, Leonello being urged to lead one-half of the pupils against the rest in mimic war. Dancing as an aid to grace of carriage is strongly pressed.

Instruction, however, is the essential factor in Guarino's

training. It falls into three stages : the elementary, the grammatical, and the rhetorical. No limits of age are associated with these groups ; class organisation was barely possible when amongst the beginners in grammar there might be, and often were, grown-up men. Nor is there any specific reference to the age at which regular instruction might take the place of home-teaching of mother or nurse.

The *Elementary* stage opens with Reading, including probably both Latin and Italian. Enunciation and right pronunciation are of great importance. Chrysoloras, following Plutarch, had always urged this, and indeed it is a characteristic of the Latin peoples in contrast with the Teuton, as Milton remarked. "When you read," says Guarino, "do not chew your words, but pronounce them with a clear voice; for this not only aids digestion but serves to impress what you are reading upon the mind." This, no doubt, is taken straight from Pliny. The rudiments of grammar follow, the regular declensions and conjugations coming first. A manual was used, owned probably by only a small proportion of boys; an abridgement, the *Donatus minor*, made in the later Middle Age and called the *Janua*, was Guarino's elementary book.

The stage of Grammar, which has two parallel sides, *Methodice* and *Historice*, follows.

The first, the formal side of Latin teaching, includes the study, gradually completed, of all the inflexions, and in addition the syntax of the verb. For the latter the text-book was the *Regulae Guarini*. This remarkable and widely-used manual, compiled by Guarino on his experience of the relative importance and difficulty of various parts of grammar, is simple in treatment and by no means a systematic or logical survey of the subject. It is drawn up to meet the needs of learners, not to afford an ordered scheme of accidence and syntax. In view of the importance, in any estimate of humanist education, of a right understanding of the place of grammar in instruction, the contents of the *Regulae* deserve attention. The manual began to take shape in his Verona days, if not earlier.

1. The introduction, defining four parts of grammar.
2. Definition of the eight parts of speech.
3. The classes of verbs (active, passive, deponent, transitive and intransitive) ; and the cases (direct and indirect objects) with which a verb may be constructed.
4. Impersonal verbs.
5. Construction of ideas of place.
6. Supines, gerunds and participles—syntax of.
7. "Figurae": prolepsis, syllepsis, zeugma, synthesis, antiptosis, evocatio, appositio, synecdoche—in order ; all regarded grammatically.
8. Patronymics.
9. Forms of the verb : inchoative, iterative, etc.
10. Relative pronouns.
11. Quis and uter and their compounds.
12. Heteroclite nouns in mnemonic verses.
13. The construction of three verbs : solvo, nubo, lateo.

Such a scheme is obviously arbitrary, illustrating the actual method by which Guarino prepared beginners for systematic grammar[1]. It is therefore a mingling of accidence and syntax ; and we are struck both by the selection and the order of the matter. We may compare it with the accidence of Ognibene Leoniceno, referred to in the previous chapter, and with the manual of Erasmus. The *Regulae* are recognised as a distinct advance upon mediaeval grammatical texts by the absence of logical encumbrances. There is little attempt to explain the laws of syntax ; Guarino enunciates them, illustrates them by usage of classical writers and there leaves them. We have an example of Guarino's method which will exemplify this : "In addressing one person," he observes, "you will write 'te oro,' not 'vos oro,' because *one* is singular in number, and *because all Latin authors follow this rule.*" This is the doctrine of Valla and every humanist.

[1] An easier book, *Floriferus Portus*, by Guarino, hitherto undescribed (B. Mus. MSS. Jul. F. 105–117) is compiled on the same principle.

Now the *Regulae* was compiled as an aid to oral exercises in composition, to which Guarino attached high importance. "It is essential," says his son Battista[1], explaining his father's method in his tract, *De Ordine Docendi*, "that every pupil be required to form oral examples in illustration of the chief rules of accidence and syntax, not only with accuracy but with a certain propriety of style, as for instance with due attention to the order of words in sentences and the position of subordinate clauses." We may add the exclusion of barbarisms in vocabulary. It need not be said that Latin is to be spoken in class.

Prosody and metre were also dealt with under this head of *methodice*; the *Doctrinale* of Alexander was relied on, but more stress was laid upon the practice of learning Vergil by heart. There were several pupils at Ferrara who could repeat the whole of Vergil.

For further exercise in prose composition, passages from the *Epistles* of Cicero were taught and committed to memory. The place of the epistolary style, as more popular than the oratorical, is to be noted ; it was even more marked in the schools of the following century. Again, such composition was worked orally with the class, not as a written exercise out of school. All oral compositions were called "Themata"; when extended and elaborated by preparation they were termed "Declamationes." The Thema was little more than a purification and an expansion of the Latin speech exacted from every scholar; the Declamatio was worked out by systematic enrichment and enlargement, the best example of which is seen in a typical school-book of the next century, the *De Copia* of Erasmus. To this stage also belongs the initiation of the pupil into the method of forming rudimentary dictionaries, and orderly collections of "excerpta": extracts from authors and commentators, with illustrative comment. Vocabulary, proper names from mythology, history, and geography, "antiquities,"

---

[1] The Tract of Battista Guarino in *Vittorino*, p. 159.

in the modern editor's use of the term, were thus slowly reduced to index shape for purposes of reference. This had been no doubt an ordinary practice with more advanced learners in mediaeval schools; but under Guarino the pupil was face to face with the author's text, and took his own share in creating his "miscellanea" or systematic note-books, whilst in a pre-humanist school the scholar was inevitably compelled to take down another's compilation, often wholly unintelligible, dictated by the master. Guarino and his contemporaries belonged to an age when each teacher had to create his own apparatus, from text-books of grammar upwards, and rarely found to his hand approved manuals built upon the professional experience of past generations. It was indeed the constant effort of humanist teachers to set aside the mediaeval guides to Latin scholarship or to purge them till they became harmless.

Guarino worked at the formation of a Greek-Latin vocabulary which did not reach completion and which has disappeared. But his abridgement, with a Latin version, of the *Erotemata* of Chrysoloras, was used in all Italian schools of the Revival for beginners in Greek. Upon the place which Greek filled at Ferrara it is enough to quote the statement (1459) of Battista Guarino, who expressly declares that he is but expounding his father's practice: "It is an essential note of an educated man to be familiar with the language and literature of Greece... without a knowledge of Greek, Latin scholarship is in the true sense impossible." But Greek, unlike Latin, was not to be taught as a colloquial language. "Yet I have known not a few pupils of my father who after gaining a thorough mastery of Latin could in a single year make such progress in Greek as to be able to translate with accuracy entire works of ordinary difficulty from that language *at sight*. Now proficiency of this degree can only be attained by careful and systematic teaching of the rudiments of grammar....In using the text-book the greatest attention must be paid to the verb, the regular form, throughout its moods and tenses; followed by the irregular verbs. When the forms of both verb and noun (noun will, of course, include the adjective) can be immediately distinguished and each inflection of voice, mood and tense recognised (and this can only be tested by constant *vivâ voce* exercises) then a beginning should be made with simple narrative prose. At this stage all authors whose subject-matter demands close thought should be avoided, for the entire attention must be concentrated upon the vocabulary and the grammar. Only when some degree of freedom in these latter respects has been secured, should the master introduce books of increased difficulty....The rules of accentuation should now be learnt....It is very important that regular exercises in elementary composition should be required from the first. The scholar will shortly be able to render a Latin author into Greek, a practice which compels us, as nothing else does, to realise the appropriateness of the writer's language and the dignity of his style. For though delicate shades of meaning and beauties of expression may be overlooked by a casual reader, they cannot escape a faithful translator."

Greek and Latin were naturally taught side by side, and in all probability, at Ferrara at least, Greek was read with the predominant motive of serving the study of Latin[1]. One important method may be noted as it was characteristic of the higher type of humanist schools for more than a century afterwards, namely the use made of the *Epistles* of Cicero. "Committed to memory," says Battista, "they serve as one of the finest possible aids to purity, directness, and facility of style, supplying admirable matter in not less admirable form for adaptation to our own uses." So far the methods of formal study of Greek and Latin.

Side by side with *methodice*, Guarino taught *historice* (the terminology is from Quintilian, i. 9), the latter including the

[1] It has been stated in the previous chapter that Greek scholarship in Italy stood on a different footing from Latin: see p. 18 above.

construing both of prose authors, more particularly the historians, and also of the approved poets. This side of classical teaching is concerned primarily with the contents of the authors read. For example, "the historians studied in regular order," will afford the pupil insight into "the manners, laws and institutions of different types of nation," "the varying fortunes of individuals and states, the sources of their success and failure, their strength and their weakness. Not only is such knowledge of interest to the student, but it is of practical value in the ordering of their affairs." Side by side with the study of history careful reading of the poets was undertaken. "The true significance of poetic fiction will now be appreciated. It consists, as Cicero says, in the exhibition of the realities of our own life under the form of imaginary persons and situations." After placing Vergil upon a plane of his own, Statius, Ovid, Seneca, Lucan, Juvenal, Plautus, were put forward as necessary to a full course of Latin reading. Terence, as possessing advantages of a peculiar kind, both as a stylist, as a model for conversational Latin, and as providing us "with a store-house of dignified judgments," was probably, next to the *Letters* of Cicero, the author principally read in humanist schools both in Italy and in Germany. Erasmus, for example, had an even higher opinion of the educational value of Terence than had Guarino. The Greek poets mentioned are first Homer, secondly the dramatists, thirdly the "heroic" poets. But it was characteristic of the humanists of this period to include a much wider range of authors than those of the purely classic epoch, consequently Plutarch, Aristotle, Theocritus, Aulus Gellius, Macrobius and St Augustine, all had their place in the curriculum of Guarino. This is explained by the fact that the use of authors for construing purposes was sharply divided or had two clearly distinguished aims. The first of these was the minute study of small portions of approved writers regarded as models of style. Such portions were learnt by heart and treated as subject-matter for imitation.

Select epistles and orations of Cicero and portions of Ovid were the material principally used at Ferrara for the purposes of exercises in composition.   But the other aim was more liberally conceived in the fifteenth century than at any subsequent time.   Writers practically unheard of in a school or even University course were construed, commented upon and studied as aids to the understanding of classical antiquity.   With Guarino one canon of selection was the moral end which an author might be led to subserve.   Edification, for example, by a process of allegorising pagan myths, or by treating Greek or Roman History upon a method of biographies, or the use of secondary writers such as Valerius Maximus, "so valuable as affording actual illustrations of virtuous precepts (sententiae) couched in attractive style," was a primary motive.   Guarino repeatedly lays stress upon the moral purport of classical study when rightly treated[1].   A second end was that of "eruditio," which included all kinds of knowledge which contributed to the interpretation of an author's meaning and an intelligent understanding of the history, geography and mythology of the ancient world.   Such "eruditio" was a source of temptation to a widely-read scholar when dealing with young pupils whose part in a lesson was too often limited to uninterrupted note-taking.   The "continuous commentary" of the earlier editions of the classics presents such an unbroken stream of undifferentiated knowledge as the humanist teacher delighted in.   Hence the importance attached to the use of the note-book by Guarino and of the practice of working up the dictated material under its appropriate headings with additions derived from the student's own reading.   We have here again the origin of that long series of "Miscellanea," "Adversaria," "Excerpta," dating mostly from a somewhat later period, which represent at least the laborious industry of humanist scholars, and are in certain cases of enduring value.

---

[1] Compare Melanchthon's attitude to classical reading, p. 234 below.

The third stage of classical instruction at Ferrara was after Roman precedent denominated *Rhetorica*. The pupil having now acquired a certain facility in speaking Latin, with a competent knowledge of accidence and syntax and some practice in the elements of composition, concentrated his attention upon Cicero and Quintilian, partly as subjects of study, but mainly as guides to systematic prose composition in its various forms. Whatever traces of mediaeval methods of study may be recognised in the sphere of grammar, the subject of rhetoric took an entirely new form in the humanist school. The *Rhetorica ad Herennium*, regarded as the quintessence of pure Ciceronian doctrine of Oratory, was at Ferrara the starting point and the standing authority. It was supplemented as the pupil advanced by the *De Oratore*, the *Orator*, and the entire range of the speeches. Side by side with works of Cicero stood the *Institutio Oratoria* of Quintilian. No modern manual of rhetoric, such as those of Barzizza or Filelfo, was admitted by Guarino; he himself provided all that was necessary in the way of introduction from his wide knowledge of Roman and Greek oratory. The *De Officiis* and the *Tusculans* of Cicero were read at the same time, the first as a manual of duties, the second as exhibiting a wealth of knowledge most valuable both as to material and expression to every modern writer. The student of eloquence, says Battista, must have his Cicero constantly in his hand; the simplicity, the lofty moral standard, the practical temper of his writings render them peculiarly fine training for a public speaker. Plato and Aristotle were also prescribed chiefly as aids to the understanding of ancient ethical standards, and, as regards Plato, as a guide to the "proper understanding of Cicero, whose dialogues, in form and in matter, seem to be modelled upon the Greek philosopher." All this obviously implies a somewhat cursory reading of the Greek writers. The importance attached by the humanists to the subject of prose composition will be touched upon in a later chapter. It will be enough here, therefore, to indicate certain methods which characterise Guarino's teaching of rhetoric, premising that Guarino accepted *ex animo* the definition of an orator as "vir bonus peritus dicendi," in whom the quality of sincerity is the crucial virtue. The practice of composition in Latin, by the way of translation from the Greek, was regarded as the most efficient way of acquiring a good Latin style. We do not hear of exercises involving versions from the Italian vernacular, but themes for declamation were set upon subjects of present-day interest as well as others drawn from antiquity. A characteristic feature was the rhetorical analysis and criticism of the poets, notably Vergil, Terence and Lucan, the latter of whom was regarded, following Quintilian, rather as the model for the rhetorician than for the poet. The grave question of the permissibility of metric passages in prose-writing was debated in this connection. The epistolary style was early recognised as important from its more practical application to daily life. Pliny, as well as Cicero, was taken as a model. Guarino himself was an indefatigable correspondent; and if his style is prolix and often far from Ciceronian yet the contents of his letters are of more interest, because of more reality, than the majority of similar productions of his contemporaries.

Such was briefly the organic scheme of literary training adapted by Guarino from the practice of the Imperial age as elaborated by Quintilian, who emphasises the three stages of grammar, composition, construing and philosophy. It was a curriculum in which the method of the school passed insensibly into that of the University. Probably the chief differences which are to be detected as between it and the instruction of Vittorino consist in the higher relative importance attached at Mantua to the teaching of mathematics, of music and of Greek.

The interest taken by Guarino in biblical learning and in religious subjects should not be overlooked. He lectured on the *De Civitate Dei*, the works of Basil, of Jerome and of Cyprian. His personal faith and his devout temper reveal themselves in his letters and in the repute in which he was held by his pupils. We may doubt whether, in respect of direct influence upon his pupil, Leonello, he had the same success that Vittorino attained with his Gonzaga boys. His nature was hardly of that peculiarly loveable type which so endeared all who came under him to Vittorino. There was little that was mystic about Guarino, as we may perhaps judge from his portrait medal by Matteo da Pasti[1], and less, perhaps, that was ascetic. But he was a thoroughly sincere and devoted teacher, a scholar single-eyed and enthusiastic.

[1] See the medal reproduced in Fabriczy, pl. xi.

CHAPTER III.

LEO BATTISTA ALBERTI AND *LA CURA DELLA FAMIGLIA*.

It is at once the attraction and the difficulty of the historical study of Education that the subject can only be rightly understood as an aspect of the social and intellectual conditions of a given age. To isolate the questions which revolve round Universities and schools, their aims, curricula and organisation, from their inevitable dependence upon the historical environment, and from the interests, intellectual and spiritual, which occupied contemporary men, is to deprive the educational facts themselves of the clue to their meaning. It is, therefore, not seldom the surest way to a just insight into educational development to pass by the man actually absorbed in schools or in the doctrine of teaching in favour of another identified rather with the fuller currents of the life and work of the community. To do this is to safeguard ourselves against that exaggeration which is the invariable risk attendant upon isolating social phenomena, and viewing them solely in the proportions accorded to them by specialists,—in this case the famous school-master or the "educational reformer." Moreover, such enquiry brings the student into contact with great personalities like L. B. Alberti, with minds of the first order like Francis Bacon, with scholarly men of the world, as Castiglione, Elyot or Montaigne.

It is upon this ground that it is instructive to supplement what has been written in the previous chapters upon the work of a famous school-master and an enthusiastic scholar by a brief study of typical representatives of such a community as Florence during the same period. In illustration of what has just been said it is undoubtedly necessary to a full understanding of what follows that the student should, by other reading, catch the atmosphere of the Florentine life and polity during the early decades of the fifteenth century. Leo Battista Alberti[1] (1404–1472) belonged to a family which exemplified conspicuously the wealth, culture and receptivity of a great Florentine house at the period when the Middle Age was yielding to the influences of the new time. He was born in exile at Genoa in 1404, and for the first twenty-four years his life was of a migratory sort, his father passing from place to place, conducting the great international commerce of the firm, now from Genoa, now from Venice, now from Bologna, but never from its original seat upon the Arno. The house had dealings with and representatives in London, Paris, Bruges, Cologne, Barcelona, the Aegean, Barbary and Syria. But whatever their domicile, or the sources of their wealth, the Alberti were always, and above all things, Florentines.

Leo Battista, from his boyhood, was marked by a persistent curiosity and a corresponding acuteness of observation, which extended to natural objects and to human and social phenomena alike. Like all the typical men of the Renaissance he possessed great strength of will: "gli uomini possono tutto quando lo vogliono," was a favourite motto with him. Hence the changeful life of exile, with its moving panorama of character and circumstance, its urgent calls upon self-reliance, its compulsory re-adjustments of opinion, tended to force the growth

---

[1] The best biography is that of Mancini, Florence, 1882. Voigt's chapter and the section in Gaspary are both admirable. In treating of so many-sided a man it has been essential to limit discussion to Alberti's views on education. The edition of his works by Bonucci is the only one which professes to be complete.

Gerini and Rösler are useful aids: see bibliographical list, infra.

of personality in such a nature as Alberti's.   Amid this
strenuous life was born that contempt of idleness, that conviction of the duty of work, that passion for creativeness which
made him the superlative example of the Tuscan men of the
Renaissance.   Further, this enforced aloofness from political
responsibility brought its consequences first in strengthening in
him that concept of the place of the family which was so
essential a mark of Florentine and indeed of Tuscan life, and
next in giving free play to the impulse to individuality, to
virtù, to the complete self, characteristic of the Renaissance
throughout Italy.   Upon such a nature the classical literatures
were bound to react with special force.   The boy learnt both
Latin and Greek, probably at Venice in and after 1414,
devouring what he read rather for its content than for any
interest of the linguistic kind.   Mathematics particularly attracted him.   The son of a distinguished musician he learnt
early to play upon several instruments ; throughout his life
music had a profound effect upon him.   Alberti had the Greek
feeling for rhythm as a law of all truly balanced action and of
right aesthetic emotion.   Like the youth of Greece and Rome
he gained much in character and in intelligence, from habitual
intercourse with his elders.   Although a fine Latinist, and not
averse to writing in Latin, he was a strenuous upholder of
the dignity of the Tuscan tongue, and from his childhood had
been practised in its careful use.   Later in his life the more
rigid humanists fell foul of him on this score, when he decried
the " mystery " of learning, fostered ostentatiously by the use
of a learned language ; for he held that wisdom should be
brought forth from laboratory or cabinet with full hands and
strewn along the open highways of life for all to gather as they
should be able.   The proficiency of the young Alberti in all
games of skill and bodily powers must be dwelt upon.   It was
not merely that it was his aim to do all things well ; but in the
grace of a free, supple carriage of the body he saw both perfect
harmony of form and physical powers exquisitely balanced.

Right culture of the body then was an integral factor in the full development of personality.

It is easily intelligible that when, at the threshold of manhood, he was called upon by his relatives, his father being now dead, to make summary choice between obedience to his eager passion for enquiry and a commercial career, he should unhesitatingly decide for learning. He was at Bologna, in 1424, when the ultimatum from the firm reached him, and he recognised that he was choosing a life of uncertainty and of probable privation. At this time the study of Civil Law mainly engaged him, but he was writing a Latin play which for many years was accepted as a recovery from lost antiquity. Soon after, brought to abject poverty, he was taken into the service of Cardinal Albergati, whom he accompanied to Paris. This led to his appointment to a post in the Vatican, the destiny of many of the younger scholars of the time, where he was fortunate to find, a little later, a patron in the friend of his student days, Thomas of Sarzana, Pope Nicholas V. Meantime the Alberti had (1428) been permitted to return to Florence, and then Leo Battista saw the home of his race for the first time. In Rome he became absorbed in the study of the architectural monuments of the city and the Campagna. Somewhere about 1432–3 he sketched there the outline of the work which chiefly concerns us in this chapter, the *Trattato della Cura della Famiglia*, in which he depicts his ideal of the social life of a Tuscan home and community and the preparation fitting for it. Florence, which, exile though he was, he knew intimately, was to him the ideal community, the Tuscan country life the perfection of wholesome stimulating environment for human activities. It would be difficult to point to one predominant interest in Alberti, so many-sided was his genius. The career of politics perhaps appealed least to him. As a result of his official connection with the Roman Curia he had taken Orders, but he in no way identified himself with clerical duties, devoting himself to art, architecture, mathematics and literature. He illustrated in his own career the principle which he invariably taught: that a man must press towards the best, in character, in intellectual acquisition, in practical achievement. "I have ever preferred true knowledge, noble studies, the lofty interests of the mind to all the worldly advantages that wealth can offer," he says, as one to whom the choice came not once only in life. No man, even in that age of marvellous personalities, surpassed him in energy and productiveness. Although perhaps best known for his genius in architecture, to which his work in Florence, Rimini and Mantua still testifies, Alberti, as a scientific enquirer, a mathematician, a writer of Italian prose, a classical scholar, a man of remarkable physical accomplishments, left the impress of his strength upon all competent to judge, a veritable "Master of those who know." He died at the height of his powers, a man of 68, in the year 1472.

The ideal of a sound education, fitted for a Tuscan of the fifteenth century, which we can draw out from the writings of Alberti, has the merit of actuality. He takes the civilisation of his time and the social order of his own country as he knows them; and he directs all that he has to say to the solution of a problem that he perfectly understands. "None of the men of the fifteenth century who have left us their formal treatises upon education gave to their theme the breadth and the touch of reality which we recognise in all that Alberti says upon the subject," says his biographer[1]. It is evident throughout the *Trattato* that he has a consistent view both of the social environment through and for which the training of youth is to be devised, and of the moral and psychological conditions which are involved. This gives a precision to what he writes which is sorely to seek in the ideal programmes for educating somewhat unreal children for an imaginary civilisation under more or less impossible conditions, with which philosophers or

[1] Mancini, p. 245.

scholars have presented the world ever since the days of Plato, and which were never more common than in the age of the Renaissance.

Alberti then took the Family, its life, its common interests, its continuity, its sanctions to self-denial, its scope for corporate and personal fame, as the *milieu* within which personality could be most fitly developed, and as the end to which each member of it must devote all that he is and has. Yet suppression of the individual is not demanded. For the personality of the individual is the adornment of the family. The fuller, the wider his individual gifts, the greater the service rendered by the son of the house to the unit of which he is a part. In the same way the special excellence of the family—its distinction, its peculiar genius—is the contribution which that family makes to the State or City. The pressure of one accepted or uniform mould upon either individual or *gens* had long been repudiated by the Florentine temper. It has been remarked that the Florence of 1400 was one of the rare cities in which fashion in dress was deliberately ignored; people wore what suited them[1]. The family, in the mind of Alberti and some other Florentines, is a more important unit than the State. It rests on Nature, on the tie of blood, and ideally upon affection, whereas the State, the union of families, is founded on advantage, for mutual defence and profit; or is the result of conquest, and its organisation an artificial device. The educative force of the home therefore is more intimate and more far-reaching than that of the State, in so far as the sense of common kinship and its mutual responsibility is in the smaller area more keenly present. Therefore, Alberti sets out to consider in what manner the family may be securely established, may increase in dignity and importance, by what arts it may attain prosperity; how it may win and retain friendly regard, by what steps it may secure present honour and

[1] Burckhardt, *Renaissance*, p. 369.

historical renown. He does not limit his view merely to the actual household of parents and children, but he is thinking also of the wider *gens*, the fellowship of blood-kindred, united in name, in territorial interests, or in a great house of commerce. The political and social condition of Florence in the fourteenth century, and within Alberti's own experience, is evidence enough that no subject could have been more real, more timely, than that of the causes of the rise and decadence of families, and the obligations of their members to a community built up on an aggregation of great houses, in an age when vengeance, faction, personal jealousies, or the ambition of a dominant clan could upset the entire social order and imperil the security of every citizen. There was indeed hardly a City State in northern Italy where this same problem was not either latent or active. It is not difficult to see the influence of his own experience as a member of a family exiled for party reasons, and the impression left upon him by the example and instruction of his distinguished father, Lorenzo, and his uncle, Antonio, in the treatment of his subject.

The enquiry to which Alberti thus addresses himself has naturally a broader scope than that of the actual upbringing of the children of the house. Important sections deal with the relations of its members to each other, friendship between families, the economy of the house and estates, the position of the father and the wife, but hardly any part of it is without its bearing upon the preparation which is to fit youth to take its due place in the home and the community.

As regards the underlying conditions, moral and psychological, of a boy's training, we shall not look for a systematic analysis in an age when the true Aristotle was still unknown and mental phenomena were interpreted in terms of scholastic theology. Alberti, indeed, like all Italian humanists, was averse to psychology, and accepted the current empirical doctrine. The dominant note is that action, not contemplation, nor speculation, is the normal end of human life ; all qualities and gifts are to be viewed as they further or hinder the fulfilment of this function. Not that the studious or religious life is to be decried, but either of these is incomplete if divorced from a definitely apprehended aim of contribution to the social good. To live for personal security in another life may be justifiable, but the duty of improving the conditions of the life we have to live *here* admits of no doubt whatever; and if the two conflict the latter is the more Christian aim. Let our end be to pursue justice—the prime social virtue—in every relation of life, then shall we be attuned alike to the duty that we owe to our fellows, and to that which we owe to our own individual excellence: "thus shall we accomplish that which is due to the Divine Power, to the community, and to the character and inner freedom which is our own true self." Yet where fortune is so determinedly hostile that a man is debarred alike from family and from country, then the individual, "padrone di se," self-reliant, self-contained, finding complete satisfaction in letters and in art, reveals himself as master even of Fortune. The theme of one of Alberti's latest works is that the highest kingship consists in the absolute control which a man possesses over the development of the entire inner life.

Human nature, as divinely created, is endowed with heavenly and with earthly attributes; in its outward form "it is the noblest and most graceful of all living things." The body as the instrument of the celestial part of us must, by all right means, be kept in health, in comeliness, in skilled aptitude, that through it a man may render most complete and prolonged service to his country, his family and himself. The maimed and unhealthy life is of necessity unequal to such due service. There is here, as with all Italian humanists, an avowed hostility to the doctrine of the worthlessness of the body and to the ascetic view of life consequent upon it. The mind, whose prime virtue is restless curiosity, with the corresponding capacity for absorbing truth, is the differentiating mark of man. For while men have in common with brutes the instincts which lead to the preservation of their kind, they alone possess the desire and the faculty for searching into "the causes of things," and for recognising action as morally good or bad. Hence the gift of intellect—curiosity, judgment, reason—involves the duty of so framing our lives as to bring these powers into most fruitful play. That this can be done is self-evident, for our will-power is equal to our real desire: *volere e potere* are only two sides of the same thing. This complete acceptance of the principle of free-will is again characteristic of the man of the Renaissance.

The goodness of human nature, its spontaneous "aptitude for reason" in conduct, as Erasmus called it, its instinctive upward look, its faith in illimitable progress, falls within the circle of Italian spiritual ideas, supported undoubtedly by classical authority. This view was, naturally enough, fiercely contested by those who regarded education from the doctrinal stand-point of the Church. The Florentine Dominican, Giovanni Dominici, in his work on the education of the home, had lately raised his voice against that tampering with the truth of the Fall of Man which he rightly perceived to accompany the new passion for classical study. There will be occasion in subsequent chapters to consider the relation between the view of the humanist and that of the rigid churchman, whether Catholic or Protestant, in regard to human nature. But it can be said of Alberti, without hesitation, that he was a most sincere believer. He differed from Carlo Marsuppini, Valla, Beccadelli, and such scholars as took just so much of Christianity as could be approved from the best moralists of antiquity. He had much in common with Dominici. But conscious of his own extraordinary powers of self-development, aware of the far-reaching force of personality in the Italy of his day, he could not doubt that the individual will had well-nigh unlimited capacity for good as well as for evil. His moral analysis, like that of all Italian humanists, was not very profound. By nature he was averse to speculative theology and to mysticism.

The contemplation of death and judgment, of sin, of the inherent conflict between God and the World, were not the dominant notes of his spiritual outlook. Probably, like many of his contemporaries, he had reached no clear reconciliation of the old faith and the revived learning, but he felt no great concern about it. The end to which the moral nature of man naturally turned was "il bene e beate vivere"—the inner harmony of a life of conscious integrity and devotion to *virtù*. Spiritual perfection, as Alberti understood it, and as he declares, is not something apart from such harmonious living ; nay, rather religious worship ought to be its entrancing expression. It is quickly proved that we have not attained to this art "bene et beate vivendi," if we obey our lower appetites, and wilfully ignore the claim laid upon us by our place in the social order. The highest good is to be one's self, but it must be the best, the highest attainable, self. The man who indulges the body, the man also who is indifferent to it, sin, both of them, against this true harmony, for each by his own fault *is* less, and achieves less, than the best possible to him. Strength, obeying the laws of rhythm and of proportion, was Alberti's moral ideal. With him the ultimate concepts of the moral life, of music, and of architecture were expressible in identical forms. "A singular and most intense pleasure affected him," says an ancient biographer who knew him, "when he came into the presence of remarkable beauty. An old man, of venerable aspect, vigorous and active under his years, had marvellous attraction for him. The genius or skilled craftsmanship of the artist, the curves and distances of landscape, the light and colour of gem or flower— in their beauty he saw something of the divine nature itself. To look upon the smiling face of the land would not seldom cure him of a malady." Certainly, in such a mood he passed beyond the precepts of the militant Dominicans, though hardly, perhaps, beyond the heart of St Francis. We must not forget that Ambrogio Traversari, the devoted friend of Vittorino, was as closely attached to Alberti, who was pressed by those who

knew them both to write the life of the distinguished Camal-
dolese scholar as the man most in sympathy with his spirit.

Turning now to his work, *Della Cura della Famiglia*, we
may discern as its initial thought that the well-being of the
house is dependent directly upon the character and ability of its
head. Just as other writers conceived their educational ideal
under the form of preparation for the Citizen, the Scholar, the
Courtier, the Orator, the Prince, the Governor, so Alberti,
strictly practical, and regarding society as he knew it, sketches
the outline of the right training of the head of a Florentine
family. He throws into the shape of a Dialogue, in which
various members of the Alberti take a part, his views upon the
conditions which make for the security of the house. The
first of the four books discusses "the duty of the elders towards
the children and of the children towards their elders, and the
principles of the proper up-bringing of the young." The second
book treats of the married life, and its basis in true affection ;
of family unity, and of the conditions which advance its common welfare. In the third he considers the circumstances
under which its wealth, estate and household may be best
administered ; and in the fourth the mutual relations of
families and their heads in their several interests, and as
affecting the stability of the State.

In complete accord with the sentiment of his time he lays
it down that the patriarchal powers of the father and husband
are at the root of the stability of the family. "Never," says
the chief speaker, "would I allow my wife to regard me as
other than the master." "It was ever a mark of honesty in a
woman to keep silence in the society of men, and to listen ; of
lightness and frivolity, to be talkative or gad-about, to put
amusement before home duties." This subordination he bases
upon considerations of physique and temperament, for woman is
by nature passive, shrinking, gentle and unstable. The difference between this view and that of the more developed
Renaissance is conspicuous.

The model of the parent-educator is Cato the Censor who spared no pains to teach his son letters as well as bodily accomplishments. So must the Tuscan father accept the same duty. He may not plead absorption in business as excuse, for what affairs are of more urgency than this? The stimulus which inheres in this home discipline with its background of tradition and example, in the unvarying manifestation of affection, trust and hope for the children, is the supreme influence in forming character. For in the home are planted the roots, and round it are grouped the ideals, of the serious life. The moral and spiritual qualities which chiefly appeal to Alberti in education are, first, religious feeling, expressed in a sense of personal allegiance to the Divine will, which is in actual fact identical with regard for the common welfare, and with self-respect; superstition is the opposite of real belief, and is baneful to the play of free intelligence. Such an analysis of the religious sanction would not satisfy either the ardent Churchman or such Protestant humanists as Cordier and Melanchthon. Truthfulness comes next; then self-control, especially in respect of anger, appetite, and, above all, the taste for gambling, than which no fault is more undermining. In the delicate problem of moral guidance the father will remember the need of tact in handling early or slight offences, and above all, will abstain from an attitude of self-righteousness and moral hypocrisy.

The father, careful in observing the temper and bent of mind of his sons, will be warranted in forecasting betimes the nature of their careers. Speech, look, gesture, quickly reveal the man; good signs are aversion to idleness, zeal to carry through what we begin, frankness, absence of obstinacy, readiness to forgive. A boy may fall short of the highest promise and yet be worthy of a career *virile ed onorato*; if below this middle standard let him be trained for the ordinary business routine. This habit of close sympathetic observation of growing capacity is a prime duty of both parents, and necessarily implies home education;

and following on that the obligation of giving to every promising intelligence its best chance.   As the son reaches manhood he takes upon himself the responsibility for his own highest development.

The purport of education is defined as the improvement of the native capacity thus recognised by discipline, by the setting forth of a high standard of duty and interest in the home, re-inforced by the study of arts and letters.   Mere precept is of no avail in forming personality.   The home influence, exerted mainly by the mother in the early years, is seconded in due course by the work of the Tutor, who shall be treated as one of the household, deservedly trusted by the parents; in the tutor the note of character is of even more import than that of learning.   The country house and not the palazzo in the City is the proper background for the training of youth.   For there the foundations of health and bodily vigour can be best secured; "temperantia," in its truest sense, be inculcated and practised. The boy is inured to fatigue, acquires out-door interests, a love of nature, learns exercises of agility, endurance and skill, and developes the practical instincts, the use of hand and finger, without interference with systematic study or with social gifts. In all training no end may be preferred to that of physical soundness.   It is the condition of moral health as well as of intellectual progress and social usefulness.   Games, therefore, should be alternated with mental work, but only such as involve activity.   Ball-play, and other games which require dexterity, endurance, strength, qualities of eye and nerve, such as fencing, leaping, riding and swimming, naturally have their place in the country life.   The tourney is not advised; it is dangerous and merely ostentatious.   Yet we must not pursue even approved exercises as though prowess in them alone were a token of serious distinction.   They are, first, an instrument towards personal efficiency, and, secondly, the graceful complement of higher gifts.   A one-sided excellence in physical accomplishments calls attention to the lack of finer qualities.

Alberti rejects the idea common in a commercial State that writing and figures are sufficient equipment for practical life, although, with reading, these form the first steps in instruction. The argument for the place of wider and nobler studies in training for a practical career is not that they have an immediate value as useful acquisitions. But starting from the principle of the innate force of curiosity as a divine gift, he holds that by suitable instruction this quality will find attractive material in arts, sciences and letters, which will thus become an object of spontaneous interest when the stage of pupilage is past. Hence one important reason why a boy should be brought, under skilled guidance, to understand and delight in history, to appreciate poetry, and become familiar with noble thoughts and deeds. No exertion has fuller reward than that by which we acquire intimate knowledge of what has been thought and achieved in time past. Letters also stand in harmony with gentle manners ; they dignify the mind, and add grace and weight to personality. The difference between an educated man and one ignorant of the past is as between a developed adult and a child. A man, therefore, imbued with the spirit of enquiry, and trained to seek the fullest sources whereby to satisfy it, is a more efficient citizen in that he is a more developed person. "Letters can never be a hindrance, but are in the result a distinct source of strength to all who follow any profession whatsoever." Alberti thus reiterates the fine humanist doctrine of the function of studies.

After a boy has learnt to read and write with ease, and has been initiated into arithmetic and the first exercises in geometry, he will enter upon Latin grammar. There is no attempt, in Alberti's programme, to treat the child as though he had been born in ancient Rome and to make him talk Latin in the nursery. The vernacular was the only language spoken in the home. In choice of books and authors it is necessary to limit the youth to the best. In grammar, Priscian and Servius are named as far preferable to the mediaevalists.   Amongst Roman writers of prose, Cicero, Livy and Sallust are placed first.   In diction as in rhythmic force, nothing excels the poetry of Homer and Vergil, and the flow of eloquence, the musical lilt, of Demosthenes is to Alberti a source of exquisite pleasure.   Xenophon, to whose book on the *Control of the Household and the Estate* Alberti was much indebted, is the third Greek author recommended.   But as he is not a professed scholar or teacher he says nothing about procedure, except that he forbids the tutor to rely upon mere selections, in which the drift and meaning of the author are wholly lost.   He lays down one common-sense instruction, that the master avoid difficult, and above all, uninteresting matter, but choose authors readily intelligible, likely therefore to remain in the memory, and when possible such as may suggest application to the present day.

But study of books alone is not a sufficient method of education.   Boys should be encouraged to mingle with those older than themselves, especially with young men just entering upon the world of affairs.   They will thus imbibe seriousness of purpose, and ambition of usefulness and fame; they will be led on to attack difficulties, spurred by the praise or reproach of those to whom they look up.   So important is the function of conversation in social life that a young man must be trained to bear himself modestly but confidently in discussion, and on this ground again it is well to accustom him to intercourse with others besides those of his own age.

As regards the "sciences," mathematics, astronomy and music, Alberti says little; but we must remember that these all came within the circle of humanist studies, the fit objects of noble curiosity.   The development and applications of arithmetic and geometry were actively advancing during this period. Arabic numerals had been introduced into Florence by Leone Fibonacci, rendering progress in arithmetic possible.   Houses of commerce adopted the new methods of calculation, and to satisfy demand a new type of school, the *Scuola d'abaco*, in which arithmetic, Euclid and elementary algebra were the staple subjects, sprang up in Florence and attracted very large numbers of pupils. Thus arithmetic was a substantial subject in Alberti's scheme. After geometry came astronomy, which covered physics, geography and meteorology, the latter two specially from the commercial point of view. Alberti was much interested in geography, as became the ardent friend of Toscanelli. Indeed, we may infer that his predominant interest lay in the mathematical sciences and the arts into which they entered. His specific allusions to the education of the aesthetic faculty in the young are unimportant. But it has been shown that the sense of beauty and of its significance coloured his whole view of life. Music was to him symbolic of all that makes for harmonious development; and in a remarkable passage he advises builders to determine the correctness of proportion by obeying the laws of rhythm as expressed in music. The educational value of fine arts, notably of painting, for men and women, he often affirms.

In this view of the training of youth to bear its part in the Florence of the new age, there is, at first sight, perhaps little that is original. But we should remember that the *Trattato della Cura della Famiglia* dates from 1431, when very little indeed had been written upon the education demanded by the growing interest in classical enquiry. Alberti writes as a man concerned with the practical side of life, and with the social welfare of his city. He is not a professed scholar, still less a school-master. He occupies rather the position of the cultivated observant citizen who points out what the community looks for from education. He records his conviction that simplicity of life, respect for parental authority, devotion to public duty, are compatible with, and are adorned by, the antique wisdom. That the new age owes much already, and will owe much more, to the restored knowledge of Greece and Rome he confidently declares; and he is not affected by the conflict of moral ideals. Florentine self-assertion, he well knew, had long been a vigorous growth enough, and had little to learn from ancient precedents.

In fine, the attitude of Alberti towards the classical past was thoroughly individual. He absorbed and assimilated, and then reproduced what he learnt in forms fit for the life of his own world, which he knew at first hand, which he desired to forward, amend and establish. Consider his relation to the use of the Italian tongue. Deeply as he lamented the loss of the great common speech of civilisation, he upholds Tuscan as, for Italians, a not unworthy substitute for Latin. The prejudice against it is an absurdity. Everyone uses it, everyone understands it; it may well attain an authority analogous to that of Latin if learned men will devote pains to its elaboration and enrichment from the ancient speech. The plea of Alberti had the approval of not a few of the humanists of his day, such as Cristoforo Landino, who regarded him as one of the chief furtherers of the Italian tongue. And this is typical of Alberti, for neither in social or political ideals, in art, or in learning, was he ever a mere imitator. Rather is he a representative of the freer, the originative stage of the Renaissance, when it was still possible for the man of Letters to keep the right sense of proportion between the old and the new, and to conceive of progress as something more than a struggle to reproduce the historic past.

CHAPTER IV.

MATTEO PALMIERI.

1406–1475.

MATTEO PALMIERI[1], a contemporary and friend of Alberti, and intimate with the same group of Florentine burghers, merchants, scholars and artists, has left in his work, *Della Vita Civile*, the judgment of an Italian citizen of position upon the training of youth. Born in Florence in 1406, of a well-to-do family immersed in politics and in business, he learnt Latin and the liberal arts under three distinguished humanists, Carlo Marsuppini, Sozomeno and Traversari. The accounts of his life show Palmieri in close relations with the Guicciardini, the Capponi, the Alessandri and other families of distinction in letters and in politics. Already in 1432 he had taken public office, and he married in the following year. He was prominent in the movement for the recall of Cosimo de' Medici in 1434; and as a friend of that powerful house was thenceforward constantly engaged in public duties, filling nearly every official post of distinction. A notable event in his career was the embassy to Alfonso, King of Naples, in 1455, when he was charged with the mission of exchanging ratifications of a treaty lately concluded between Florence and the Kingdom. Palmieri addressed the royal Court in Latin, Spanish and Italian, and by his combination of scholarship and skill in affairs so impressed Alfonso that he exclaimed: "What must

---

[1] For authorities see under *Bassi, Messeri*, in list of writers. Evidence of his repute amongst men of letters is afforded by the choice of Palmier to deliver the funeral oration upon Carlo Marsuppini in April, 1453.

the Medici be, if this be but a simple citizen-trader of Florence!" Again, as representative of his city, he negotiated with Sixtus IV. (1473) a league for the defence of Italy. It is characteristic of the Florence of the great Age that Palmieri, merchant and diplomatist, should be the friend of such an artist as Botticelli, should write a history of his native city, a treatise on citizenship, and a religious poem of a quasi-platonist sort, dull but "suspect" as to its orthodoxy. Just at the time when his friend Alberti was busy upon the *Cura della Famiglia* Palmieri was planning his dialogue, very similar in form and scope, introducing the same Agnolo Pandolfini, the typical figure of the dignified Florentine citizen, upon the "method of ruling the household and the state," or, as the title ran when the work was printed in later years, *La Vita Civile*[1]. The date when it was first put into circulation may be fixed between 1435 and 1440. The scene of the dialogue is laid at a country house in the Mugello, an Apennine valley north of Florence, during the plague of 1430. The theme is propounded "in what consist the virtues to be desired in the perfect citizen?" and is discussed in four books, the first of which treats of the training of the child up to the threshold of manhood.

Palmieri occupies ground very similar to that adopted by Alberti. The scholarly man of affairs is his ideal. He aims at exhibiting the education and activities of a serious citizen of an Italian city, and not those of an imaginary State without centre in time or space. His humanist feeling is remarkably expressed. Pandolfini asks why progress in knowledge and culture has been for so long halting and uncertain. Why but that men have been disposed to rest satisfied with what has been handed down from the generation before them, careless of possible advance in wisdom or in arts? "Thus the noble achievements of our far-off ancestors (i.e. the men of ancient

---

[1] The first edition is dated 1529; from this the quotations in the text are cited.

Rome) are forgotten, and have become impossible to modern men. Where was the painter's art till Giotto tardily restored it? A caricature of the art of human dilineation! Sculpture and architecture, for long years sunk to the merest travesty of art, are only to-day in process of rescue from obscurity; only now are they being brought to a new pitch of perfection by men of genius and erudition. Of Letters and liberal studies at large it were best to be silent altogether. For these, the real guides to distinction in all the arts, the solid foundation of all civilisation, have been lost to mankind for 800 years and more. It is but in our own day that men dare boast that they see the dawn of better things. For example, we owe it to our Lionardo Bruni that Latin, so long a bye-word for its uncouthness, has begun to shine forth in its ancient purity, its beauty, its majestic rhythm. Now, indeed, may every thoughtful spirit thank God that it has been permitted to him to be born in this new age, so full of hope and promise, which already rejoices in a greater array of nobly-gifted souls than the world has seen in the thousand years that have preceded it. If but our distressed land enjoy assured peace, most certainly shall we garner the fruits of the seed now being sown. Then shall we see these errors, deep-seated and long reputed, which have perverted every branch of knowledge, surely rooted out. For the books which an age of darkness puts forth into the world are themselves—how otherwise?—dark and obscure, and in their turn darken all learning by their subtleties and confusion....But I see the day coming when all philosophy and wisdom and all arts shall be drunk from the pure fountain head—the great intelligences of old....By way of illustration, it is not so long ago that a man would spend a large portion of his working life in the intricacies of Latin grammar. Inferior masters, teaching from perverse manuals, mingled grammar with philosophy, with logic, with heterogeneous learning, reducing it to an absurdity. But now we rejoice in seeing our youth entering on the study of Latin by such order and method that in a year or two they come to speak and write that language with a fluency and correctness which it was impossible that our fathers could ever attain to at all[1]."

Such is Palmieri's confident hope for the future of learning and for human progress through learning; typical indeed of this passionately sanguine era of the Revival.

We perceive the same spirit in another, and even more, instructive utterance. "Men," he declares, "fail to realise the true end of art and knowledge, which is the satisfaction—a thing of exquisite pleasure—of the desire to know and to understand Truth for its own sake: whereas the common view is that men should pursue Art and Wisdom for personal advantage or repute[2]." The eager spirit of the Florentine Renaissance here proclaims self-development as a sufficient end. Yet the reconciliation of this motive with the social aim is readily seen. His Christian spirit is undoubted: it is even more clearly manifested than with Alberti. Cicero and St Jerome stand together in his judgment upon the same pinnacle. With unconscious humour he regrets that his great master of vernacular prose—he means Boccaccio—had not chosen to write rather in the vein of the great Churchman. The collocation of the Roman orator and the father of Biblical study is a mode of claiming the reconciliation of antiquity and the Church in the genuine humanist manner. Palmieri, indeed, partly on account of the frequency of his reference to the future life, is recognised with Vittorino and Traversari as a typical example of the "believing scholar."

The first book of the dialogue *Della Vita Civile* treats of education, intellectual and physical, up to manhood. In the second and third books Palmieri expounds the moral life, showing how the good citizen exhibits "onestà," or justice, as he often calls it, in all relations of life. In the fourth the interaction of the "useful" and the "virtuous," i.e. of the

[1] *Della Vita Civile*, pp. 27, 28.
[2] *Ib.* p. 29.

motives to social well-doing and to individual perfection, is set
out.   Dante[1], Petrarch, as well as the Greek and Roman
moralists have been avowedly laid under contribution, but the
Greek writers are known only at second-hand, and superficially.
Certain treatises of Cicero, of Xenophon, and of Plutarch,
with an incomplete Quintilian, are all that he seems to have
read from classical prose.

Upon the ultimate educational aim he states the following
conclusion.   There is no human activity nobler than that
which has for its aim to secure the safety and prosperity of the
community, and to unite in mutual trust all classes of its
citizens.   He reviews the various forms of excellence characteristic of man, and enquires in what way each conforms to
the cardinal virtues of Prudence, Courage, Temperance and
Justice.   The claims of the "religious" as against the secular
life are thus disposed of.   The solitary life—the life which has
no concern for outside responsibilities—is essentially lower
than the civil life—the life of conscious citizenship.   "Undoubtedly some men are called to find their happiness in this
way by devoting themselves to the contemplation of heavenly
wisdom"; but it is with regret that he speaks of talents
imperilled by a life of lonely ease, removed from all public
activity, discharged of duties to the social life of mankind, and
intent upon personal salvation.   No one knew better than
Palmieri how great a peril to the independence and the
freedom of a small Italian state lay in the indifference of
leading citizens to public responsibilities, whether from absorption in money-getting, from cultured exclusiveness, or from
religious aloofness.   It is one more mark of the analogy, so
far-reaching and instructive, between ancient Greece and the
autonomous communities of Italy.   It remains then for him
finally to affirm that "no activity is so acceptable to God as
that of sharing in the task of guiding communities of men

---

[1] *Della Vita Civile*, p. 21: "il nostro glorioso poeta."

organised on the basis of social justice ; to those who fulfil this duty He has given the promise of assured felicity hereafter." The relation of individual to social virtue is this: the youth learns to exercise rational control over his lower self; this same faculty or disciplined capacity he carries, later, into the sphere of family life and its interests, ordering the home upon those foundations of temperance and justice which characterise his personal life. He has then approved himself worthy to be joint ruler in the Community, and applies the qualities which he has thus made his own to the defence and furthering of the common weal. Thus, as with Alberti, so with Palmieri, the Home is the training ground of the virtues which make for the health of the State.

In psychological analysis Palmieri is, like Alberti, crude and defective, as were all humanists before the true Aristotle became available much later in the century. The "anima" has two parts, the rational and the irrational, of which the first is the citadel of personality, controlling bodily impulses and setting the faculties free to attain knowledge. The rational soul has three factors : memory, intelligence and prudence. Memory, though a natural endowment, can be trained by history, by the practice of composition, by recitation, by repetition and reflection. By intelligence we not only acquire knowledge, but we judge of facts, and of motives to conduct in ourselves and others. Prudence is intelligent forecasting from cause to effect. But no view of human nature is complete which does not recognise in the "anima" an immortal quality.

As concerns the curriculum, the ideas of Palmieri are original only in so far as they represent the correlation of humanist enthusiasm with the traditional training of a Florentine youth for practical life. He never forgets that he writes for a modern community : he is proud to express his views in the vernacular, which he desires to see cultivated and developed. The capable head of his house, the active man of business, the keen politician, yet inspired with a passion for personal culture, such a man, placed in the environment of the civic life of Florence, is the ideal which Palmieri has before him. The environment, indeed, is that created by the best citizens, by those in fact who have been trained upon the lines of a sound education as set forth by Palmieri. It is the inevitable qualification of all ideal moralities to postulate the conditions which it is desired to create. Macchiavelli alone had the courage to look facts squarely in the face and describe the "Governor" exactly fitted to things as they were.

What then are the disciplines by which a boy may be trained to live the serious civic life as Palmieri conceives it? Two factors are always of first-rate importance in determining the choice of instruction : the first is Environment, to which, as has been seen, both Florentine writers ascribe the chief weight in education. The next is Nature, or inherited capacity. Yet even the most promising disposition if left without guidance is a weak and ineffective thing, and skill therefore is requisite to make the best of natural gifts. The conformity of training to nature he illustrates from physical development. Every gesture and exercise which is out of harmony with natural action, and which therefore is ungraceful, must be wrong. In walking, a boy must obey the conformation of the figure to secure dignity and attractiveness of carriage. The boy's instinct being towards activity, such games only as involve energy and versatility should be admitted : but Palmieri demands universal training in military exercises. The argument for these is specially enforced by urgent patriotic duty, and rightly, for the Florentine trader lacked military spirit and left defence to a hired foreign soldiery with disastrous effect. Vanity and ostentation in dress are to be repressed as dangers peculiar to a state where personal rivalries run riot.

In respect to the first steps in teaching, Palmieri follows Plutarch as to the duties of the mother and the choice of nurses and companions. He offers one curious piece of advice, alien in temper from the mind of Alberti and of the humanists generally, viz., that little children should be steadily imbued with a fear of hell, and that impressive stories of the fate of bad boys should be driven home on suitable occasions. As to the subjects of instruction, Palmieri obviously relies much upon Quintilian, whose treatise upon the *Education of the Orator*, never wholly forgotten in the Middle Ages, had been for some twenty years circulated in a far more complete and exact form, and was thenceforward the text-book of every humanist in the matter of classical instruction.   He has evidently read Vergerius, *De Ingenuis Moribus*, possibly, but not probably, M. Vegius, whose treatise *De Liberis Educandis* is the fullest manual of education produced in the fifteenth century.   The end of the first book of the *Vita Civile* is largely a reproduction of passages from the *De Officiis*, and elsewhere Guarino's translation of Plutarch's treatise on Education is in evidence.   But Quintilian is the more important authority and it is possible to quote parallel passages as between him and Palmieri which indicate direct borrowing from the ancient writer; and, indeed, this is possible with most humanists[1].   But it is of profound importance to note how these incorporations, confined mostly to matter of instruction, fit into the ideal and end of education as Palmieri formulated them for the Florence of his day.   The spirit is modern; the antique world is drawn upon, not for imitation but for assimilation.   It was the more possible to utilise Quintilian in this manner in that the public life of Rome offered certain genuine analogies with that of Florence as Palmieri knew it.   The tradition of political service, the importance of oratorical gifts, an acute national and civic self-consciousness, the relative positions of the Julian house and of the Medici, the modification of a native culture by the intrusion of external influences,— the effects of Greek civilisation upon Augustan Rome being

---

[1] See Bassi in *Giorn. Storico d. Lett. Ital.* xxiii. 191.

parallel to that of the antique world upon Italy of the Quattrocento,—are all suggestive of such parallelism. When we remember the anxiety of the man of education of the Revival to recognise the ideal of his social and intellectual life in that of ancient Rome, we do not wonder that the humanists, whether professed students or just cultivated men of affairs, seized upon the one systematic manual of Roman education as the authoritative guide for an age in which the virtues and glory of the ancient civilisation were to be re-born. Thus the humanist reproduced Quintilian, or Cicero, or Plutarch, without concealment. Where there was no pretence there was no plagiarism. It was not necessary to mention Quintilian ; he was to every humanist a free quarry, and every scholar recognised the rock from which each new building was hewn. Who will say that Vergil " plagiarises " Homer, or Milton Vergil? It was useless to improve upon Quintilian ; as Erasmus said seventy years later, where Quintilian had stated a principle it was presumptuous to alter it. The essential fact to note is that Palmieri uses Quintilian because he recognises in the *Institutio* the one systematic treatise on the subject, carefully and eruditely elaborated from experience ; the experience, moreover, was that of the golden age of antiquity which was, to the Florentine humanist, at the same time the ideal of a restored Italian culture. The "ottimo cittadino " of Palmieri is in reality identical with the " perfect Orator" as understood by Cicero or Quintilian. And Palmieri succeeded in fitting what he drew from Quintilian into his scheme of an ennobled Florentine society. There is in the *Vita Civile* hardly a trace of awkward working-in of borrowed material. For the book is the genuine product of an original mind, stating and solving a problem, special to the time indeed and with its own peculiar conditions, yet one which is in the nature of the case common to all civilisations at a similar stage of development. It is characteristic of this particular period of the Renaissance that one absorbed in mercantile business and in municipal affairs should accept without defence the higher education of Imperial Rome as directly and literally fitted to mould the ideal training of a Florentine citizen. And for nearly five centuries the education of the governing class in Western Europe has followed the lead which the Italy of the Quattrocento originally gave.

Turning to the details of Palmieri's scheme of instruction we notice the importance which he attaches to the first steps. The habit of speaking clearly and fluently is to be acquired before writing. Letters should be recognised and named, and then follows easy reading in the vernacular. All this is taught by way of pastime, whilst the niceties of speech with proper intonation, gesture and bearing as part of it are carefully inculcated. These, with reading and the elements of drawing, cover the more important factors of home teaching up to the age of ten years. It is often stated that the Italian humanists were indifferent to the claims of the vernacular speech in education. It is true that no specific place is given in schemes of school study to the grammar of the language or to the great masters of Italian prose and poetry. But every Italian master would be expected to lay great stress upon fluency and refinement in *spoken* Italian. The function of conversation as an instrument of cultivation and of actual linguistic acquirements has been adequately recognised in France and Italy alone.

Next come music and singing, which latter is valuable as a training of the speaking voice in enunciation and right pronunciation; both serve as mental discipline through rhythm, and as a physical exercise have their effect upon personal health. In the third place arithmetic and geometry—"the order of numbers and the distinction of forms"—are needed both as practical arts and as rational disciplines. The boy next enters upon systematic classical study. The preparation for it has been laid in and through vernacular speech. There is no attempt at forcing unreal familiarity with the ancient languages as spoken tongues, so that Latin grammar, the basis of all serious intellectual progress as he holds it to be, is not begun until the eleventh year of age. The " doctrina dell' ornato parlare," or eloquence in the broad sense, is of profound importance to a citizen of a self-governing state; it is, indeed, only a development of the quality which distinguishes man from the brute. But it is certain that Palmieri regards as a chief part of the value of close study of Latin and Greek the resulting improvement in the power of expression in the vernacular.

There can be no doubt that the great majority of humanist teachers in France or England, hardly less than in Italy (excepting the purists, like Erasmus), were concerned with rhetoric not as training in Latin only, but as an essential instrument for the acquisition of a sound and cultivated vernacular style. It was certainly so with the Florentine men of the world of whom Palmieri is the type ; it was true, at a subsequent stage, of the historians and men of letters, Macchiavelli, Capponi, or Poliziano. Francesco Patrizi, a citizen of Siena, writing, like Palmieri, upon the virtues essential to a free community, and in the same century, urges the study of Roman oratory as the needful preparation for civic eloquence. "No quality is of more vital concern to the State than that of public speaking, especially that aspect of it which relates to civil discussion. For the entire business of the State is dependent on the ability of the men of affairs to persuade to, or dissuade from, a proposed course of action…to the end that the citizens be not led into a wrong policy, which after sorrowful experience, they will be forced to undo." Only second in importance in the public economy is the art of the debater and of the advocate, whereunto all young citizens thereto disposed should be encouraged. Such eloquence obviously means command of the vernacular, and Patrizi makes it clear that the foundations of it are to be laid in " Grammatica," or Latin reading and composition. That poverty may be no bar to promise the State is urged to set up public masters in this fundamental subject whose schools shall be free to the sons of all citizens[1].

Moral philosophy must be inculcated from Roman writers, of which Cicero and Seneca are the chief, and from the Greeks, meaning Plutarch and possibly Xenophon. Such moral instruction should be full of example, of intimate application to family life and to individual self-respect, and bear upon the future duties of the citizen. After moral comes " natural," philosophy. This latter is of much less utility to man. " It consists in the investigation of the secrets of nature ; certainly in itself a not unworthy study, but none the less one of much less service to mankind than that of moral wisdom, upon which is based the well-being of the race. Therefore admitting that the causes of Rain, Hail, Snow and Ice, the origin of the colours of the Rainbow, the secrets of Lightning and Thunder, are in themselves matters of marvellous significance, and deserve enquiry, we hold them still of the minutest interest in the supreme task of solving the problem how to live[2]."

The curriculum which Palmieri here indicates is far in advance of that usual in the education of the son of a Florentine merchant, whose instruction would consist chiefly of arithmetic in its practical shape, and astronomy, as understood at the time. So it was necessary to face the criticism that he propounded too great variety of subjects. Palmieri meets it on the common humanist ground that change of instruction, like variety of food, makes for health ; that the old dismal monotony of instruction in the dry bones of grammar repelled eager intellects, whereas if teaching be of a kind to stimulate the learner's interests, both amount and variety of matter will allow of liberal increase.

Punishments may not be brutal, such as will injure self-respect. This is, indeed, fairly secured by the fact that the scene of education is the home, where the father's control is

[1] *Discorsi*, pp. 44, 51.
[2] *La Vita Civile*, p. 20.

supreme. Should a boy be incurably idle or dull he must be transferred from higher to lower disciplines, to spend his time upon manual arts rather than upon liberal studies[1]; such a boy, prepared for a mechanical or industrial career of lower type, with restricted outlook upon the world, cannot expect to become an influence in the community; and therein consists, as Palmieri holds, the sufficient stimulus to a boy to perseverance in higher studies. Already we trace the conviction which was deeply fixed in the minds of the humanists of the following century that the bent and force of youthful wits could be accurately estimated by the observant teacher at a very early age, and the future career of the pupil thereupon determined. To this corresponds the belief that personality was within the power of every man to create or mould as he would. "Let everyone by careful weighing of his capacities determine what line of development he shall consciously follow out, and devote himself to that." We are reminded of Alberti's dogma that "to will a thing and to achieve it are two terms for the same thing."

The chapter may fitly close with an utterance of Giovanni Rucellai[2], a distinguished contemporary and friend of Palmieri and Alberti, in which a typical merchant-citizen of Florence at the height of its dignity, expresses the noble pride in his city which the new education has engendered. "La fortuna non tanto m' ha conceduto grazia nel guadagnare, ma ancora nello spenderli bene. E credo che m' abbi fatto più onore l' averli bene spesi ch' averli guadagnati, e più contenta-

---

[1] A boy of this lower type might be punished upon methods unjustifiable in case of boys of keener wits.

[2] *Zibaldone* (1466), by Giovanni Rucellai, quoted by Biagi, *La Vita Italiana nel Rinascimento*, p. 83. The dignity of the man of the Renaissance, who has developed an ideal which rises beyond that of *masserizia* (the prudent family economy, which characterised the old Florentine life) is here admirably expressed. It is the Aristotelian μεγαλοπρέπεια. See infra, p. 262. There is evidently reminiscence of Plutarch's *Life of Marius*, s. f., as Dr Sandys suggests.

mento nel mio animo,…massimamente delle muraglie ch'io ho fatte della casa mia di Firenze, del luogo mio di Quaracchi, della facciata della chiesa di Santa Maria Novella, e della oggia nella vigna dirempetto alla casa mia." He proceeds to give thanks to God that He has made him a "rational creature, a Christian, and not a Turk, a Moor, or a barbarian"; that He was pleased to grant him to be born "nelle parti d'Italia, la quale è la più degna e più nobile parte di tutto il cristianesimo, e nella provincia di Toscana la quale è reputata delle degne provincie ch'abbi l'Italia." And further that he can claim as his native place the city of Florence "la quale è reputata la più degna e la più bella patria che abbi non tanto il cristianesimo ma tutto l'universo mondo"; and lastly that his "lot fell in the present age, which all who understand aright know full well transcends in splendour every age that has passed since Florence was first built."

CHAPTER V.

RUDOLPH AGRICOLA.

1444–1485.

WHENEVER German humanists look back from the sixteenth century upon the origins of the New Learning in their own land they, with one accord, claim as their forerunner Rudolph Agricola[1], the wandering scholar of Friesland. It is not, however, altogether an easy matter to determine the precise grounds of the high repute as a restorer of learning which he acquired in his own short life-time, which, however, was a commonplace amongst scholars of the subsequent generation, and which has ever since been accepted. The recorded facts of his life are few though full of interest. If his active achieve-

---

[1] The life and letters of Agricola have been the subject of much enquiry. The chief sources are: the *Lucubrationes*, the *Opuscula*, the *De Inventione*, all printed in the sixteenth century. In addition the *Serapeum*, vol. x., contains extracts from the Stuttgart MS., which Hartfelder has supplemented (*Unedierte Briefe*, etc., 1886). The *Vita Petrarchae* of 1477 (Monac. Cod. Lat. 479) has never been printed. Prof. F. von Bezold's *Festrede* (1884) upon Agricola and Morneweg's *J. von Dalberg* (1884) are valuable modern authorities. Dr Kan (1894) has printed from a Vienna MS. an interesting but imperfect and not always accurate life of Agricola, composed by an anonymous friend of Melanchthon. Tressling's *Vita et Merita R. A.* is of no original value. There are probably further unedited Letters in German libraries. Mr P. S. Allen of C. C. C. Oxford has contributed an important article on the printed "sources" for Agricola in the *English Hist. Rev.* for April, 1906, to which the present writer is much indebted. See also his *Op. Ep. Erasmi*, i. 579 seqq. Geiger's biography in the *Allgem. Deutsche Biogr.* is, like his section on A. in the *Humanismus*, hardly worthy of his undoubted learning.

ments were not striking, his literary product is hardly of
marked significance.   He was not a great teacher like Vittorino
or Hegius; nor an administrator and organiser like Melanchthon;
nor a hero of controversy like Reuchlin.   He left little now
recognised as of distinction in criticism or scholarship, in
theology or philosophy.   Yet by consent of men of the stamp of
von Dalberg, von Langen, Hegius, Wimpheling, Melanchthon,
and above all of Erasmus, Agricola was a dominant influence
in the transfer of the new light from Italy to northern Europe.
"Incredibile vero, quam multa divinarit vir ille plane divinus,"
says Erasmus of him; and again, "si fatorum invidia superesse
voluisset, haberet Germania quem Italis opponeret, qualem
nunc habet Gallia Budaeum."   In the *Ciceronianus* Erasmus
pronounces him to be a man of recondite erudition, of
remarkable power as a writer of pure, forceful and translucent
Latinity; worthy to be compared with Quintilian whom he
even excels in clearness of effect.   In his rhetorical gifts he reminds Erasmus of Isocrates.   He instances particularly his wide
reading in Latin and Greek literature and his sound scholarship.   "Inter Graecos Graecissimus, inter Latinos Latinissimus";
in his knowledge of oratory and poetry and of the learning of
the ancients he demands highest respect.   Erasmus longs for
the appearance of his literary remains, and asks that all works
by Agricola as published may be sent to him.   His treatise on
Logic he regards as worthy of a commentary, which he himself
would be proud to attempt.   As regards Agricola's power as a
textual critic Erasmus singles out his work in the text of
Seneca as of noteworthy acumen.   "I myself have heard
Erasmus say that both in eloquence and in all regions of
learning he stood distinctly below Agricola," relates one who
knew them both[1].   "Cogitatis," says Melanchthon, "quantum
Germaniae, quam bene de literis meritus sit."   "Cum Germania

---

[1] "Audivi Erasmum fateri Agricolam se longe cum in eloquentia tum
in omni genere eruditionis praeire."   Kan, p. 9.   These are the words of
an intimate friend of Agricola writing to Melanchthon.

tanta literarum inscitia esset, ut quid esset recte loqui ne quidem suspicari nostri homines possent,…unus Rudolphus primum auribus atque animo sentire illa vitia et desiderare meliorem orationis formam coepit." In especial he commends him as the founder of the new education in Germany. For nothing less than this is involved in his enlightened reform in dialectic, based on the real Aristotle; the "ineptae persuasiones scholae "—so baneful in their effect on the development of intelligence—gave way to a dialectic which truly aided thought and exposition. With the one exception of Erasmus no scholar had so effective an influence in the moulding of Melanchthon's humanism as Agricola. The Reformer alludes to the charm of his personality, itself the outcome of his intellectual devotion which again was guided by an enlightened patriotism. For Agricola, a spiritual child of the Italian Renaissance, brought into his humanism an intense zeal for the advancement of German-speaking peoples in the field of learning. The epitaph composed by Hermolao Barbaro, the distinguished Venetian scholar, Patriarch of Aquileia, is quoted as a token of the respect with which Agricola was regarded in Italy: "Scilicet hoc uno meruit Germania laudis Quicquid habet Latium, Graecia quicquid habet." Testimony from this source Erasmus holds as final. Pietro Bembo, a still more notable authority in Italian scholarship, writing thirty years after Agricola's death, records the marked impression he had left behind amongst scholars who had known him. Even Guicciardini expressly notes his distinction.

Agricola was born at Bafflo, near Groningen, in northern Holland, on February 17th, 1444. As a child he displayed remarkable gifts in music and in drawing, modelling and wood carving. His first instruction was gained in the town school of Groningen, where he passed rapidly over the heads of his fellow pupils. It is uncertain whether he came under the teaching and influence of the Brethren of the Common Life. His earliest biographers make no mention of his presence at their famous school of Zwolle ; and it is an unverified tradition that he was taught by Thomas of Kempten, better known to the world as Thomas à Kempis. Nor was he ever a pupil of the school of St Lebuin at Deventer.

This is perhaps the place to insert a short notice of the Brethren whose work at this period began to acquire a dominant influence in the educational progress of Holland and the lower Rhine. The schools organised by the Brethren of the Common Life, described sometimes from the names of St Jerome, or St Gregory the Great, the traditional patrons of learning, as Scholae Hieronymitanae or Gregorianae, owed their origin to the work of Geert Groot of Deventer (1340–1384) who founded an Association, or Brotherhood (it was never a monastic order under vows) of devout men who consecrated their lives to industry, teaching and learning, to which he gave its well-known title. In the period of the close of the Middle Ages and the beginnings of the Renaissance, which north of the Alps may be said to fall within the century 1430–1530, no schools were so well frequented or enjoyed so wide a reputation as those connected with certain houses of the Brethren. From the Netherlands, their place of origin, the schools spread to the Rhine, to Westphalia and to south-west Germany. Before 1500 those of Zwolle and Liège were large establishments of 800 scholars, and eight or ten others planted in large towns had attained hardly less renown. They were of the type of the "Latin" or "Trivial" school; "Trivial" as teaching the subjects of the Trivium—Grammar, Dialectic and Rhetoric. Such schools, whether civic or ecclesiastical in organisation, provided the middle or "secondary" education of that age. In the best of them, the upper forms, as in a modern Public School, did work not distinguishable from that of the Faculty of Arts in a contemporary University. We are not to suppose a special affinity between the Brethren and the humanist spirit abroad in Italy; for at best we can discern in certain of their Houses, Deventer or Zwolle, an absence of distrust of learning, and a sympathy with higher aims and methods of education.

Indeed, the relation between the Frater-house and the school must have differed in various cities. Paulsen's[1] conclusion does not correspond to that hitherto accepted. "The Frater-house was not a school, the brothers were not a body of teachers in the sense that the Jesuits afterwards were; certainly they were not humanist teachers. From humanism, indeed, the earlier brethren, of the time of Groot, or even of Kempis, were far removed. These particular men were ascetic and devout, and not concerned with mundane knowledge. The relation of the Brothers to the school of any town where they had set up a House consisted chiefly in this: that they received as boarders into their house pupils attending as day boys the civic or parish Latin schools, watching over them spiritually and morally and no doubt aiding them in their studies. Only in a few cases is it known that the Brethren themselves taught in schools. On the other hand there were some amongst the masters of secular or ecclesiastical schools who were in sympathy with the Brothers without being members of the order." At Deventer, for instance, Hegius was not one of the Brethren; though he was obviously in close relations with them and several of his teachers belonged to their body. The school of which he was Head was attached to the church of St Lebuin, as a corresponding school in England might be part of the Minster of Beverley or the Cathedral of Lincoln or Wells. Yet we have evidence of much closer association of Brethren and school in other places at the end of the century, and the influence of the Brethren was shown in a certain uniformity of type in the schools with which they were connected. There were special reasons for a more rapid progress in educational ideas in the Low Countries at this time. The practice of frequent change of posts, of short engagements of teachers, who often stayed but two or three years and then moved on elsewhere, the visits of

[1] Paulsen, *Geschichte*, i. 159.

merchants and ecclesiastics to Italy where the new schools made due impression upon the least observant,—such causes led to an interchange of knowledge and of methods within the schoolroom, and silently moulded public opinion upon desirable learning. The accident of individuals and of situation counted for much. Humanism affected Deventer earlier, for example, than it affected Bois-le-Duc; for Hegius found in the Brethren and in his staff intelligent co-operation in his reformed methods.

Alexander Hegius, the Rector of the Deventer School, prided himself on having sat at the feet of Rudolph Agricola. "Although," he confesses, "a man of forty, a Master of Arts, I was but a novice in true learning up to the day when I fell in with my youthful teacher Agricola." This was in 1474, when Hegius was at Emmerich, and Agricola home for a time from Pavia. Agricola was ten years his junior : "from him I learnt all I know or what men suppose me to know." Under the stimulus of Agricola, Hegius made progress in the study of Greek, wherein like all earlier humanists he was mainly self-taught. He tentatively introduced it into the work of the higher forms at Deventer, where Erasmus got some smattering before he left, and worked at a reform of the apparatus and methods of Latin teaching throughout the school. Before his death (1498) he had placed Deventer in the first rank of the schools frequented by German-speaking youth. The contribution of Hegius to the advancement of the Revival lies chiefly in his work as a reformer of schools. Erasmus, indeed, looking back upon his school days at Deventer, spoke slightingly of the efficiency of the teaching judged from an advanced humanist standpoint[1]. But it is necessary to remember that ideals and practice are but slowly brought into line in a large school. Assistants, text-books, available methods, attitude of parents or clergy, had to be reckoned with. Still, by the close

---

[1] Cp. Nichols, *Epistles of Erasmus*, i. 7.

of his career Hegius had in large part achieved his end. By incorporating Greek into the school course he established its place in German education. The amount actually learnt by the pupils was small enough, for the difficulties involved in the lack of texts and grammars, and of methods tested by experience are readily perceived. But in his tract *De Utilitate Linguae Graecae* Hegius set out the value of Greek for the study of divinity, and, in true humanist spirit, its indispensable importance to a sound knowledge in every region of enquiry. In regard to Latin his chief concern was to reduce grammar to its right place by relieving it of its dependence upon logic, and by treating it as an aid to the study of classical texts and to composition. He was a most efficient and inspiring master, the spiritual father of a long series of humanist teachers who owed their illumination to the school at Deventer, whilst he was gifted with notable powers as an organiser. His pupils numbered, at the time of his death, over two thousand. He divided the school into eight classes; he himself taught the senior boys, and by way of lecture read Latin poets and gave moral instruction based on Cicero and Plutarch. Erasmus records that, though in the third class, he occasionally had leave to attend such courses, to his great delight. With Hegius character took precedence of learning, though like a true humanist he believed that sound learning, rightly applied, conduces necessarily to moral worth.

The town of Deventer became through the school a centre of intellectual interests. The activity of the two printers, Paffraet and Jacob of Breda, indicates a demand for classical books, although we need not suppose that the whole list of their issues had reference to the school needs. Cicero, Vergil, Plautus, Persius, Seneca, with Latin versions of Aesop, Hesiod, and Agricola's translation of pseudo-Plato, find a place in the Deventer issues. The town was a recognised centre of humanism for all north-western Germany as well as for Holland, and wandering scholars found their way thither as to a famed seat of learning.   The teachers who went forth from it carried the spirit of humanist education throughout Germany, and in Murmellius, Caesarius, von Busche, and many others the methods and aims of Hegius lived again in the following century.

The school at Liège was founded by the Brethren in 1496. In all probability its organisation was based on that elaborated by Hegius.   John Sturm, the great Rector of the Strassburg school, was a pupil there.   The school order is worth quoting, for it no doubt reproduces the organisation of Deventer at its best, and was certainly the basis of that propounded by Sturm for the reconstitution of the school at Strassburg in 1538.

As at Deventer eight classes were constituted.   In the Eighth the pupil learnt to read Latin, to write, and to repeat the declensions and conjugations; in the Seventh an easy Delectus was used and exercises framed upon it, and a beginning was made with sentence structure.   The Sixth class began to read a simple Latin author; grammar was systematically learnt; prose composition and prosody were included. In the Fifth syntax is completed; historical writers are read for the first time, their style noted and imitated; verse exercises attempted, and first steps taken in Greek.   In the Fourth more time was given to Greek; the rudiments of logic, principles of rhetoric from Cicero and Quintilian, and original prose are taught.   Not until the Third was Greek composition begun, and along with the close study of Greek grammar and authors, mainly poets, logic and rhetoric were continued, with regular exercises in composition after ancient models. In the Second the *Organon* of Aristotle was read in Greek, and also Plato; Euclid was read in Latin and the elements of Roman law.   Orations were composed in strict accord with the laws of structure as laid down by Cicero; and disputations on classical subjects were practised.   In the First theology was introduced, and increased use was made of disputation, in which the two senior classes joined; and the study of rhetoric was completed. We note that rhetoric involved the constant use of authors, Greek and Latin, of various types as examples of style. Probably no University in Germany in 1500 afforded so advanced a course in Letters as is implied in this curriculum of the two upper classes of the school at Liège.

To return to Agricola, whose school-days fell in a period when humanist influences were but beginning to penetrate to northern Germany, although even so early there were, here and there, individual masters who urged their pupils to study the classics as literature, and inspired in them an ambition to make their way to Italy as the source of all sound learning. From Groningen Agricola passed (1456) to Erfurt at the age of twelve, and from Erfurt, after a stay there of two years, to Louvain, which was rapidly advancing to the front rank amongst the new Universities. At Erfurt he had, after two years' residence and under the age of fifteen, obtained his "laurea," and "commenced Bachelor"; at Louvain, before he was seventeen, he gained, "stupore omnium," his Mastership in Arts. His principal studies lay in mathematics and philosophy, but he also took the opportunity of the presence of students from France of learning French. From Louvain in May, 1462, he went to Cologne, the seat of scholastic theology, and always regretted the waste of time upon the "ineptiae" of the logical and metaphysical doctrine there dominant. He would admit in later years that an interest in historical divinity was born in him at Cologne, by way of reaction from the spirit of the current theology, and was never altogether abandoned. He seems to have spent a short time in Paris, whence dates his life-long friendship with Reuchlin; although beyond the bare fact nothing is recorded. But in the prime of his early manhood, in 1468 or 1469, the opportunity of his life befell, and he found his way to Italy. To him, as to so many others in every age, the years spent there were the truly formative years of his life. He seems to have lived in Italy, with some interruptions, probably brief, for a period of ten years, a longer residence than we can ascribe to any other northern scholar of distinction. From his letters we trace him first at Pavia, where not a few of his fellow-countrymen were working, like himself, at classics or law. Agricola earned money, as Erasmus and many others on their travels, by becoming tutor to youths of distinction, the sons of a Count of Ottingen, whose studies at Pavia he directed, and with whom he formed ties of lasting affection. At Pavia also he first met Johann von Dalberg, to whom he acted also as preceptor. Dalberg, though only nineteen, was elected Rector of the University in 1474. Later, as Chancellor of the Elector of the Palatinate and Bishop of Worms, he was instrumental in establishing Agricola at Heidelberg. Agricola apparently delivered the oration at the installation. The friendship between the two men is one of the most pleasant incidents in German humanism. He spent some time in acquiring knowledge of Roman law, but a feeling of repulsion for the career to which it pointed grew upon him; he abandoned the Faculty and devoted himself entirely to the classical tongues. But not finding at Pavia the opportunities he needed for due advance in Greek, he yielded to the universally-felt attraction of Ferrara, "the very home of all the muses," as he described it, and in the summer of 1475, when Dalberg had left Italy, entered himself as a pupil of Battista Guarino and of Theodore Gaza. Guarino was the distinguished son of the yet more famous Guarino da Verona, and Gaza was the old colleague of Vittorino at Mantua, and the ablest teacher in Italy of the Greek language and literature. From this time onwards Agricola's chief interest on the side of letters lay in Greek. Ferrara, indeed, was at this period the best reputed University of Europe amongst foreign scholars pursuing the humanities. It had been the aim of its founders and subsequent benefactors—the d'Este princes—to develope the University as a school primarily of the liberal arts rather than of professional studies. Ferrara, therefore, had attracted all those occasional

English scholars who, chiefly from Balliol, found their way across the Alps in search of classical learning. The reputation of Guarino and of his son after him appealed in particular to students of Greek, such as Agricola. From Ferrara he wrote many letters which reveal his characteristic interests. We find him busy upon translations from Lucian; on Isocrates, in whose style he felt the delight of an artist, "ea enim suavitas est dicendi, is ornatus, et, ut ita dicam, sculptura orationis...": his version of the *ad Demonicum* had an extraordinary popularity for nearly a century; perhaps his principal pre-occupation was Aristotle, the *Logic*, the *Metaphysic*, and the works on Natural History, parallel with which he read Pliny's *Historia Naturalis*. Of Quintilian he made a complete copy with his own hand; the text of Seneca, still corrupt, was corrected with an insight and skill in conjecture which provoked the admiration of Erasmus. Theodore Gaza was expressly noted as his guide in the study of the true Aristotle, but he learnt much from Guarino, of whom he speaks with respectful regard in his later letters from Germany. Translations of pseudo-Platonic dialogues, and an edition of selections from Priscian, were also amongst the products of his studies at Ferrara. Under Guarino, we may suppose, he laid the foundations of that knowledge of Thucydides, Xenophon, Diodorus Siculus, and Polybius, which he was to turn to account later. But one work which was perhaps begun, and certainly finished, at Pavia, in 1477, during a visit he paid to it from Ferrara, is of peculiar interest. The MS., which has never been printed, has for title *Vita Petrarchae, illustrata per eruditissimum virum Rudolphum Agricolam, ad Antonium Scrofinium Papiensem: Ann: Sal: 1477, Papiae.* It is not a substantial contribution to the knowledge of Petrarch's career; it is rather of the nature of an "appreciation," and was possibly delivered as a public declamation in the University. But it gives evidence of the profound admiration which, as we know from other sources, he felt for the proto-humanist: "quem cunctis ingeniis seculi sui haud cunctanter praetulit, cuique, sua sententia, omnis eruditio seculi nostri plurimum honoris debet." It is to be noted that he has in mind Petrarch, mainly, if not entirely, as the Latinist and the inspirer of the Revival of Learning, rather than as the poet. Yet that aspect of the great Italian was by no means alien from his interest, for Agricola, unlike many humanists, held vernacular languages in due esteem. He had brought with him a working knowledge of German and French besides his own Low Dutch, and at Pavia and Ferrara set himself diligently to acquiring Italian. For, in contrast to Erasmus and many other Teutonic scholars, it was his desire to enter completely into the spirit of the new age in Italy, and to gain that intimate communion with it of which a thorough knowledge of the language was the first condition. So, as his pupil and biographer, Johann von Pleningen says of him, he applied himself to the Italian vernacular, "non quemadmodum vulgo sciri tenerive solent, quo vitae necessaria coemere posset, verum ut versu et oratione soluta in singulis concinne apteque diceret."

Northerner though he was, there was that in Agricola which rendered him peculiarly sympathetic in the presence of the Italian Renaissance. For he was possessed of a finely receptive nature, which enabled, or rather impelled, him to absorb something of all the spiritual influences by which he was beset. The intimate harmony of the outward and inward in things of the soul touched him profoundly. He was himself of noteworthy presence. His biographers remarked his vigorous type of face, his rich chestnut beard, the breadth of shoulder, the dignity of carriage, which made him a figure to note in the distinguished society of Ferrara. Such details as the singular grace of his hands, and his fine baritone voice, are specially recorded. The attractiveness of his bearing was not wholly a matter of natural gift, for in true Italian spirit he cultivated such exercises as tended to suppleness of frame and ease of gesture. He was a skilful fencer and an adept with all military weapons, whirled the disc, and excelled in ball games. Thus in spite of severe intellectual work he maintained the fine bodily proportions which marked him. "He was," said one who knew him at Ferrara, "built on splendid lines ; verily a man goodly to look upon."

To such an outward form the essentially artistic temper of the man was in true correspondence. His many-sidedness struck all who were intimate with him. Especially did he cherish that passion for an unfettered life which, in various forms of expression, characterised the genuine son of the Renaissance. It must be remarked that it is a wholly incorrect view of Agricola which represents him as an industrious grammarian bent on uplifting Germany by aid of scholarship in Greek and Latin. It was on the contrary the marvellous personality of Agricola, in whom the genius of the Italian Revival stood forth with more completeness than in any northern man of his century, which made him so significant a force. His brilliant conversational gifts enabled him to hold his own in the most exacting Court in Upper Italy, and his command of graceful language, coupled with his well-trained voice, was a standing rebuke to the time-honoured sneer at the uncouthness of the "barbarians from beyond[1]." In such a society too, his musical gifts enforced his personal distinction. For Agricola was a scholarly musician, a skilled singer, a performer upon the organ, the flute and the violin, and was even more interested still in musical theory. It was said of him by his contemporaries that he could hold his own at a performance with the best reputed masters of his time. In the history of Renaissance music Agricola has an established place. A year or two after leaving Italy he built an organ, in which perhaps for the first time the vox humana stop was introduced, for

[1] Such, for example, as the remark of the Mantuan chronicler Schiva-noglia, who describing the entry of Margareta di Baviera into Mantua as bride of the heir Federigo Gonzaga (*Cron.* p. 153) says : " vene con deii assaii todeschii e todesche...del vivere et di chostumi soii non digo niente." This was in 1463, a few years before Agricola's arrival in Italy.

the Church of St Martin in Groningen.   Further, in Italy he developed that other native bent, a serious taste for Fine Art. He was not merely, as we might naturally assume, a dilettante, a stranger superficially affected by the unwonted cult of art and beauty which dignified his new environment.   He was, on the contrary, a serious student of design, devoting much time to work in the studio, and, as in the case of music, concerned to master the principles of Art.   He insists, for example, upon the crucial significance of a right understanding of anatomical proportion in painting the human figure, without which, he declares, all decorative treatment is but a clumsy attempt to mask technical weakness.   He was said to have been gifted with a peculiar power of recalling feature : he would paint a portrait from memory without the aid of sketch or memoranda. "When he desired to produce a portrait," says his biographer, who was his most intimate friend at Ferrara, "he would watch his subject unawares, say in church, and take note of his attitudes, his way of standing, seizing thus his natural self, the complete man.   Then at home he would record his impression in charcoal; and when I saw such a drawing in the rough I would say that the very man stood there before me on the paper."   Agricola used to say that to get a true portrait he must draw his subject as a whole, and not the face only, for nothing less than the entire figure was the real expression of the man.   It may be suggested that had he chosen painting as his life work he might, in this region also, have proved the transmitter of the Italian Renaissance to German lands.   The characteristic note of his artistic interests consists in the thoroughness, the reality of his work.   His personality was thus suffused with the Italian spirit[1]; it was moulded and enhanced by the absorption of the best which that favoured land could offer to a nature impelled always to select only

---

[1] A phrase of Marsilio is thoroughly characteristic of Agricola : "Gratiae et Musae a Deo sunt atque ad Deum referendae."   With a strong vein of seriousness he still set himself to enjoy life.

what is finest. Only when we realise this remarkable receptivity of Agricola, and the personal force which welded his
manifold experience into a strongly marked individuality, can
we understand how a man who achieved so little in action or
in letters should have left the masterly impression which he
did upon the first-rate intelligences of his time. Agricola
could transport Italy to Germany in virtue of the truth that he
had made the strongest factors of the Italian spirit his own.
The comparison which has often enough been made on
shallow grounds between Petrarch and his Teutonic disciple
gains new significance as we learn to understand what Agricola
really was.

During his stay at Ferrara Agricola had the distinction of
being invited to deliver a public Declamation in praise of
sound philosophy and liberal learning at the opening of the
University session, before the Duke Ercole, the Rector and
the students. We may forgive the Orator something of his
loudly pitched encomium upon his patron when we recall the
contrast, which was so vividly present to him, between the
brilliant court of Ferrara and the boorish ignorance of the
petty magnates of North Germany. Yet, for all that, Agricola
was beginning to feel the call to carry home the light to his
own people. "Barbari, indocti, elingues," he admits, are not
unfair epithets in the mouth of Italian scholars and courtiers
when criticising the Teutonic race. It is the duty of German
scholars to see to it that their land become the home of taste,
of eloquence, and of sound learning, fit to rank with Italy herself. He is anxious to take the lead in vindicating the
competence of the Rhineland to this great trial of wits.

In 1479 Agricola crossed the Alps after a period of nearly
ten years spent in classical studies. He had now a good
command of Greek, a Latin style of true humanist standard,
though far from that, say, of Poliziano ; but he had acquired
under Theodore Gaza—and it was a still rarer accomplishment—a first-hand knowledge of the true Aristotle. By

temperament he had, as has been shown, the gifts of a student rather than of a teacher, of an inspirer rather than an organiser or administrator.   When still not more than 38 years of age, and of modest means, he had refused two offers of important posts—one at Antwerp, whither he was invited to reform the Latin school, and another at the Court of Burgundy, a position of influence and dignity.   But, as we can easily understand, he refused to bring himself to face the monotony of a teaching career or the fetters of a Court.   To be master of his own time, to contribute to the world that which he best could, to pursue his own ideals,—this is the invariable note of the humanist Agricola.

The precise occupations which filled the first four years of his life after his return to Holland in 1479 are not easy to determine.   He held an administrative post of distinction under the Municipal Council of Groningen (1480–1484) which permitted of considerable absences.   He was sent upon official missions by the Emperor Maximilian, and took the opportunity of visiting schools and seats of learning during such journeys. He was in frequent correspondence with teachers and scholars, stirring up enthusiasm for the new light, and basing his appeal upon the motive of patriotism.   He had recognised the national spirit which underlay in part the Italian Revival, and himself foreshadowed the Germanic Revival as it found its later expression in Hutten, Luther and Melanchthon.   Yet we cannot but perceive the longing for Italy which beset him : a veritable nostalgia which became unbearable during his later years.

His letters of the period, 1480–1485, afford instructive insight alike into his interests and his temperament.   First and foremost he longs to be back in Italy : he wonders how he will manage to carry with him his great accumulation of books. There is a library of Greek MSS. at Basel which he means to go to see, though the journey will take a week or ten days.   He hears with anxiety of the uncertain fortunes of Duke Ercole, and asks for all news of affairs in Italy. He congratulates a correspondent on the privilege of hearing B. Guarino ; or he reports progress in translating Lucian, and asks for notice of any classical MSS. or printed books which may be available for purchase ; sends urgent requests for copies of Columella, Statius, Celsius, Macrobius, Silvus Italicus, authors as yet apparently not issued by German printers. Elsewhere we have news of the sad interference of studies caused by the plague in South Germany ; of the dangers and expense of the Italian journey ; a scholar friend of his wishes to join a party going south, for mutual protection, but also for economy ; and we have vivid light thrown upon the risks and anxieties attendant on illness or disablement which might befall on the way. Agricola was held up on this account for some weeks in 1485 in the great heats of Trient. These letters, it should be noted, are wholly different in character to the formal epistles so popular with the Italian humanist, which tell us so little amid all their ingenious display of the grand style. Agricola writes as one having something to say, and records plain facts and experiences in perfectly sound and readable Latin, after a fashion which brings us very near to the real man[1].

During the period of his residence in Holland, in which he paid a visit to Heidelberg (1482) and planned a further and longer stay in Italy, he was persuaded to accept, at Dalberg's instance, a post purposely left undefined in the Palatinate capital. His old pupil was now Bishop of Worms and Chancellor. The appointment was offered him expressly as a position allowing leisure and freedom. The Electoral Prince, von Dalberg, and their friends pressed upon Agricola to consider the support which his presence would afford to noble studies. All his wishes would be carefully respected ; he would never ask in vain for anything he might desire. Dalberg expressly added that he fully understood and esteemed

---

[1] A complete edition of Agricola's works and correspondence is much to be desired.

Agricola's passion for independence, and his determination never to be the servant of strangers. Wherefore he begged of him to take up his quarters in his palace, where he should live absolutely at his own will and pleasure as though it were his own. As to teaching, no demands would be made upon him except that he would, of his own goodness, read with Dalberg himself in the humanities, and this he hoped he might be willing to do out of the affection he bare him. As to his liberty of movement, he should come and go as he would. Such were the arguments used, in 1482, to induce Agricola to transfer himself to Heidelberg; and they so far succeeded that he accepted the invitation promising to fulfil it so soon in the following year as opportunely offered. But it was not until March, 1484, that he was free to leave Groningen; he stayed on his journey at Deventer with Hegius[1], where somewhere between 7th and 12th April Erasmus saw him. On May 2nd he reached Heidelberg.

"Agricola," says Morneweg, "no doubt began some teaching work at Heidelberg soon after his arrival. For Melanchthon makes it clear that the Bishop induced him to act as instructor not only to himself but also to certain youth" (whether of the city or of the University is not indicated). Whether he delivered his praelections upon logic, physics, astronomy, Aristotle's history of animals, and upon Eloquentia and the Greek and Latin literatures in the University itself is not definitely known. The fact is that the records of Faculty and University contain no mention of him. But during the Heidelberg period Agricola accompanied Bishop von Dalberg to Worms, where they looked into the local antiquities and

---

[1] The chronology of Hegius is not yet finally determined. If he took up his post as Head of the school at Deventer as late as 1483 (so Vienna MS.) the transfer of Erasmus to the school of Bois-le-Duc upon his mother's death must be placed in 1484, as he certainly was at Deventer during Hegius' headship. See Nichols, *Epistles of Erasmus*, i. 17, and P. S. Allen, *Eng. Hist. Rev.* Ap. 1906, p. 315.

mediaeval monuments. There also he repeated many of his lectures upon classical subjects, at Dalberg's request, to audiences of which teachers formed a large part. He complains, in a letter to Hegius, that these have so little time to spare from their dreary toil of words that it is hard for them to enter into Letters. At Worms, also, he delivered an address to the clergy of the diocese, whom Dalberg was anxious to win over to sympathy with the new studies. Agricola, it is evident, enjoyed ample freedom under the patronage of Dalberg; and there is no doubt that he had opportunities of imparting his enthusiasm to the circle which gathered round the Palatine Court. The fame of the two men began to draw scholars from all quarters to the University, among them Konrad Celtis, later the centre of humanism in Vienna. But there is no reason to suppose that he held a definite chair, with established duties and status; and the facts of Agricola's position at Heidelberg show how inappropriate are the assumptions as to university practice during the Renaissance which are based upon modern experience. Agricola taught after the independent fashion of the humanist masters in Italy. But he took part, with acceptance, in the disputations[1] of the Schools, and offered advice upon the general business of the University. There is an allusion in one of Melanchthon's references to Agricola (1539) to the project, in part at least realised, of a work to be undertaken at Heidelberg by Agricola, dealing with the history of the ancient world[2], and we have evidence of great activity amongst his group in producing translations from the Greek and Latin classics. Just in the same way the beginnings of the Renaissance in France and England were marked by the rapid issue of the classics in the vernacular.

[1] The popularity of these disputations was recalled when Melanchthon was a student at Heidelberg twenty years afterwards.

[2] The *Chronicon* has disappeared; its nature and its fate have formed the subject of much fruitless enquiry.

It is characteristic of the typical figure of the northern Revival that Agricola should reveal a drift towards divinity and Hebrew studies. Immediately upon his arrival at Heidelberg in 1484 he began to learn Hebrew from a converted Jew, whom Dalberg found for him. Agricola had never felt a contradiction between humanism and religion. Like Reuchlin and Erasmus after him, he held that conduct mattered most; and like them, too, he realised the function of scholarship in relation to the sound and impartial enquiry into Christian origins. His excursion into the region of devotional verse was not significant otherwise than as revealing the temper of his mind; neither as poetry nor as Latin does it correspond to his reputation. Yet he ardently desired to make a new and independent version of the Old Testament as an aid to a purified Christianity[1].

Agricola was, in spite of all, too restless to remain content with his post at Heidelberg. Very soon after his arrival he complains that he is afraid that he is unfitted for it. Probably he was already in bad health; more certainly, the Renaissance spirit rendered him (as it did Erasmus) impatient of narrow activities when so much remained to be learnt. Ferrara was other than Heidelberg, Italy than the Rhineland. But suddenly the longed-for opportunity arrived. Sixtus IV had died in August, 1484; the news of Innocent's election reached the Electoral Prince on the 12th of September. A legation to congratulate the new Pope was decided upon. Von Dalberg was naturally chosen, with Agricola as secretary. Starting in the spring they crossed the Brenner, and spent a night in beloved Ferrara, where the desolation wrought by the Venetian war was still only too apparent. On May 30th the mission reached Rome. Six weeks at most were passed amid the marvels of the city; and we sorely regret that not a word is left to us of Agricola's impressions of this, his only visit. The necessary Oration was delivered at the Vatican, and the return made by Verona in

[1] On the Heidelberg period Morneweg, *Dalberg*, is the best authority.

July. There Agricola fell ill of intermittent fever, and after a long halt recovered sufficiently to reach Heidelberg, but within little more than a month the trouble recurred and Agricola died in the arms of his sorrowing friend on the 27th of October, 1485.

A letter from Agricola (Heidelberg, 1484) to one of his friends, Barbirianus, is often referred to under the title *De Formando Studio*. It is a slight composition, hardly to be regarded as more than a sketch for a fuller treatment of so great a subject. Agricola died young, and out of his forty-two years he had been able to devote scarcely more than twelve to adequate study of the new learning. Moreover he was evidently, like Vittorino, a man by temperament averse to much writing. This tract is, however, of interest on various grounds ; amongst them, that it is the first of the long series of German compositions on the same theme. He begins by excluding from the new education the entire discipline of the mediaevalists ; the controversy upon the reality of ideas was to him an insignificant thing compared with the content of ideas. The ingenious verbal subtleties, the logical fence, which lead to nothing, the preposterous dilemmas, which constituted the exercises in dialectic and corrupted the study of language—all this, as mental discipline, he rejects with contempt, as did every humanist. Man has, indeed, in Philosophia the ultimate end of all education, but to "philosophy" he gives a modern interpretation very different from the one then current. It consists of three divisions : moral philosophy, rerum cognitio, and ars commode eloqui : or, the art of conduct, the circle of the Liberal Arts (including nature[1], history, Letters, politics), and the art of expressing our ideas.

---

[1] Agricola especially required a knowledge of Geography and "Natural Philosophy," but the latter was, characteristically, to be found only in Theophrastus and Aristotle, and the former undoubtedly implied the study of Strabo, an interest in whom he would have derived from B. Guarino at Ferrara.

"Mores," conduct and principle, are placed above knowledge. They are the end to which all else leads up. But the
place of Letters in relation to conduct is all-important. For
character is moulded and strengthened by the study both of the
great examples and of the judgments of those wise men of antiquity, whose survey of action and verdicts upon it are full of
instruction. Not only are professed moralists, Aristotle, Cicero,
or Seneca, of weight as guides to conduct, but historians,
orators, and poets rank scarcely below them as teachers of the
worthy and the unworthy in life. If we will treat the great
ancients as our comrades we shall find that the new generation
inspired by them will be braced to grapple with the problems
of the modern world[1]. For antiquity offers ample instruction
and encouragement to action, both individual and social.
It places at our disposal an unworked quarry in history,
geography, science, in politics, in thought, in Letters, in
medicine, in the fine arts. Hence Agricola unhesitatingly
declares that this second aspect of wisdom, "rerum cognitio,"
or "eruditio," as it was usually called, is to be found only in
the classical writers, and as a consequence of the ignorance of
the present age, is not to be won by mere observation; which
is only of use to confirm the authority of the great past. To
be distinguished from the scope of this erudition are the strictly
professional studies of law, theology and medicine, which
stand outside of his purview except in so far that they can be
accurately understood only by those who have laid the foundations in the antique wisdom.

The place of the great authors is thus distinctly marked
out. They are to be scrupulously read in that they are
authoritative upon every branch of secular knowledge; and as
providing examples and models in character, manners, personal
and national cultivation, their study makes us "paratiores ad

[1] The comparison with Elyot, infra, pp. 286–28 is obvious: but the
point of view is consistently humanist.

virtutem." We can almost hear Guarino speaking through Agricola in this formulated claim for the function of humanism in life. There is, too, a forecast of the Erasmian hatred of the mediaevalists in his solemn advice : "regard as suspect all that you have been taught hitherto ; ban and cast away as an imposture anything and everything that professes to be know-ledge, unless its title can be vouched for by the evidence of the great writers of old."

The third factor in Philosophia is the art of *expressing* truth. To every humanist truth was, in the first place, incon-ceivable unless defined in exact terms, and in the next, useless to man unless communicated and recorded. Eloquentia[1], then, with Agricola as with others, was much more than the ornamental garb of "eruditio," it was an essential condition of its utility. Agricola's contribution to rhetoric is thrown into the form of an introductory manual of logic, *De Inventione Dialectica*. It was at Ferrara that he first learnt to see the right function of logic as an aid to perspicuous expression and exposition, and to detach it from the abstract study of grammar. Just as "rhetoric," in the proper sense, includes literature—to be a poet or orator one must be steeped in the poets and orators—so also it assumes the laws of right reasoning. Rhetoric and logic meet in "inventio," which is the ordering of matter to produce conviction. And this will apply to description, narrative, exposition, forensic, or religious persuasion. The argument, as he lays it down, is this : in all speech, written or spoken, there are three factors : the speaker, the selected subject-matter, the hearer. In all successful speech, therefore, these must be present : intelligibility in the speaker, reason in the subject-matter, and favourable attitude on the part of the hearer. To ensure the first is the object of the teaching of grammar ; the second, orderly exposition of facts, is

---

[1] The influence of Agricola upon Melanchthon may well be illustrated by a comparison of this passage with p. 238 below.

secured by logic, the third by rhetoric. It is thus in relation to expression that Agricola views logic: it is an instrument of proof, but of proof which is to be recorded, communicated and enforced Logic, therefore, like grammar, is a factor in style, in the very widest sense of that word, in which perspicuity of argument is of more weight than ornament or variety. The treatise, regarded as a contribution to the development of logic, is of no great value. Agricola has read Aristotle and has understood him; he knows the scholastic dialectic and has rebelled against it. The Italian humanists had for half a century held his views; though none of them had excelled him in clearness of treatment and strength of conviction upon the subject. The book, however, had important influence in Germany, to whose teachers and scholars it was, in many cases, the first introduction to a new concept of dialectic. Melanchthon, for instance, found in it the stimulus to a fresh intellectual departure; he cannot exaggerate its effects upon him; his own significant attitude towards logic was based upon Agricola's doctrine. That it is a comparatively simple manual its author allows, indeed, with some pride. Melanchthon devoured it when he was fourteen. Every teacher, he said, would be a stronger force for a diligent reading of it. In their view of the value of such logic the humanists were right, for it is one of the marks of the expounders of the new learning to exhibit the art of laying out their theme and of building up argument, as they build up the sentence, in sequences which reason recognises.

Such a view of logic saved the German Revival from a misconception of style as a thing apart from content. Certainly for Agricola a style of pure imitative artifice, laborious, empty, never had attraction; nor did it, in the region of prose, at least, become a fashionable exercise in German lands. As we shall see, the "Oration," so dear to the Italian scholar, early gave place in the north to the "Essay" as an educational device, to the increase of reality.

One more factor in true education must be recalled. Agricola insists that a study of architecture, painting and modelling, in practice and in theory, is of the highest weight in the equipment of a cultivated man. Such stipulation is evidence of the breadth and dignity of the educational concept which Agricola had developed in Italy and now urged upon his co-workers in the cause of the Teutonic Renaissance. It is this breadth, and the enthusiasm of the personality which enforced it, which may give us the clue to the secret of the profound influence, which, in his lifetime and afterwards, Agricola exercised upon the strongest intelligences of the age of the Revival.

CHAPTER VI.

ERASMUS. 1466–1536.

THE transfer to foreign soil of a complex culture so eminently characteristic of the Latin genius as the Renaissance is a subject of study hardly less subtle than the Italian Revival itself. It is true that the movement was already approaching the last stage of its evolution in the country of its origin before other nations were ready to receive it. This, in a certain degree, simplifies the enquiry. But on the other hand no civilisation of alien birth makes, or can make, just the same appeal to different peoples. Whenever a new way of regarding knowledge, or a fresh mode of viewing life, presents itself in developed shape for admission to a strange environment, a problem of profound interest is at once set up. There has never been in history the simple phenomenon of a civilisation merely "borrowed." To receive, in such a case, means to select and to adapt. To discern the variations in the mode of such reception, in the consequent processes of assimilation, and in the spiritual result, as expressed in art and letters, in ideals of belief and action, is an essential task of criticism.

The purpose of this chapter, as it was, in part, of the last, is to attempt some understanding of one aspect of this problem, viz., as it is concerned with the first steps in the adaptation of Italian humanism and its educational ideal to the Teutonic world. The enquiry is obviously one of wide range in respect both of facts and of persons. The student approaching it for the first time will wisely look for his avenue to the subject in the life and teaching of certain of its out-standing figures, amongst whom the most notable personality of the northern Revival claims the first place.

Erasmus was born at Rotterdam on October 27, 1466[1]. His boyhood was passed under the care of his mother, who, in 1475, took him to Deventer, to attend the school of St Lebuin in that town, where he came under the instruction of certain masters belonging to the Brethren of the Common Life. Before he left (perhaps in 1484) Hegius had been appointed head-master. To him Erasmus looked back during his later life with a reverence which he rarely acknowledged as due to any one, excepting always Rudolph Agricola, whom he saw, apparently in 1483, when the great humanist passed through Deventer and stayed with Hegius. Soon afterwards Erasmus, his parents being dead, was taken from the school and placed in the monastery school of Bois-le-Duc. The contrast which his new surroundings presented to the freer and more stimulating atmosphere of Deventer was undoubtedly keenly felt by the studious youth. Probably he had real grounds for the distrust with which he always regarded conventual places of instruction. In later years he resented, in particular, the pressure which was brought to bear on him to contemplate the "religious" life as the career obviously marked out for him by destiny. He entered in 1487 (with what degree of voluntary assent we cannot now determine) the Augustinian House at Stein near Gouda ; after a short novitiate he made full profession (1488) and in

---

[1] The chronology of the first thirty years of the life of Erasmus is even yet uncertain. Mr P. S. Allen and Mr F. M. Nichols differ in some important points. Mr Allen now fixes the Deventer period at 1475–1484, including an interval of absence at Utrecht. The later limit is dependent upon the date allowed for Hegius' succession to Deventer (1483). The period at Stein is also abbreviated. But this scheme has its own difficulties. From 1495 onwards the correspondence of Erasmus renders the record of his movements much more definite. Mr Allen's *Op. Epist. Erasmi* i. is the best available authority for the period to 1514.

1492 was ordained priest. This period of his life was of moment in determining the bent of his talent. There was much leisure available for study, and this he divided between two main interests, classical reading and theology. In 1493, or the year following, Erasmus entered the service of the Bishop of Cambrai, with whom he anticipated to make a journey to Rome. Circumstances, however, compelled the abandonment of this alluring prospect; instead, he was sent to Paris by his patron, and resided there from 1494 as a student of theology in the Collége de Montaigu. Although the dominant interests of the University were logic and scholastic Divinity, Erasmus seems to have spent all the time he could spare from compulsory reading of theology and the occasional tutorial work by which he eked out his resources in Latin scholarship. He made also some effort, though to no great profit, to teach himself the rudiments of Greek. Already his drift towards a historical rather than philosophical treatment of Divinity was perceptible to himself, and he further realised the significance of classical study in relation to the interpretation of Christian origins. He had already acquired special regard for the writings of Lorenzo Valla, from whom he gained not only a concept of the function of grammar, but something also of the method of historical criticism as applied to ecclesiastical claims.

At Paris Erasmus fell in with a group of English students pursuing studies in the University, and at the invitation of one of them, Lord Mountjoy, made a journey to England in the year 1499. From London he went in the autumn to Oxford, and formed acquaintance with Colet and Grocyn, and the small circle of men of humanist leanings gathered round them.

These men had returned from Italy filled with zeal to imbue English learning with the new spirit. Grocyn had publicly taught Greek in Oxford; Colet was busy upon the Pauline Epistles. Outside Oxford, More and Warham, Linacre, Fisher, the elder Elyot, were in their several ways widening the intellectual interests of thoughtful society. These men were the true founders of the English Revival. The early scholars who had, before the last decade of the fifteenth century, found their way from this country to Italy were like this latter group, predominantly Oxford men. It is not difficult to realise their objects, and we can follow their journeys to Florence or Rome, and note the almost invariable attraction which Ferrara had for them in its palmy days, when the elder Guarino and his son drew the ambitious intellect of Europe to the Court of the D'Este princes. Gray, Frea, Gunthorpe and Fleming were all clerics ; they gained preferment by their pilgrimage, but their learning left little impress on their contemporaries. They started no tradition and founded no humanist school of thought. It is questionable whether the valuable library of MSS, which Gray brought from Ferrara, and which ultimately he gave to Balliol, evoked any particular desire to read them in the fortunate College. There were other influences at work in Oxford which foreshadowed the new impulse. Vitelli, an Italian scholar, was teaching Greek, as a private tutor, in New College, about 1470–1475. In Magdalen the humanist bent became pronounced early in the new century under Claypole, and Colet himself may have been a member of the same society. But the association of Erasmus with the Oxford group was destined to prove a stimulus to a definite humanist movement in England, which was even more effectual than that which originated with Agricola at Heidelberg. For example, the foundation of the avowedly humanist college of Christ's at Cambridge, by Fisher, was probably due to Erasmus' influence. Erasmus indeed, had he chosen, might have found a permanent home in England. Probably no country appealed so strongly to his taste. But he resembled many other humanist scholars in resenting all suggestion to tie himself down for long to specific work or fixed residence. A contract of this kind irked Agricola, as has been seen ; and all his life Erasmus would hold himself free to come and go as he chose. But he had a further reason for cherishing liberty.

He realised his ignorance of Greek, and believed that in Italy only could he attain his desire. Seven years were to elapse before his wish could reach fulfilment; and during this interval he devoted himself to a serious study of the less difficult authors. He would sell his coat for Greek texts, he declared; but competent teachers were not to be found in France or the Low Countries. Yet he made rapid progress. His industry and power of reading were extraordinary. His health was neglected; he begged, with little reserve it must be said, for means to live a student's life. Paris, Orleans, Louvain, Holland, London again, were in turn his home. He collected Latin adages, translated Lucian (in company with More) and tried his hand at Euripides. Efforts were made to keep him at Louvain as Professor of Rhetoric in the University. At last, at the age of 40, already perhaps a better-read Latinist than France or England could show, he started (1506) for Italy. He was consistently indifferent to much which was characteristic of the living Italy which lay before his eyes—the Italy of the zenith of the Renaissance. Florence, Padua, Venice, Rome, were to him merely the homes of learned men and of ancient libraries. The throbbing pulse of the fullest, most eager life the modern world has known left him unaffected. At Venice he buried himself in the printing-house of Aldus; at Florence he would hold no intercourse with people who talked mere Tuscan; in Bologna and Padua he devoted himself almost exclusively to Greek. For a few months (1509) he saw the brilliant and dignified exterior of Roman humanism. He abandoned the monastic dress. On a sudden invitation from Mountjoy he returned to London to congratulate the young King Henry upon his accession.

Erasmus was now one of the acknowledged leaders of European learning. For the next five years England was his home. He lived in or near London, where More's house at Chelsea was open to him. It was there that he wrote the *Praise of Folly*. Grocyn, now in London, made him welcome for a year or more. By advice of Fisher, the Chancellor of Cambridge, he accepted the offer of a lectureship in Greek (August, 1511), unendowed however, and by no means well-secured, and delivered lectures in divinity on the Lady Margaret foundation. His influence at Cambridge (1511–1514) was by no means limited to the work he did with the occasional pupils who came to him to read Chrysoloras and Gaza—disappointed, we may conjecture, with the great scholar's impatience of rudiments—nor even to the direct effect of his readings of Jerome. Erasmus gave standing to the new learning, and more than any other single person created the atmosphere in which humanism could flourish.

During his Cambridge period he was greatly occupied with the fortunes of the new school of St Paul's, which Colet (since 1505 Dean of the Cathedral) was planning when Erasmus reached England in 1509. It may well be that the scheme would never have been realised but for the stimulus and zealous activity of Erasmus. He looked for masters, and helped to find Lily. He edited and amended the fragmentary Latin accidence which the head-master drew up for junior pupils under the title *De Octo Partium Orationis Constructione.* He completed the *De Copia* at Cambridge and offered it as a contribution to the teaching of composition—and a very valuable one—in the new school. His concern for the problems raised by this experiment in true humanist education set him upon thinking out systematically the principles of a curriculum, which were formulated in the *De Ratione Studii* (1511); and the *Colloquia* (1516) were a product of the same interest. "I am now all but an Englishman," he wrote in 1512, "such is the welcome I receive." But like most humanists Erasmus was conscious of his deserts, and found the benefactions of his English friends unequal to his expectations and his needs. So in spite of the dignified leisure which Cambridge afforded for the prosecution of historical divinity, and the pleasure he derived from his opportunities of advancing learning and education, he decided (1515) to go to Basel to arrange for the publication of the New Testament and the Jerome, the product of his English residence. He was back in London for a brief visit during the two years following, but until 1522 his principal place of abode was Louvain, where he was concerned with the project for the new humanist school, the Collegium Trilingue, in which several of his personal friends (in part at his instance) were engaged. But he himself declined a post as professor, just as he had refused an opening suggested by Budaeus at the Court of Francis I. He became, however, Counsellor to Archduke Charles (1516), a post with the indispensable quality of involving no services.

The shadow of the Reformation controversies now began to loom over western Europe. Louvain and its University were plunged into the conflict. Erasmus was a reformer, but no fanatic; above all no separatist. His was the temperament which sees two sides to a great question. No one had more bitterly denounced the obscurantism of the average ecclesiastic and the irreligion of the Papal court and policy. His instinct was for flight to a region where he could continue undisturbed his classical and patristic studies, and thus contribute material for the true solution of those grave issues whose importance no one realised more clearly than he. He cared far more for education than for dogmatic encounter, for peace and unity than for nationality, whether in Church or State. Thus in 1522 he betook himself to Basel, where, with an interval spent at the neighbouring Freiburg-in-Breisgau, he passed the years that remained to him in editing and translating, in elaborating his ideas on education in the *De Pueris statim ac liberaliter instituendis*, in the *Institutio Matrimonii Christiani*, in which he developed his views on the up-bringing of girls, and in the *Ciceronianus*, which is in essence a dialogue upon the true function of Latinity in modern life. Through correspondence he remained in close touch with the world of affairs and of scholarship, and watched, with ever-growing discouragement, the drift of the ecclesiastical crisis towards the disruption of Christian unity. He died, after many years' suffering from chronic illness, in 1536.

It might be expected, perhaps, that an acute contemporary observer, viewing the Italian Renaissance from without, might be better placed for appreciating its content than those actually absorbed in its development. But it is certain that, with the qualified exception of Agricola, no son of the northern Revival grasped or expressed the many-sided significance of the Quattrocento in the sense that Poliziano, or Castiglione, and, indeed, hundreds of cultivated citizens of Florence or Venice typified it. Therefore, in accepting Erasmus as a representative personality of the age of Revival in Teutonic Europe, it is with the qualification that he expresses in part only that which the Italians had elaborated during the century which was closed by the French invasions from 1494–1501.

Erasmus, in fact, views the forces of the age as a man of Letters. Antiquity laid its spell upon him not less stringently than upon Bruni or Poliziano. To him, as to them, it stood for a Golden Age. Humanist scholarship did not, as yet, admit of a critical judgment of the actual conditions, moral, social, or economic, of the great age of Athens, or of the Augustan empire. The Roman world was, it is not unfair to say, presented as the ideal, once realised, of a universal state ruling in peace and justice the entire human race, adorned with arts, Letters, and achievements of practical skill, which mankind had lost through barbarism and was then struggling to recover. Hence, to Erasmus, antiquity was not a subject of liberal study alone, but partook of the nature of a working ideal of social order, to be adjusted to modern conditions, chief among which was the supremacy of the Christian faith. Hence the passionate note discernible in all that he has to say concerning the function of ancient literature in the education of the new generation. To deny the claims of antique learning was to take stand against human progress. For the illumination that the age craved for in every department of life lay there. Progress meant, therefore, to hark back to an ideal once perfectly realised in a historic past.

As a training for life the antique culture lacked, for northern humanists, one special sanction which it possessed for the Italian, the sanction, namely, of patriotic feeling. The Rome of Scipio or Augustus belonged to the new Italy as it did not belong to Teutonic Germany or England. The history and the tongue of Rome were, to such nations, those of a foreign people. This affected the point of view and inevitably drew with it differences of method. The use of Latin speech, and the modes of acquiring it, were, due exceptions made, a different thing north of the Alps. In spite of all the skill and the pressure which went to the teaching of spoken and written Latin, the results were never proportionate; and when once the vernacular attained literary status and knowledge advanced Latin and Greek became just mental disciplines or aids to taste. Reaction, whether from the standpoint of Montaigne, or of Bacon, or of Locke, was inevitable.

We discern in Erasmus an obstinate refusal to admit the inevitable difference in the position of Latin as between Italy and northern countries. He has four main lines of proof which converge to enforce the acceptance of humanism as the one possible training for life in the modern world. First, the study of the classical languages and literatures strengthens religion. It does this in various ways. The study of the Bible or the Fathers in the light of knowledge, which is attainable only by students of classical antiquity, tends directly to more intelligent views of the grounds of faith, and dissociates Christianity as a living force from current superstitions and corruptions. Further, the study of the moral teaching of the finer minds of the ancient world is in itself a support to true religion; indeed, in certain of these we may recognise the working of the Divine Spirit. The opposition to humanism on religious grounds, proceeding mainly from his bitter enemies

the monastic orders, Erasmus took in hand with the thoroughness characteristic of his controversial method. For a question
of religion or morals had more weight behind it in northern
opinion than south of the Alps. So Erasmus is at pains to
show the means by which suspected perils may be evaded.
The Fathers, he explains, quote Pagan writers with approval.
Some classical myths are edifying to all Christians, others are
to be read allegorically. Approached in the proper temper—a
condition which parents and masters can secure—ancient lore
will yield its honey even from flowers wherein something of
poison may lie hid. As to the pretended danger to belief
Erasmus flatly disbelieved the good faith of the accusation.
In sum the northern scholars, Catholic and Protestant,
accepted humanism as an aid to Christian life, and the able
men among the Reformers soon recognised in it a powerful
instrument in their cause.

In the second place, Erasmus found in antiquity a politico-
social ideal of supreme importance for his own age. Imperial
Rome was, he argued, a standing witness to the reign of law
and peace, with the resultant benefits of the spread of knowledge and of the well-being of the helpless part of mankind.
His hatred of war and of the personal ambitions which in his
experience were the standing cause of war, was, perhaps, his
one fixed conviction in the field of politics. Any force making
for international accord was welcomed by him. Enthusiasm
for sound learning might well lead rulers towards higher aims
before which bounds of State or language might be disregarded.
To secure peace, as Rome had enjoyed it, Erasmus would
have sacrificed much that, though he was unconscious of it,
did actually constitute the modern world. Nationality he
disliked, vernaculars he despised, racial creeds and churches
were utterly abhorrent to him. For each involved divisions,
antagonisms, in the last resort, war. A universal language—
Latin, a universal church, a uniform standard of culture, and
perpetual peace formed his social ideal. To weld together

a reformed Catholicism and a rational humanism was, as he conceived it, the highest contribution which he himself could make to progress.

(3) In the third place, only through systematic study of ancient writers could human knowledge be purified and advanced. "Within the two literatures of Greece and Rome are contained all the knowledge that we recognise as vital to mankind." In Melanchthon's words, "a world in which the monuments of Greek learning are unknown is a world where men are always children, or, to put it in another figure, are for ever groping their way through blinding mists." Every department of knowledge is instanced by Erasmus and his successors as demanding reform through enlightened study of antiquity. Not only is this true of religion, of literature, of the arts, of history, and of oratory, where proof is easy, but it holds good also of applied knowledge, and professional studies: law, medicine, education, mathematics, the sciences, politics, war[1]. Hence the importance of first-hand acquaintance with ancient books. Melanchthon, in strictly Erasmian spirit, would refuse a medical diploma to a candidate unable to read Galen or Aristotle in the original. There was much truth in the contention that in most branches of knowledge, especially in applied science, the level of Greek and Roman attainment had not been recovered. The bearing of this conviction upon the scope and method of classical education as understood by Erasmus is obvious.

(4) Lastly, Erasmus perceives, like the Italians, though with an inevitable difference, the intimate relation between humanism and behaviour. The ancients had developed a social code and standards of personal bearing to match the worthiness of their ideal of the inner life. It was, as will be shown later, one of

---

[1] Upon this characteristic of the humanist educational ideal, cp. Woodward, *Vittorino*, p. 182 sqq. and infra p. 286 for a definite application to English politics by Elyot.

the characteristic tasks of the Revival in Italy to work out the ideal of the modern man in society. Erasmus also, in far less favourable surroundings than those of Mantua and Urbino, sees the same correspondence of mental refinement and the courtesies of intercourse. He pours out his scorn upon the petty lords of the soil whom he knew in German lands, their arrogance and their boorishness, their mean concept of life, their coarse self-indulgence. True, he expects no more from them, for they ridicule learning, despise education, and hold a scholar on a lower level than their groom or their cook. He has, therefore, no difficulty in explaining their manners. For behaviour follows interests. Hence a boy, privileged to walk in the company of the great minds of old, is quickly taught how to adjust his outward bearing to such society, and how to manifest in his whole personality that inward civility of the mind which is the product of noble studies. On such grounds Erasmus wrote his little manual, *De Civilitate Morium Puerilium,* for the behoof of the boy, and insists repeatedly that the duty of both parents is to provide for him such home environment that unconsciously his earliest impressions will be of gentle sort.

It is evident that this beneficent influence of classical culture could only operate through the education of the young generation. Erasmus therefore put his best efforts to the task of stimulating the spread of a truer concept of what education implied. He has an intimate knowledge of the problems involved. His insight into child-nature is remarkable ; he perceives the need of reforming the education of women ; he deals in a spirit of sound common sense with the first stages of teaching, and with the possibilities indicated by boy-nature. He adopted the best ideas or curricula current in Italian schools. He has considered the methods of teaching language, the place of grammar, of construing and composition, and the kind of books likely to be helpful. Organisation and administration of schools, qualifications of masters, co-operation of parents with teachers, companionship, boy-interests, were subjects of long observation and reflection. Though never actually engaged in the teaching of children, Erasmus was essentially a practical "educator," whose advice no schoolmaster in Europe would have dreamt of disregarding.

The Erasmian psychology was that of most humanists who stood outside the influence of the Reformation. The body counted for less with Erasmus than with the great teachers of Italy; he was after all a monk, and a student. Mental activity was determined by the co-operation of Natura, Ratio and Usus. Natura is the given, innate, endowment; *general*, as "aptitudo quaedam ad discendum," possessed by every one; *special*, as the bent of the individual, almost always discernible by the skilful teacher. Ratio is the faculty of thought which differentiates man from lower creation. Its native tendency is to truthful judgment. It is not clear how Erasmus placed Ratio in respect of observation and imagination. Usus is the application and practice of what is learnt. Natura is, therefore, bare capacity, not developed skill; a ploughed field ready for the seed; soft clay prepared for the potter. It is eager to respond to external impression. Hence the fundamental doctrine of Erasmian education. "Efficax res est natura sed hanc vincit efficacior institutio"; "educatio superat omnia"; "homines, mihi crede, non nascuntur sed finguntur." There is no limit to the effect of wise education, and at the same time, neglect, or perverse training, may drag down even a nature of promising capacity. This was a view of human nature which, as Luther saw, was perilously Pelagian. It postulated innate goodness, and a complete freedom of the will, and was scarcely consistent with a conviction of original Sin.

The broad ends of education, as conceived by Erasmus, are laid down in the following passage: "Sicut prima [pars], ita praecipua, est, ut tenellus animus imbibat pietatis seminaria, proxima ut liberales disciplinas et amet et perdiscat, tertia est, ut ad vitae officia instruatur, quarta est ut a primis statim aevi

rudimentis civilitati morum adsuescat[1]." It may be safely
affirmed that to Erasmus, as to the great Italians, education
was training for social service in church, state, city and family;
yet the merely professional studies make little appeal to him.
The development of individual capacity and erudition through
the study of a great civilisation is the true means to effectiveness in every honourable walk in life. Practical experience is
not an adequate preparation for the practical life itself. A
liberal education is one common to all men whatever their
career. It is analogous to the training of the "Orator" as
elaborated by Quintilian; it is practically identical with that of
the "Governor" as described by Erasmus' own disciple,
Thomas Elyot.

It may be noted here that the humanist education implied
"an order of the learned[2]," to use More's phrase. The
Utopians made choice of a few "which be exempt and discharged of all other labours, and appointed only to learning;
that is to say, such in whom, even from their very childhood,
they have perceived a singular towardness, a fine wit, and a
mind apt to good learning." "All in their childhood be
instruct in learning....in their own native tongue." This
expresses the attitude of humanism to the question of the dis-
tribution of education. From the nature of the case their
ideal was for the few, a privileged minority, in no way determined by birth or wealth, but by capacity[3]. Yet its tendency
was to set up a class, not narrow or professional in type, rather
an educated upper-middle class, upon which were falling the
responsibilities now slipping from the feudal society. It is,
therefore, true to say that the Renaissance offered little in the
way of an educational hope to the people, except on condition

[1] Cp. Woodward, *Erasmus*, p. 73: and *Op.* i. 1033 B, C.

[2] *Utopia*, Book II. p. 128, Camelot edition of Robinson's translation.

[3] Mulcaster more than fifty years afterwards was anxious lest this class
should outgrow the economic need.

that the individual rose out of his class to receive a training for a rank above it.

It has often been said that the humanists had no contribution to offer to the problem of the education of the young child. It may be admitted that they had, like most teachers to-day, but an empirical knowledge of appropriate material and methods of instruction. But at least they recognised the existence of the problem, and some of them tried their hands at solving it. Erasmus devotes the most important of his specifically educational writings, the *De Pueris*[1], to questions of the first steps in education. He realises the force of heredity, of unconscious imitation, of early impressions — aesthetic and moral. The direct function of the mother he rates low, like many humanists, partly as a consequence of his knowledge of the poor equipment which women received in his day. He is willing to allow to her the oversight of the child up to the age of six or seven, when matters of health, habits, religious impress, exercise and control of appetite, are of main concern. He attaches high significance to bodily fitness in early childhood as the basis of future intellectual vigour. But it must be allowed that he had little or none of that Greek feeling for physical perfection which in a degree marked Vittorino, and which was an essential factor in the "complete personality" of the Italian Renaissance.

To the home properly belongs the duty of laying the first foundation of instruction; for systematic teaching is not desirable before the seventh year. The elements of Christian faith, observance of Church order, and the moral basis of life, are inculcated at the mother's knee. Side by side, training in refined speech (he would prefer that it should be Latin), elements of reading, drawing and writing, find their place. Letters are to be modelled not on German script but,

---

[1] Versions (with abbreviations) of the *De Ratione Studii* and the *De Pueris* in Woodward's *Erasmus*.

with sound instinct, on the fine lettering of an imperial sestertius. The use of natural objects, such as animals, or the garden, and the furnishings and ceremonial of the home, will provide exercise for vocabulary and instructive conversation. Everything is done "per lusum"; attractiveness, spontaneity, parental co-operation with the tutor, are the marks of all that is taught at this stage. Erasmus is severe upon fathers who threaten and drive, and who cannot control temper in discipline. He understood that the art of watching sympathetically the action and thought of childhood is a difficult but most necessary condition of success. "Non mediocris artis est instituere primam aetatem." Least of all is it a function to hand over to the failures of life.

With the seventh year the boy reaches the stage of systematic instruction. In the abstract Erasmus would prefer home tuition under the father's direction. Failing that—few fathers have the leisure, fewer still the necessary capacity—the choice lies between a civic day-school, should such be available, and a highly qualified praeceptor engaged to teach a small group of boys in the home of one or another of them. Erasmus has a low opinion of the average school-master of the time (1520–1530) —as had Elyot—and judges still more severely the schools carried on in religious Houses. The qualifications of the praeceptor are carefully reviewed and pitched at a high level. Thorough mastery of Greek and Latin, wide reading, and conversational power in Latin are especially requisite. Success in instruction will depend upon the extent to which the tutor is capable of discerning the "natura" of his charge, the taste, bent, and special powers which distinguish him. Erasmus hopes to bring into existence a new type of master; he was scoffed at in his Cambridge days for urging the teaching career upon men of standing in the University, and defended himself with feeling. He never mentions Vittorino, but it is clear that in his personality he would have found the ideal he had formed.

The beginnings of school-work consist chiefly of Latin but

not of Latin grammar. The position which Erasmus allots to grammar is significant of the trend of the new education. The mediaevalist had treated grammar as an end in itself: to Erasmus, emphatically, it was but an instrument: to the School-men it was indistinguishable from the laws of thought of which it was the expression: to Valla, and all humanists after him, it was but a summary of classical usage. " Ego pro lege accipio," said Valla, "quicquid magnis auctoribus placuit." Erasmus has special praise for the *Rudimenta* of N. Perotti, a pupil of Vittorino, which was the first systematic text-book on humanist lines. The method of approach which Erasmus lays down is that of tentative conversation, object teaching[1], dialogues, reading easy texts, oral and written prose. Latin was treated as a living tongue, in which the facts of modern life, as well as those of classical times, were capable of expression. Like Cordier he urges parents to talk Latin at home, as did the Estiennes, the elder Montaigne, and Thomas More, for the children's good, as one might to-day plead for French at meal-times. Grammar was not to be disregarded, but proportioned strictly to actual needs at each stage. Logical completeness was by no means to be sought; let such rudiments be taught and in such order as are necessary to the understanding of easy authors. But forms unusual or anomalous must be ignored where possible. The actual arrangement of a first manual of accidence and syntax will accord with the method of teaching followed by the compiler. The order of Guarino, of Ognibene, of Lily, of Melanchthon presents marked divergences. Not until the influence of Melanchthon became dominant in humanism did grammar of the logically complete type begin to impose itself upon the school. Erasmus postponed such study of the subject until the later stages of education, when he required it to be learnt with thoroughness.

---

[1] Cp. the Colloquy *Convivium Religiosum*; extract (in English) in *Erasmus*, p. 226.

In the *De Ratione Studii* he has sketched the reading which he considers proper to a humanist school, and the course in rhetoric which should accompany it. He apologises for treating a subject which Quintilian has made his own. In the region of moral instruction he would supplement the Gospels and *Proverbs* by selections from Plutarch, Seneca and Aesop. It is a prime object with him to exhibit the moral content of the ancient authors, and to draw lessons in political and social judgment. "Postremo ad philosophiam veniat et poetarum fabulas apte trahat ad mores," is his direction to the master. The hints given upon the mode of reading an author deserve comparison with the method contained in the *De Ordine* of B. Guarino[1]. That Erasmus had clear intuitions upon sound psychological principles of teaching, though without arriving at them by way of mental analysis, is obvious to the careful student of his writings on education.

The place given to the study of Orators and the technique of rhetoric is characteristic of humanism as developed in Italy, and the reasons for it need not be repeated here. But whilst in Italy and still more in Germany and England, rhetorical exercises tended to the development of vernacular facility (e.g. in political writing and in preaching), Erasmus, contemptuous of all modern languages, regards Latin oratory as an end in itself. Quintilian and Cicero are naturally the high authorities, and by senior pupils select orations of the latter will be minutely studied as illustrations of the formal rules. Livy, Sallust and Tacitus, Demosthenes and Isocrates, with Lucan, the rhetorical poet, will be read as models in composition. The importance of the epistolary and declamatory styles is dwelt upon; and it appears that all humanists urged a laborious study of the *Epistles* of Cicero upon beginners. The chief modern aids available were the *De Copia* and *De Conscribendis Epistolis* of Erasmus, and the *Elegantiae* of Valla.

---

[1] B. Guarino, *De Ordine*, etc., in *Vittorino*, p. 117.

This pre-occupation with rhetorical skill carried with it certain obvious perils, particularly did it affect the humanist judgment of historians. Erasmus was, it must be admitted, deficient in historical perception. He was too alert in his search for persuasiveness of style and for overt edification to be a sound judge of historical writing or an instructive teacher of history. He insists no doubt upon its study as necessary to a man of education: Plutarch, Livy, Sallust, Herodotus and Xenophon, are often named by him in this connection. It is, however, true that the more the historian displays the artifice of the stylist the more sure he is of humanist applause. And we can see from the *De Ratione Studii* how imperfectly Erasmus realised the proper content of history by the themes he proposes for senior pupils. The habit of treating history mainly as a body of moral illustration Erasmus shares with most humanists. That in an uncritical age the personalities and striking incidents of history should be primarily seized upon was inevitable, and a further explanation may be found in the ever present fact of the importance of outstanding individualities in the contemporary world. The development of the art of history, critical and constructive, was not in the result the achievement of the scholar, but of the diplomatist and the politician.

It is obvious that the study of Greek was pursued with aims and upon methods differing materially from those accepted in the case of Latin. "Ex instituto omnis fere rerum scientia e Graecis oratoribus petenda est." Roman culture, moreover, is only half intelligible apart from a knowledge of Greek civilisation. Hence all sound education involves acquaintance with both languages. But the end in view was chiefly a knowledge of the content of Greek learning and literature. There is little stress laid on minute linguistic study, on composition, and none at all on conversational power; but much on wide reading, and a grasp of the thought and poetry of the Greek world. A first-hand knowledge of Greek spread broadly through the professions and the Church would prove a reforming force of the first rank.

As regards logic, Erasmus had so profound a distrust of all that savoured of scholastic methods, whether in grammar or theology, that he has rarely a word of approval for this subject in modern education, with the conspicuous exception of his respect for the *De Inventione* of Agricola. On the question of the place of natural and mathematical studies in education, Erasmus has the usual limitations of the humanist. He is indeed desirous of a wide range of information upon nature and geography, but the sources he commends are "sound authors"; from them the orator, i.e. "the educated man," will have at his command for public speaking or for conversation "all that varied mass of material which the curiosity of antiquity has handed down to us. To such belongs, first the natural history of birds, quadrupeds, wild animals, serpents, insects, fishes: this will be chiefly derived from ancient writers, with additions from our own observations. Next we shall prize the accounts of singular adventures handed down to us by trustworthy authorities, such as the story of Arion and the dolphin, of the dragon who rescued his deliverer from danger of the lion, who returned kindness for kindness, and others which Pliny vouches for. There is also, in the third place, a vast body of facts concerning geographical phenomena, some of which are extraordinary, and these are of peculiar value to the scholar; though even the usual occurrences of nature are not to be passed over. These again are partly drawn from antiquity, partly are within our own experience. I refer to rivers, springs, oceans, mountains, precious stones, trees, plants, flowers: concerning all of which comparisons should be derived and stored away in memory for prompt use in description or argument[1]." The result of such knowledge of plants or animals, even if gained at first-hand, cannot be called a scientific apprehension of

[1] Erasmi *Opera*, i. 389 c.

facts; it is shown chiefly in increased Latin vocabulary and a better understanding of classical allusions to nature. Three colloquies, the *Convivium Religiosum, Amicitia* and *Problema* provide apt illustrations of this attitude. As to arithmetic, music and astronomy, a slight modicum of information suffices. In truth no subject which does not directly appeal to the human side of existence had much interest for Erasmus. It has been seen, moreover, elsewhere in this volume that natural studies had, in the first decades of the sixteenth century, barely begun to acquire that precision and systematisation which are indispensable to the effective use of learning for purposes of instruction.

The education of girls was a subject which occupied Erasmus in the later years of his life. The Italian ideal of a woman's training and status was familiar to him. But Erasmus was aware that the reasons for the neglect of girls' education in German lands were deeply rooted in the social order. Public opinion, according but a low place to woman in society, was content with an instruction to correspond to it. Erasmus seems to have approached the question from the point of view of the uplifting of the home influences which mould the boy's early years. He demands a new standard of training for motherhood. Much as he deprecates the evil effects wrought by uneducated and frivolous women upon the mind and character of young children, he recognises to the full what is implied in the loss of the finely-tempered affection of the mother. Hence he looks upon the training of girls as necessarily marching with that of boys. Further, he believes that amongst the worst enemies of character stand triviality and indolence, which again are the consequences of lack of opportunity for the cultivation of lofty interests. The fuller life is the better life. He urges, therefore, that type of women's education on classical lines which was elaborated a century before by Lionardo Bruni, and was current in the more refined society of Italy. Erasmus had been impressed by the intellectual atmosphere of the More household at Chelsea, and desires to see home surroundings wholesome and cheerful, yet marked by sober decorum, the mother's wise and unselfish patience guiding rather than repressing the hopes and vitality of youth. The method of training girls accepted in German society of the time he holds up to scorn, as producing the worst faults which mark feminine nature—capriciousness, vanity, shallowness, love of intrigue. There is much in common between this criticism of Erasmus and the opinions of Bercher referred to in a later chapter[1]. Upon one point Erasmus lays especial stress. He makes a striking appeal to parents to respect the judgment and the feelings of their daughters in the momentous decision between the "religious" and the married life. The personal note here struck is unmistakable.

Finally, to Erasmus as to Vittorino, training in moral duty and religious obedience were the highest ends of all right education. The home alone can lay the foundations of character: the dignity of humanist training appears not least in this, that it fittingly equips those upon whom such high responsibility falls. The fatherhood of God, the brotherhood of men, are the sanctions of the family bond. By example, by kindly discipline, by direct instruction, the young boy will be led to realise the law of the Christian life. Especially must he learn to control temper, to check maliciousness, and to scorn lying. By the fourteenth year the bent of the rightly trained child should be definitely towards good. The systematic teaching of morals, from ethical writers, from historians, and from poets, forms no small part of a classical education. In this connection Plutarch stands only lower than the Fathers. Cicero, Seneca, Terence and Vergil, are all worthy to bear part in the task of moulding character. Not that Erasmus founds moral teaching on a purely literary basis. Its roots are

---

[1] Infra, ch. xii. p. 261. The Colloquy of *The Learned Lady and the Monk* is thoroughly characteristic of Erasmus' attitude.

securely twined through and through the fabric of home life and example. There is the further stimulus of intercourse with well-reputed elders, for the man of the Renaissance had no thought of confining youth in modern fashion to society of its own age and interests. Individuality should be encouraged by all available agencies: travel in particular is urged as a needful instrument for widening the mental horizon and inducing tolerance. The common end held out as the crown of all was the development of personality for the due service of the community and of God.

CHAPTER VII.

GUILLAUME BUDÉ'S *L'INSTITUTION DU PRINCE*.

REFERENCE has already been made to the high anticipations for the progress of learning aroused by the accession of Henry VIII, an event which brought Erasmus post-haste from Rome to London in 1509. The two other great powers of Europe passed within a few years under the sovereignty of young princes of no less promise who aroused no less vivid expectation of a brilliant future for themselves and their States. Francis I a youth of twenty succeeded Louis XII of France in 1515, and Charles the young King of Spain became Emperor in 1518. To such acute observers as Erasmus and Budé these happy events were fraught with significance for the cause of intellectual progress. Though in different, and in some respects, wholly unexpected ways, these three monarchs were in actual fact destined to be gravely concerned with that new world of politics and belief which was the unforeseen birth of "sound learning."

The Renaissance reached France from Italy in the train of the returning armies of Charles VIII and Louis XII. The romantic expedition of 1494, with Naples as its dazzling prize, which was in truth the beginning of the end of Italian independence, was, no less truly, an originative moment in French history of the first importance. The military procession—it was little more—of 1494-5 revealed Italy to France,—Italy, too, at a critical period of her development. In the last decade of the fifteenth century Italy was, it may be safely argued, at her apogee. In outward brilliance of life, indeed, Rome, Venice, and Milan were to attain the full measure of distinction in the century to follow. But that which expresses the Italian Renaissance, that which in truth it *is*, the spirit and the fashion of the men who were by turns its creatures and its creators, unfettered as yet by convention or by the constraining force of the stranger, lacked nothing of completeness. That the Frenchmen in their King's train should be profoundly impressed with the Renaissance man as they found him declared in Rodrigo Borgia, and his enigmatic son, in Ludovico Sforza or Ercole d'Este, is no cause for wonder. But they carried with them also across the Alps impressions, no less enduring, of men and of ideas of a different order. The grace and verve of the life both of the city and of the Court, the dignity of its outward setting in palace and villa, in civic hall and piazza, the instinct for beauty in art and in Letters, the high level of technic knowledge—in a word the refinement, the modernness, the forward impulse, of the Italian race awoke an alert response in the French spirit. When in the last years of the century Louis XII won for a time the Dukedom of Milan and became a standing factor in the world of Italian politics the influence of the classical Revival beyond the Alps grew to a steady, resistless current, carrying with it new inspirations in architecture, in fine art, and above all in Letters.

The bulwark of mediaevalism in France was the University of Paris, a force in the region of theological opinion not less powerful than the Papacy itself. At this period the University was far more narrow and intolerant, gifted with a much keener scent for the encroachments of the lay spirit than Renaissance Rome. It was the position of the University of Paris that rendered the task of French humanists peculiarly difficult. In Provence and in Burgundy the soil was already prepared for the new order of thought, but the intellectual and spiritual dominion of all France lay in Paris, to which was attracted the

studious mind of every province of the Kingdom. This vast
organised authority was put forth in unhesitating fashion on
behalf of the philosophy, logic, and theology of scholasticism.
Whatever be the particular knowledge, or teaching, which
Italian humanists or Protestant reformers from time to time
denounce, satirise, or cast from them, we are certain to find
that in the colleges of the University of Paris it had its chief
citadel and its most powerful defenders. Yet so universal was
its renown, so strong its attraction, that, amongst the men of
northern race at least, its critics and its fiercest enemies are
often those who have passed through its doors. Agricola,
Reuchlin, Erasmus, Vives, Calvin, Dolet, Cordier, Sturm, were
all students or teachers in its colleges, and all spent the best
years of their lives in fighting its most cherished ideals.

It was natural that the humanists north of the Alps,
watching the brilliant progress of the new learning in Italy
should be struck by the parallel between the attitude of their
own Universities to classical enquiry and that of the Italian.
Not from the traditional schools of Law or Theology but from
the Courts or the free communities had come the first and
strongest impulse to humanism. Padua, Bologna and Pavia
had been but as grudging hosts to uninvited guests and their
functions as leaders in intellectual advance had been abandoned
to Venetian patricians, or Florentine bankers, to the petty rulers
of smaller despotisms, or to popes like Nicolas V and Pius II.
Before such patrons, who did but represent an ever-growing
body of lay opinion, the obscurantism of professional interests
perforce gave way, and before the fifteenth century was out the
Italian Universities had granted to liberal learning equality of
opportunity and new foundations had come into being avowedly
in response to classical enthusiasms. Hence in England, in
Germany and above all in France the hopes of the humanist
scholar centred in the person of the Sovereign, Duke, King, or
Emperor, and later, and less securely, in the enlightened civic
Corporation. In France the commanding position of the great

national University rendered any influence less powerful than the King's of no avail as a protection to the weak and scattered forces of humanism.   It was to Francis I, therefore, young, ardent and ambitious, that scholars turned in their fight with scholasticism, professional privilege and ecclesiastical suspicion.

Guillaume Budé was born in January, 1468, his father being a citizen of Paris.   Of his education we know only that it was of a perfunctory sort.   He studied Law at Orleans as a young man and was much hampered by his meagre powers of reading Latin.   But in his twenty-third year he devoted himself to the classics in a sudden access of intellectual ambition. He taught himself Greek, and read widely in Latin.   Like Erasmus his contemporary, and Scaliger his successor in Greek scholarship, he owed his skill in Greek to his own efforts. Besides the ancient literatures, he acquired a knowledge of mathematics, theology, philosophy and medicine.   He was possessed of means sufficient to enable him to pursue the life of a scholar unfettered by professional work.   Soon after his thirtieth year he was busy upon translating Plutarch and St Basil, then followed a work on Roman Law, and in 1514 his first important treatise, *De Asse et partibus ejus*, primarily a study of the Roman monetary system, but branching out into a much wider enquiry into the economic aspects of ancient civilisation.   He put ten years' work into the treatise, which was at once recognised as the product of a scholar of the first rank both in France and abroad.   In 1516 he wrote in French his tract *De l'Institution du Prince*, addressed to the young King Francis I; in 1527 a slight and not significant treatise *De Studio Literarum Recte et Commode Instituendo*, and finally his monumental work, *Commentarii Linguae Graecae*, a vast collection of solid yet unorganised material, dictionary, criticism and syntax in one, which established his fame as the first Greek scholar in Europe.   Certain other translations and a considerable correspondence with learned men complete the tale of his production.   Francis I promptly recognised his distinction.   The young King was in no sense a well educated youth, but he was quick, receptive, and had fine artistic feeling. He was eager to place himself as a patron of art and learning abreast of the Italian princes with whose achievements he had already no slight acquaintance.   Scholars and artists were welcome in his Court ; and humanists became ambassadors or secretaries.   Budé was made Royal Librarian (1522), and had the King's promise to found a great College of Letters such as Wolsey was meditating at Oxford and Erasmus and his group at Louvain.   The elder Montaigne rejoiced to see the day when sound learning received so notable an impulse ; Erasmus congratulated France and her scholars in their happy lot under a prince of such promise.

Budé therefore was not without congenial elements in his environment.   But he was a poor courtier, and at Fontainbleau, though the royal collection was growing under his hands, and was especially sumptuous in respect of the beauty as well as the rarity of its Greek MSS., he pined for greater freedom.   But his influence with Francis gave him opportunity of aiding in the establishment of the Royal Press (1526), to which Robert Estienne became first printer, and of the long contemplated Collége de France.   The warrant of foundation of the Press runs thus : "We are persuaded that these sound studies will give birth in our Kingdom to theologians who shall teach the sacred doctrines of religion ; to magistrates who shall ad-minister justice without partiality and in the spirit of public equity ; and finally to skilled administrators, the lustre of the State, who will be capable of sacrificing their private interest to affection for the public good....Such are among the benefits that may reasonably be looked for from sound studies and from them almost exclusively."   The Royal Press was the instrument through which the noblest achievements of French scholarship were given to the world.

The Collége de France was initiated by the establishment of new Chairs in Greek and Hebrew in 1530, followed by similar foundations for mathematics and Latin (1534). This modest but significant beginning was due to the unwearied urgency of Budé in the teeth of an opposition which he denounces with an eloquence reminding us of Erasmus girding at the obscurantist Orders. Budé outlived Erasmus by a few years, dying in 1540. But when he died humanism had won the day, and was fermenting within the intellectual life of France, already, indeed, transforming it. It has often been remarked that the humanists had no difficulty in perceiving the importance of the education of the Prince both for the spread of the new learning and for the securing of their own maintenance. The Prince was idealised as Maecenas and Augustus in one. The Italians had set the fashion; Vergerius, Aeneas Sylvius, Filelfo, Patrizi (1494) had all put their hands to the task of presenting treatises on the subject to their patrons. Erasmus imitated them, though the *Institutio Principis Christiani* treats of the royal duty rather than the training needed to teach him what it is. Budé wrote immediately upon the accession of Francis I (1515), but the work was not printed until 1546, one possible reason for the delay being the publication of the tract of Erasmus just mentioned, with which Budé did not desire his less impressive vernacular piece to come into critical comparison.

Budé has, as his aim, to win over Francis I to humanist sympathies, for the sake of the glory of France in the world of learning. He is convinced that France will be advanced by the possession of a King who is also a philosopher. That philosophers should be Kings is of course forbidden by the hereditary principle. Like Erasmus he couples national happiness with assured peace. The Prince must cultivate "sapientia," practical wisdom, rather than "contemplatio." Abstract and absolute knowledge are for a King less desirable than such as concerns itself with economic and political well-being. It is necessary to presuppose a King born with full average ability : such a one by education will rise above the average, and will so command the widest intellectual horizon. This is attained by enlightened experience, the study of good examples, and intimate intercourse with men of learning by whom he will be guided to the fruitful interpretation of the great past. Hence the importance of history in Budé's scheme. It is worth a whole College of Professors.

The form in which Budé presents his ideal of the qualities and duties of a Prince is not analytic but hortatory. Hence it lends itself to much trite illustration and second-hand generalisations drawn from ancient books. The first part of the Tract consists mainly of general reflections upon the knowledge and virtues desirable in the good ruler, who is an abstraction, belonging to no time or place, and not realised as King of France. In the second and larger part, he arranges for contemplation a gallery of historical and traditional figures which serve as texts for the author's views upon moral and political wisdom.

But there is a note of the special purpose of the treatise in the remark that "Every man, even if he be a King, should be devoted to philology." Philology is interpreted as the desire for and love of Letters and all liberal learning, which is so-called because for its pursuit a man must be independent and free. Such learning again is called by the ancients "human" or "humanistic," for without interest in it, without "eruditio," the world would become animal and not human. But such learning is attainable only by such as know Greek and Latin. Budé sets forth the claim for the study of Greek as above all other knowledge. It is more important than Latin learning. As a language, as the embodiment of ideas, as the essential instrument of expression of philosophical truth it is unique. It is the necessary key to Latin, as the Romans readily allowed. Nay in the study of Roman history itself, one need not go outside Greek writers for a sound knowledge of the great periods. No element in Budé's personality is of so great moment as this passion for Greek learning, and he did not fail in his effort to enforce a due sense of its importance upon Francis.

Eloquence, the command of style, is necessary to a King, though less so than to the chief of a democratic State who has to uphold his policy by arts of persuasion. Pericles is quoted for the four conditions needful to a true leader of men ; the second is eloquence, without which knowledge is but a sword stuck fast in its scabbard. Now such eloquence cannot have been limited to Latin ; and Budé's own example in composing his tract in French is evidence of the relation of training in classical composition to skill in vernacular speech. Nor can we forget how, as a matter of history, the French tongue gained its fullness, its precision and flexibility by the aid of that process of translation from the classics which characterised the French literary activity in the latter years of the life of Budé.

Budé is conscious of that intimate connection between thought and expression which was always acutely present to the mind of humanists. Without clear speech definite thought is impossible. The scholastics of the University "will not understand that the function of eloquence is to serve as the instrument of knowledge in its relation to life, without which truth cannot be translated into action ; just as a mechanic engine which no one knows how to work is no engine at all but a mere mass of metal." "For all their Faculties, deprived of the aid of Letters, are scabbards without swords, which may serve to scare children but nothing else." An elaborated language is necessary not only to record and communication but to thinking. Now such highly organised speech can only be found in the Greek and Latin tongues, in their classical usage. Accuracy, promptitude, and security of thought demand a language which has reduced the various logical propositions, and all possible relations of affirmation, with such distinctions as those between concrete and abstract terms, to grammatical expression in rules. This is achieved in the classical languages. Hence, as Budé with all humanists affirms, the fact that the scholar, the man of affairs, the lawyer, doctor, theologian, had an instrument of exact thinking ready to hand made the great civilisations of antiquity possible. The grava- men which he lays against the Universities is that they refuse to perceive that progress in science demands above all a purified and enlarged instrument of analysis, viz., logically ordered language.

Next to eloquence stands history. To use an Elizabethan phrase, the Prince must be well-seen in languages, and so qualify himself to be their advocate in the struggle for sound learning. So, too, he must be trained in the reading of histories that he may encourage historians. The space which Budé gives to history in his tract shows the importance which he attached to it. His position is as follows. A knowledge of the past enables a man to judge more securely concerning the present, and to forecast the future with less vagueness. A Prince fortified by historical reading is a Janus or Argus: he will not be taken unawares. The gallery of examples which history affords through its incidents and personalities "excites to courageous and fruitful activity the sleeping germs of nobility which lie hidden in every sound nature." Thus to the responsive soul the path to fame and immortality is laid open and made smooth. But not every historian is competent to fulfil this function. The writer worthy of regard must with attractive presentation combine seriousness and dignity of purpose, so that pleasure and conviction alike result. Partisan- ship disfigures truth. Thus Augustus required that none but historians of accepted repute should treat of his reign. Plutarch is the finest model of historical treatment, even in Roman history, a claim which indicates the uncritical and limited concept of the historian's function characteristic of the Revival. Budé gives a large space to historical disquisition, particularly on Roman statesmen. He goes out of his way to declare that Pompey as described by Lucan stands foremost in the range of great names whom he commends for study. Budé no doubt thinks rather of historians than of history; it was indeed inevitable from his concept of the relation of truth to expression : history can only be conveyed through luminous exposition. But he believes that the approved historians are trustworthy. Modern court annalists and panegyrists are to be ignored, and a new type of historian raised up under the influence of patrons who know what true history is. France cannot boast of any writer of eminence in the sphere of history who has done anything to secure for his characters abiding fame. This will not be remedied until the King protects and rewards scholars who devote themselves to historical research and composition. So great has been the lack of liberality in France in encouraging and supporting such authors ! How different from the practice of the Greek world, nay of the Persians, Medes, Egyptians, and above all of the Romans. Through the works of ancient historians the fame of kings of old is enshrined in literature which neither fire nor wars have been able to destroy ; and now printing has rendered such monuments eternal.

It may be observed that Budé never rises to political philosophy. There is no discussion of the best form of State ; he accepts as beyond dispute that a well administered monarchy is the ideal constitution. He is struck by the long continued existence of the French kingdom. Nor could he well throw open to debate the basis of his patron's throne. Peace, good laws, honest finance are the marks of a " good Prince " and of happy subjects.

This leads him to consider how the lessons of history may best be brought home to his ideal pupil. The direct and systematic reading of historians is only effective when the student is a man of ripe experience. In other cases a learned teacher is needed, who can concentrate the attention of his pupil upon salient matter, and expound it to the adequate comprehension of the intelligence. Such a teacher can hardly be offered too high inducements, when the training of a Prince is concerned; for upon the tutor the fortunes not of one life but of millions may turn. Philip and Aristotle are, as usual, taken in illustration. The season of youth is not disposed to sustained attention to things of the mind; hence the need of one who shall by his talents command respect and by his character be strong to enforce it. Learning is a perennial treasure. It imparts in the stage of youth, moderation, in age self-reliance; it is in poverty a new wealth; in wealth a priceless jewel. To a prince, above all, it is a crowning gift.

Yet Budé was probably aware of the exceeding difficulty of winning and retaining the young King to his views. For his favour was not easy to secure. Francis' own education was scarcely of the kind to induce serious views upon higher learning. It was doubtful if he would prove strong enough to withstand the forces brought to bear against all interference with established privilege. Budé therefore attacks the obscurantists of the University in whom he recognises his chief foes. In particular he combats their pretence that the study of Greek and of classical Latin is tainted with heresy. He then enters upon the argument, common to humanists, both Catholic and Reformed, that the true beauty and meaning of Holy Scripture is perceptible only to those whose training rests upon the basis of antique learning. The precedents of Moses and Daniel, skilled in the wisdom of the Gentiles; of Basil and Gregory, pillars of the Temple in virtue of their classical scholarship; of Hilary, Jerome, Augustine, who move familiarly amongst the old authors. There is no antagonism between antiquity and religion. Yet Budé does not apparently realise the deep ethical-religious problems which a comparison of the Greek with the Christian temper suggests to the student of moral ideals.

He can plead that the Collége de Navarre has sheltered a teacher of Greek. Hieronymus Balbus, a Venetian, probably a very moderate Greek scholar, had gained a subsistence by teaching there (1485–1492) and Erasmus had found someone to help him in the early years of the century, but Budé aimed at the establishment of a College, with endowed Chairs of a status equal to the great professorships in Philosophy and Theology. This was attained partially at least by 1534. But in that very year a hardly less significant forward step in the progress of humanist teaching was taken in the famous provincial capital of south-west France, Bordeaux, which with Lyons was destined henceforward to be a notable centre of classical activities.

CHAPTER VIII.

LE COLLÉGE DE GUYENNE. MATHURIN CORDIER.

THE teaching of Budé in Paris, the development of humanist influences in the University through the new Chairs founded by Francis I, and, not least, the increasing activity of the Estiennes and other learned printers sensibly affected public opinion upon the education of children. As in Italy, a century before, the spread of interest in classical antiquity re-acted directly upon the aim and spirit of school life, producing schools of a new type in Venice, Mantua, and Ferrara, so it happened in France. Bordeaux as the commercial port, administrative and social centre, of south-western France, was naturally amongst the first of the great provincial towns to feel the impulse of the new movement in education. In 1534 the corporation of the city, in which stood a University of some repute and an ancient school in connection with it, both under control of the magistracy, applied to Andre Gouvéa, then director of the Collége de Sainte-Barbe at Paris, to undertake the re-organisation of the boys' school, in the hope that it might rank with the foremost schools of the humanities in France[1]. Gouvéa, " le plus grand principal de

---

[1] The best accessible authority is Gaullieur's *Histoire du Collége de Guyenne*. L. Massebieau has reprinted the *Schola Aquitanica*, the Programme d'Études drawn up by Vinet in 1583 on the basis of the traditional practice of the school. This is amongst the most valuable documents upon the actual organisation and curricula of 16th century schools which we possess. The same editor's *Les Colloques Scolaires* is full of interest as a review of methods of teaching Latin at that period.

Professor Foster Watson's *Cordier*, in the *School Review*, of Chicago, vol. xii., is an attractive sketch.

France," as Montaigne, who was later on a pupil of the school, calls him, invited certain colleagues to transfer themselves with him to Bordeaux; amongst them were three teachers of distinction, Budin, Grouchy, and Mathurin Cordier. Under the guidance of a succession of able principals supported by a broad-minded body of lay governors (Montaigne as Mayor was chairman in 1580), the Collége was able to attract a teaching staff of marked capacity. Amongst the assistants we trace many Scottish names, Boyd, Barclay, Robert Balfour (who rose to be principal), and George Buchanan, the most considerable Scottish humanist of the century.

At the period of the Reform the humanist scholars of France were in large part inclined to sympathy with the new doctrines. The group round Gouvéa typified this trend of opinion. He himself with the assent of the Governors or "Magistrates" proclaimed on arrival that he would recognise no differences of creed amongst the pupils or the staff. Cordier, for example, was already an ardent disciple of Calvin, who had been his pupil in the Latin classes as a student in the Collége de la Marche in Paris. The Church, however, had by 1535 succeeded in persuading Francis I that the new teaching was inimical to the stability of the state, and the tolerance hitherto accorded was gradually withdrawn. Perhaps to save embarrassment to his colleagues Cordier determined to accept Calvin's invitation to co-operate with him in the foundation of his great Protestant school at Geneva, and after barely two years' work he bade adieu to Bordeaux. Cordier had, however, left an abiding mark upon the Collége de Guyenne, for he had fixed the methods of organisation and of instruction of the lower forms of the school upon the lines which they retained for the rest of the century.

The subsequent fortunes of the Collége followed, as was inevitable, the varying currents of the political and theological controversy of the century. Two points stand out in clear relief: the keen, intelligent co-operation of the civic governing body in the management of the school and the distinction of the teaching staff. Such a scholar as Muretus was an assistant master in 1550. Gouvéa, it is evident, was a commanding personality, energetic, liberal, intensely sincere; he left the impress of his spirit upon the school, which for nearly a century was administered upon the methods which he evolved in the course of his headship. It was a characteristic of the school dating from the first days of Gouvéa's control that the principal should regard himself as "primus inter pares" in relation to his colleagues. We are expressly told "that he made no distinction between different colleagues, showing to all equal consideration. When they met in conference the first to arrive took the chief place at table. In this way each was assured that he had the like regard. Each alike was entitled to reprove, commend, or punish his pupil, and thus it was that each was held in esteem little inferior to that paid to the principal himself." It resulted from this that he could count upon the hearty co-operation of every member of his staff, whilst suggestions from all sides were welcomed and considered. It was possible for a principal to step down from his position in order to devote himself to a specific department of teaching, gaining leisure thereby for original work of his own. Élie Vinet, a former regent, i.e. professor or master, under Gouvéa, in this way resigned his post of principal in 1560 in order to confine himself to the functions of professor of Greek and of mathematics. It was during the period of Vinet's connection with the school that the Collége reached the high water mark of its prosperity (1556–1570) as a teaching institution. Between these dates, however, the Collége de Guyenne was, like France itself, distracted between the rival faiths. Almost did the controversy end in actual disruption in the years 1557–1562. But under Vinet's control the school weathered the storm, and the year 1570 may be perhaps taken as the culminating period of its efficiency and renown. In that year, however, when Vinet resigned the

direction to one of his colleagues that he might secure leisure
for the completion of his edition of Ausonius, there occurred
an event of much significance for Bordeaux. The Jesuit
Order despatched certain fathers to the city in order to secure
the countenance of the authorities, if not for the transference
of the Collége to the Order, at least for the establishment of
a rival school. In 1572 the situation, complicated by the
adhesion of the Archbishop to the intruders, became more
acute upon the arrival of a papal Legate and a large benefac-
tion to the Order made specifically for the purpose of a new
school. Before the close of that year the Collége de la
Madeleine, with a staff of eight masters of admitted ability,
was opened in the city. Vinet had now resumed his principal-
ship, and by his educational zeal and his earnest though broad-
minded Catholicism carried the city with him. His school
suffered little from that of the Jesuits, and when the Order was
expelled by Henri IV part of their educational revenues
lapsed to the Collége de Guyenne. In 1598 the famous Edict
of Nantes by its Article XXII expressly secured that special
privilege of tolerance and equality of creeds in education
which, sometimes avowedly and always in intention, had been
the mark of the Collége of Bordeaux since the arrival of
Gouvéa. The words are worth quoting : *qu'il ne serait fait
aucune différence ni distinction pour le regard de la dite religion*
(i.e. the Reformed) *à recevoir les escholiers pour estre instruicts
ès universitéz, colléges e escholes.*

The services of Élie Vinet to his great school have reason
to be remembered on one other ground. As has been said, he
had been as a young man a colleague of Gouvéa and had
frequently urged upon his chief to reduce to writing the
scheme of studies and of class organisation which Gouvéa in
conjunction with his staff, and with Cordier in particular, had
worked out in practice. But it had never been done, although
in effect the original school plan of Gouvéa, modified of course
in detail with the growth of experience, had governed the

school ever since. Vinet, however, the depository of the tradition of the heroic age in the history of the school, determined to draw out in documentary shape the " disciplina et ratio docendi " of the Collége as he had known and had followed it since the days of his great principal. As an authoritative programme, curriculum, time-table, and scheme of organisation of a great high-school of the flowering time of the French Renaissance, this " Ratio " deserves careful study. It should be compared with similar school plans by Melanchthon and Sturm, which moulded the classical instruction in Protestant Germany during the same period, as well as with the still better known " Ratio " of the Jesuits, which reached its final shape in the last year of the same century.

The interest of this document is enhanced by the fact that it is not an ideal programme written by one unacquainted with actual school work, or propounded by a teacher for use in a school yet to be created, like so many tracts *De Ratione Studii* which date from this century, for in it we have before us the record of a method which has fifty years' experience behind it. It is indeed one of the very few pieces of evidence of daily school practice which we possess. Attention may at the outset be called to certain general characteristics. There is no reference to the question of boarders, though probably most of the masters, several of whom were married, took a few boarders into their homes and acted as tutors to them. This we know also to have been Melanchthon's custom at Wittenberg. But the majority of the pupils seem to have been drawn from resident families in the city and neighbourhood, burghers, petite noblesse, landed gentry and the like. Again there is no reference to the disciplinary punishments in vogue, though much stress is laid upon the stimulus of disputation, marking, examination, promotion, etc. The existence of higher groups in philosophy and of public lectures in Greek and mathematics indicates the overlapping of school and university, which amounts to the absorption of the less advanced work of the faculty of arts in the school organisation. This throws light upon the co-ordination of what we should now describe as preparatory, secondary, and academic stages of education—a comprehension which has been noticed as characterising the first humanist schools of Italy. Lastly attention should be called to the practice of " disputation," or questioning between master and pupil, or between one pupil and another pupil, which is extended to the junior classes. As a method of working from wrong as well as from correct answers, and as an exercise in ready oral expression this was in skilled hands a useful adaptation of mediaeval practice to elementary classical teaching.

The aim of the school is declared in the programme in the following words : " Latino sermoni cognoscendo haec schola imprimis destinata est." This did not hinder that beginners were taught the rudiments by aid of the vernacular, and that good reading in French was requisite as a qualification for promotion from the junior to the middle forms. The lowest Form, the Tenth, the Classis Decima, consisted of the boys of seven years and less, who were called " Alphabetarii," or " Abecedarii." Two books were provided for this class : the *Alphabetum*, which contained the alphabet in small and in capital letters ; the Pater Noster, the seven penitential psalms, and the Ave Maria ; and the *Libellus Puerulorum*, a little summary of inflections of regular nouns and verbs. The pupils were arranged on benches without backs, placed five deep. The front row contained the more advanced scholars who were able to read and could learn by heart the penitential psalms. The method of teaching is set out in some detail. The front bench was divided into groups of two or three. The word *miserere*, for example, is pronounced by the teacher and then repeated by the first group. The master next spells the word by letter and by syllable. The next group of boys follows him. Another word, *mei*, is treated in the same way, and thus every boy of the front bench has his turn. The second row is then put on, new words being taken but the method remaining the same. The third row in its turn spells out the Ave Maria ; the fourth row the Pater Noster. When they have finished the fifth bench follows with the finger the letters of the alphabet, read or pointed out by the master. In the meantime children in the groups not actually reading follow as they can the work of the rest. Each pupil is put on at least once during the lesson, which is followed by half an hour's exercise by the front bench only in the *Libellus*. The morning school-period finishes with the recitation by the same boys of the Creed, the Lord's Prayer, and the Hymn to the Virgin, to which the entire class listens reverently. The same procedure is repeated both at the midday and at the afternoon school. Throughout, the school-periods begin each day at eight, at noon, and at three. The writing lessons are not attempted until some facility has been gained in reading. Letters, words, and edifying maxims are written in copy books and handed in for correction as soon as done. The master is instructed to overlook attempts at drawing which he may find in the margins ; a boy will draw a man, a horse, a dog, but if the writing is not neglected the teacher may regard such inventions leniently ; often they are early signs of true artistic feeling. And generally the pressure upon children at this stage must be gentle, as Quintilian insists : memory work apart from such as results from repeatedly hearing sentences read aloud is not to be required. This applies both to spelling and to inflections.

Promotion to the Ninth Form may take place quarterly, the tests being ability (*a*) to read all that is contained in the two manuals referred to, (*b*) to decline and to conjugate, (*c*) to write legibly. The principal examines and determines promotion ; he personally delivers the successful pupils to their new master, a formality observed with each form. The Ninth was the largest class in the school, and occupied the Aula or "big school" of the Collége. The boys were seated on a gallery in six rows. The course required reading and writing with fluency and speed both in French and in Latin, Latin accidence of noun and verb, the *disticha de moribus* of Cato with a French parallel version and a small handbook of grammar, such as Cordier's *Exempla partium orationis* (1540) and Estienne's French manual of Latin grammar, in which the method of treating rudiments is set out very fully. The intimate connection between French and Latin teaching at this stage is laid down in Estienne's book : " Le Maistre accoustumera aussi l'enfant à bien prononcer le François et le bien escrire autant que le Latin. Par ains adviendra que tant en Latin que en François il sera accoustumé et bien instruit pour aller plus oultre."

First lesson begins at eight. The front row reads by groups two or three sentences from the Cato, the other rows other sections of the same text, such as the sayings of the Seven Wise Men, each bench having as in the form below its special set work. Following each passage the French version of the Latin is read from written copies made by each pupil for himself, or recited from memory. The midday lesson consists of repetition of Latin grammar, each bench doing different work, the upper boys covering much more ground than the lower group.

In the afternoon at three the lesson was confined to learning moods of the regular verbs, and on Fridays the entire verb is written out and handed in. On Saturdays fair copies of all lessons said and written have to be sent up, this constituting the week's home work.

Two things stand out : the class is divided for construing and for accidence into six benches, with obvious risk of loss of time and of distracted attention of teacher and of scholar alike. Next the stress of preparation falls upon the written work, for text, version and notes are copied at home into exercise books for class use, the actual printed manuals not being brought into school at all.

Promotion from lower to upper places in the form and from the Ninth to the Eighth Form is decided by oral tests, in particular by ability to repeat Cato and the accidence, and also by fluent reading and legible writing. In the Eighth the textbooks employed were a selection of Cicero's letters, selected scenes from Terence and, in Vinet's time, the *Colloquia* of Cordier. The latter were divided into daily portions to be learnt by heart. The pupil buys a copy of each of these books, and a plain manuscript book into which the daily sections are to be copied. The printed text of the grammar, however, is now allowed in class. In a construing lesson each passage involves three pupils. The first boy put on reads the text; the second explains it, and gives a paraphrase of it in Latin; the third states the argument and the logical analysis. A second group of three then takes the next passage, and when this has been done for the whole lesson the class takes up the parsing, boys being put on in turn to conjugate the verbs and to explain constructions. " Locutiones," or conversational phrases, and the Latin equivalents for familiar French expressions—"Je me porte bien," "Tu m'a fait plaisir,"—are to be learnt. We see the beginnings of systematic Latin conversation exercised through Terence and colloquies. A passage of French prose is dictated as the weekly task in Latin composition to be done at home. Two construing lessons are taken daily, the third lesson consisting of the repetition of the grammar. Promotions to the Seventh are made partly upon examination, partly upon the form master's report.

Instruction in the Seventh Class is marked by an important step in advance. Although the select letters of Cicero are still the principal text the procedure is different. The master reads aloud the Latin text, indicating by his intonation the general lie of the passage, as for example the distinction between the principal and the dependent, or parenthetic, clause. He points out the orthography of an unfamiliar word. He then begins to explain the passage, rendering each word of the original into literal French, but, where idiom requires, doing something more. This done, the parts of speech are taken in turn as the passage may serve to illustrate them, the verbs especially being questioned upon and any compounds or derived forms being treated at length. This part of the lesson is followed by revision ; by groups of three the text is read aloud, a French construe or Latin paraphrase is offered, whilst the third boy puts selected words through their inflections and repeats " locutiones " and other phrases useful for conversation or prose. On Wednesday and Saturday a subject for Latin composition is dictated, such as a free rendering in French of one of Cicero's letters, the matter of which is very carefully explained. This exercise is brought up on Thursday and Monday and all faults are corrected in Form. This retention of French as the vehicle of instruction in Latin is to be noted. Pupils at this stage were presumably between eleven and twelve years old.

The amount of construing required consisted as a rule of four lines of a small octavo text which were copied into an exercise book, a blank line being left below the text for the French version inserted in class. The above lessons were taken at eight. The midday lesson was prescribed as the Latin grammar of Despautère, a book for middle forms based upon Alexander de Villa Dei, and like it written in Latin hexameters, with long comments intended for the use of the master. The book was something like Sintheim's simplified *Doctrinale*, to which Erasmus gave a grudging approval. The Despautère was in common use in French schools from the opening of the sixteenth century, and though highly praised as an introduction to systematic accidence and syntax was in reality a forbidding book. Two or three verses were learned at a time and then elaborately explained and illustrated. This excessive comment, a defect in grammarians which Erasmus and Vives so frequently denounce as pedantic ostentation, made progress very slow.

The Sixth and Fifth Forms were still mainly occupied with Cicero's letters as the standing prose text. Parts were learnt by heart, and the master's explanations reduced to notes were also committed to memory. In the Fifth we find added an entire play of Terence, and a book of the *Epistolae* of Ovid. The practice of many humanist schools of beginning with the poets and then passing on to the prose writers was not followed at Bordeaux. In the Fifth Form also the rules of prosody are learnt for the first time.

Not until the Fourth was reached (boys of thirteen or fourteen) did the pupils attack an oration of Cicero, with which was used a little manual of rhetoric such as that of Barzizza, or of Sulpicius, or the *De Copia* of Erasmus ; the *Tristia* of Ovid is the chief poetical work read. These authors are made the text for grammatical questioning in which Despautère is always referred to. Composition exercises are more frequently demanded and are of greater length ; simple material for Latin verse is dictated as a home exercise. Boys attending the Fourth Class, as will be shown later, make their first acquaintance with Greek.

The Third Form, the usual age being thirteen to fourteen, read at eight, for one term, the *Epistolae Familiares* or *Ad Atticum* of Cicero, with a commentary by the master in French. The two terms following were devoted to one of the speeches of Cicero and a substantial manual of rhetoric by " some good author." The midday lesson was, for part of the year, given to syntax, verse composition, and the section of Despautère upon " Figurae " ; for this was substituted later on a play of Terence. The *Fasti* or *Metamorphoses* of Ovid were read in the afternoon ; the first part of each lesson consisted of repetition of the text treated upon the previous day and the master's comment written up the evening before, with special stress upon the constructions involved. Latin composition from the French in prose and in verse is of increasing difficulty.

The substantial work of the Second Form was constituted

of one or more of the oratorical treatises of Cicero, illustrated by one of his speeches, the *Letters* being now laid aside. The lesson at noon was mainly devoted to ancient history, Roman no doubt, although we have no particulars as to the aim or method of teaching the subject. Its inclusion at this stage seems to have been peculiar to this particular school, its usual place being the Classe de Rhetorique, or highest form. The regular afternoon lesson at three o'clock was given to construing Vergil, Ovid, or Lucan. The passages read in form are all learnt by heart as before. Prose compositions worked at home include for the first time "Declamations," alongside the customary themes worked from French originals. An additional hour was now imposed. At five o'clock a form exercise in verse composition was dictated, the finished copy to be handed in before the boys left the class-room.

In the three classes last described a gradually increased stress was laid upon rhetoric, which is still more markedly typical of the First or highest form. The position is expressly said to be based upon the usage of the Roman schools of the time of Quintilian. The school day begins in the First Form with an hour's lesson upon the precepts of the art of oratory after Cicero or Quintilian, followed at nine by one of the speeches of Cicero in illustration, and as a model for exercises in declamation and forensic prose. At noon followed the history lesson, from "Livy, Justin, Seneca, Eutropius, P. Mela, or other author." The poets were read at three; Vergil, Lucan and Persius coming first in the school year, followed by Juvenal, Horace or Ovid, these latter with careful attention to the canon of edification. At five, composition was set as in the form below. Each construing lesson opens with repetition of passages treated the day before. Written copies of such passages are handed in to the master when school opens. Declamations are now prepared for recitation before the whole school on Sundays at one o'clock, and for private recitation, i.e. before the form alone, on Saturdays. Latin compositions in prose and verse, it is expressly stated, are to be set to the First Form well in advance so as to enable due thought to be given to these most important exercises.

The ten classes in grammar, so far summarized, are crowned by courses in the *Faculté des Arts* open to all boys who have passed through the First Form. The lectures are delivered by the readers in philosophy and cover two years. The first year's course, the age of the pupils being presumably about eighteen, consists in the main of Aristotelian Logic, taught from Latin versions made direct from Aristotle. The *Isagoge* of Porphyry is mentioned as well. For the second year's course, the students in which are called " physici," the chief text is still that of Aristotle, namely the *Physica*, the *De Caelo*, and such other works as are usually read in the subject of philosophy. An introductory book by N. Grouchy, a distinguished master of the Collége under Gouvéa, was added. Broadly the topics treated are those styled natural philosophy, based, however, wholly upon antique learning.

The entire course, from admission to the completion of the second year in the faculty, thus covered about twelve years. Boys of more than average ability might pass under the Praeceptores Philosophiae one or two years in advance, as promotions, in the lower forms at any rate, might apparently be won half-yearly. But in addition to the regular work of form and faculty above described, all pupils of the Fourth, Third, Second and First Forms were required to attend a concurrent course in Greek, and all above the Third a further course in mathematics. It is interesting to notice that these two subjects were dissociated from the systematic teaching methods of the form and were imparted by what appears to have been mere dictation.

The reader in Greek lectured at one o'clock, beginning on October 1st in each year. As the pupils would in the ordinary way attend him for five or six years from the day on which they entered the Fourth, we may assume that he delivered parallel courses of lectures of advancing difficulty, and thus an individual pupil would attend one hour only in each week. We are told that the first half-hour was devoted to the elements of grammar, and a second half-hour was given, in which "Demosthenes, Homer, or authors as nearly like as possible," were read, construed and explained. An elementary grammar was published by Millanges, the Bordeaux scholar-printer, and at a later stage the grammar of Theodore Gaza, written originally for Vittorino's school, was employed.

We may conclude that the resulting knowledge of the language was somewhat meagre, and the insight into Greek thought and life gained by such a process wholly unsatisfactory. The contrast is marked when we recall the practice of the best humanist teachers in Italy, and the emphatic dictum of the younger Guarino that no one is entitled to the term "educated" who does not move freely within the circle of Greek scholarship. Moreover, the ideal of Erasmus, Melanchthon and of Vives, with their insistence upon an early initiation into Greek for all boys of intelligence, seems much in advance of the practice of Gouvéa and his successors. Yet we may conclude with some confidence that in actual practice the curriculum of the Collége de Guyenne, with its relegation of Greek to a position of distinct inferiority, was typical of the grammar school both of France and of England during the sixteenth century.

Attendance at the courses of the reader in mathematics was limited to the pupils of the Second and the First Forms and of the two classes in philosophy. Instruction began with arithmetic in which Vinet published a school manual covering simple proportion, square and cube root, and vulgar fractions. This was followed by the *Mathematicorum Breviarium* of Psellus, an eleventh century writer, which was a dry compendium of arithmetic, music, geometry and astronomy, translated from its original Greek by Vinet for use in the school. Proclus, *de Sphaera*, a favourite author amongst Italian teachers of mathematics and astronomy, was also in use.

We have interesting light upon general methods of class instruction as pursued in the school. The retention of the mediaeval Disputation, in the rational form of mutual questioning under the control of the form master, was a safeguard against the prevalent fault of lecturing or dictating to the class which Erasmus so frequently ridiculed as the practice of the unskilled teacher or of the pedant parading his erudition. The construing lesson lasted as a rule for one hour, and was followed by such disputation : the pupils asked questions of each other, propounded difficulties, discussed the matter of the text and the notes given by the master. This exercise occupies half an hour. On Saturdays, in place of a set lesson at midday disputations were arranged in which form was pitted against form. Six pupils from each brought up as many compositions in prose or in verse which had been worked in advance. These were written out in large text hand and pinned to a screen or on the wall of the class-room : below each line of the script was left a clear space for interlinear correction and criticism. Thus the opposers could make careful examination of each exercise, detect errors and propound improvements. This disputation lasts an hour.

Although French, as has been shown, was regularly employed for an instrument of Latin construing and composition it was not allowed to be used in school or play-ground except by the juniors : "nemo nisi parvulus idem elementarius vernacule loquatur." Elder boys were required to use Latin in addressing little boys, and only when not understood were they to repeat their words in French. The words of the statute of the University of Paris as revised in 1599 show that to the very end of the century the same principle was upheld in the authoritative seat of French learning : "nemo Scholasticorum in Collegio lingua vernacula loquatur, sed Latinis sermo eis sit usitatus et familiaris."

The school hours were from 8–10, 12–1, 3–5, with an extra hour twice weekly in the case of pupils reading Greek and mathematics. Sunday was, apart from one exercise for the upper forms, a whole holiday, as were certain Saints' days. On some important vigils, about fifty during the year, a half holiday was allowed. Mass was attended daily by the entire school. The school year began in September, and continued till the beginning of August.

The Collége de Guyenne, it is easily conceivable, might have developed its usefulness as a high school of a liberal Huguenot type. The trend of opinion, however, at once represented and furthered by Francis I, gradually, but surely, took a line antagonistic to the Reform. Between 1520 and 1540 French humanist scholars and the men of position who shared the spirit of the Renaissance were so far in sympathy with the freer and more intelligent attitude to theological and ecclesiastical doctrine that it was by no means certain whether they would not, like the similar class in the Rhineland and in North Germany, frankly accept the breach with Rome. As regards the school at Bordeaux, although at the outset, as already noted, maintaining complete tolerance in matters of faith, and in later years the object of bitter antagonism at the hands of the Jesuits, it remained definitely Catholic. It was, however, throughout the century conspicuously free from ecclesiastical control, and preserved, like Colet's school of St Paul's, its civic and lay characteristics both as regards its government and as regards the guiding aim of its curriculum.

It is instructive to follow out the career of one of the most attractive figures grouped around Gouvéa who had been compelled to quit the school at the time of the parting of the ways. Mathurin Cordier attracts attention as the most notable representative of a Huguenot education. Born in Normandy in 1479 he found himself drawn to the priesthood, partly at least by an instinct for mysticism and for religious ceremonial in which he found its expression. He came as a student to Paris where he was ordained. We hear of him as a secular priest in Rouen, which he left in 1514 in order to return to the University, where he studied theology and taught Latin in more than one of the colleges in Paris. He was of grave, studious temper, yet always with a fund of kindly humour and of real sympathy with young people. As a scholar he was as enthusiastic as Erasmus himself for sound classical learning, while as a teacher of Latin he soon discovered, as did Melanchthon a little later, that the higher range of study was hampered by defective grounding in accidence and syntax. It is indeed easy to see that the Erasmian not less than the mediaeval method of teaching Latin, might alike militate, though in different ways, against thoroughness; the latter as being too abstract, too much involved with dialectic, and too laborious, and the former as superficial and less systematic than is necessary for absolute security in reading and in composition. To remedy this Cordier abandoned his Chair of Rhetoric in the Collége de la Marche, 1527, and stepped down to assume the function of a master of grammar. Here his real force and peculiar gifts manifested themselves, notably his earnest sympathy with beginners, and his capacity for understanding the mind of youth. The monument of this stage of his activity is his well known book *De Corrupti Sermonis Emendatione Libellus*, an attempt to impart to French students the standard of purity in classical diction. "Of the reasons for the present work," runs his preface, "the first is that every learned person may hereby be led to write the better; the next, that boys may not only be brought to a ready use of Latin conversation, but stimulated to lead a noble life. For throughout this book we have scattered, as due occasion offered, exhortations to a devout and Christian life. For this comes before purity of speech. Without piety there can be no true progress in learning." We see here the twin aspect in which classical instruction presented itself though obviously in varying proportions to the humanist of a serious type; whether to Vittorino, to Agricola, to Sturm, or to Cordier. "Pietas literata," "eloquens et sapiens pietas"— with Cordier the combination was a vital one, as with the school-master of Mantua : it was typical of him as a man, not as a Huguenot. The work just mentioned treats of the expressions used in French and in Latin for most of the forms of speech needed in daily conversation. The strictly literal Latin version of the French is often placed first, and the classical equivalent follows. The following is a typical instance of "pious exhortation on Christian conduct."

> " Imprecationes.
>
> *Gallicè*, Mauldissons, Maledictions.
>
> Le diable te puisse emporter.
> Pro Scelus !

But should there issue forth from the mouth of a boy, who ought to be innocent, an expression so wicked ? What if the Devil should seize thee ? which indeed he would do were he permitted by the Lord.

'But,' you say, 'I do not say it in seriousness.'

So be it. Yet that is a bad saying, even if uttered in joke. If anyone annoy you, either you should answer him not at all, or reply, 'Friend, may God forgive you.' Be good words, not evil, always in your mouth."

Of a purely grammatical sort is the following[1] : the first line in each example being the "Sermo corruptus."

> "XXI. Cicero nunquam locutus est de hoc.
> Jamais Cicero ne parla de cela.
> Huius rei Cicero nullam mentionem fecit.
> De hoc nulla mentio a Cicerone facta est.
> Huius rei Cicero nusquam meminit. Nusquam :
> Id est, Nullo in Loco.
> Nunquam de hac re meminit Cicero.
>
> Loquitur optimum Latinum.
> Il parle très bon Latin.
> Latine optime loquitur.

[1] *De Corrupti*, etc. p. 243. Ed. 1538.

Tu es nimis longus ad loquendum.
Tu es trop long à parler.
Nimis longum loqueris.
Prolixior es, quam par sit, in loquendo.

Opposui illi unam quaestionem et ipse ignoravit.
Je lui ai demandé une question, à laquelle n'a pu respondre,
ou, qu'il n'a pu souldre.
Proposui illi quaestionem, cui non potuit respondere.
Varietas: ad quam respondere non potuit. Quam solvere
nequivit. Quam dissolvere non potuit. Quam explicare non
potuit."

It has been suggested that Cordier was peculiar amongst
humanist school-masters in the stress which he laid upon the
vernacular. For it is evident that he took French as the
instrument through which Latin rudiments were initially taught.
The book just quoted not less than the practice of the lower
forms of the Collége de Guyenne is sufficient evidence of
this. Herein he agrees with the practice of Vives and differs
from that of Erasmus and probably most other German humanists. Yet the practice was common enough in the Low
Countries and in England where it was, probably, the usual
method. This is proved by the popularity of such books as
the Louvain version of the Grammar of N. Perotti, and of the
various "Vulgaria" and rudimentary abridgements of accidence
compiled by Horman, Stanbridge and other English school-
masters of this period. But it is certain that beyond the
earlier stages the vernacular was not encouraged, and in
conversation actually prohibited. "We must," says Cordier
in the work just quoted, "bring children not only to love
Latin, but to be so enchanted by it that we become ashamed
to use the vernacular and slip back into the habit of it against
our will."

Later on when master in Geneva (1560) his rule was that
boys should speak Latin both in and out of class, and that
offenders should be reported. We can perceive the weight which

he attaches to the consistent habit of Latin speech in the Colloquy between a monitor and another boy (Bk iv. 13): "I have heard, said the master,"—the monitor is quoting him—"that there are some among you who talk in French ofttimes, and in the meantime none of you doth tell me anything; which is an argument of the consent of all of you....Whereupon (quoth he) I admonish you that each of you exhort diligently to speak Latin, and that you bring unto me the names of them who will not obey, that I may add a remedy (punishment) to this evil."

The monitor being asked by another boy: "May we not therefore utter any word in French?"

"The master," is the answer, "doth not understand the matter so....He is not so very severe or exacting that he doth punish straightway if any word escape any by chance, as they are talking together. He hath said before the whole school sometimes that his edict apperteineth to those only who, when they know how to speak Latin, yet always seek holes that they may talk in French."

The rule is that boys speak Latin in school and out of it; and that monitors report offenders. The *Colloquia* (1564) contains no word of French: the much earlier *De Emendatione* (which represents his method in his Paris days) is framed on a basis of instruction *through* French. Yet when we examine the curriculum of the Collége de la Rive at Geneva, as set out in the constitution of 1559, in part the work of Cordier and certainly the school order under which he taught for the last five years of his life, it appears necessary to admit the regular employment of French as a vehicle of teaching Latin, in spite of the presumptions against such a practice afforded by the *Colloquies*.

The reputation of Cordier, greatly enhanced by his success in the school of Nevers, where he was principal from 1530–1534, led to an invitation from Gouvéa to join his staff at the Collége de Guyenne in the latter year. Cordier, like most of his colleagues, had already attached himself to the party of Calvin and rejoiced therefore in the freer air of Bordeaux. The result of his co-operation was seen in the curriculum of instruction for the junior classes of the school, a task in which his peculiar gifts of insight and sympathy in all that concerns child-life found full scope. Yet only for a short time ; for before the end of 1536 he was pressed by the magistracy of the city, fearful of complications with the Church, to quit Bordeaux. He had received an urgent appeal from Calvin, his old pupil, and now a refugee at Geneva, to join him there. So from that year to the day of his death in 1564 Cordier spent his life in Switzerland, always teaching, organising, or reforming schools. His last years were lived at Geneva, where he taught in the great Collége de la Rive, the public school of Geneva which was governed and inspired by Calvin himself, and by him framed into a most effective instrument of his propaganda. The following abstract of the curriculum, referred to above, of the Geneva school is instructive for purposes of comparison with other similar schemes propounded during the same century. There are seven "classes": classis VII is the lowest.

Classis VII. In this class the pupils will learn the letters, and write them to form syllables, using a Latin-French reading book. Reading French, and afterwards Latin from a French-Latin Catechism : drawing, and writing letters of the alphabet.

VI. Declensions and conjugations are begun ; this occupies the first half-year. Parts of speech learnt in French and Latin : more practice in hand-writing : easy Latin sentences learnt orally and repeated as practice in conversation.

V. Parts of speech finished : elements of syntax : the *Eclogues* of Vergil read : first steps in written Latin composition : Latin and French employed side by side.

IV. Latin syntax continued. Cicero's *Letters* begun ; composition exercises are based on these. Prosody, with reading of Ovid in illustration. Greek begun : declension and conjugation ; elementary construing.

III. Greek Grammar systematically learnt, with comparison of the two languages. Cicero, *Letters*, *De Amicitia*, *De Senectute ;* these two treatises to be turned into Greek. The *Aeneid*, Caesar and Isocrates read.

II. Chief stress laid upon reading: Livy, Xenophon, Polybius, Herodian and Homer. Logic begun : propositions, syllogism : to be illustrated from Cicero's orations. Once a week the Gospel narrative in Greek.

I. Logic systematically taught from approved compendium (such as Melanchthon's) ; the elements of rhetoric in connection with it, and elocution. The whole doctrine of rhetoric illustrated from Cicero's speeches, and from Demosthenes (the *Olynthiacs* and *Philippics*). Homer and Vergil also analysed for rhetorical purposes. Two original "declamationes" are prepared monthly. Once a week an Epistle of St Paul or other apostle is read in Greek.

The choice of authors and the place of logic deserve attention, not less than the acceptance of the vernacular in junior classes.

Cordier was a fine example of a long and notable succession of French school-masters—devoted, thorough, modest, full of zeal for character, full of sympathy for childhood. The man stands out sharply in his two principal works ; a short reference to his *Colloquia* will supplement what has been said above respecting his earlier book.

The object of the *Colloquia* is set out in the title : *Colloquiorum scholasticorum libri IV ad pueros in Sermone Latino paulatim exercendos recogniti.* Like that of the dialogues compiled by Vives or Mosellanus their purpose was to enable boys to speak Latin by providing them with examples of conversation upon the common life of the day as it presented itself to the young. Cordier realised that the fact that boys were not allowed to talk to their masters or their fellow-pupils in their own tongue tended inevitably to stifle thought and to make conversation sterile and artificial. The purpose of the *Colloquies*, therefore, was to remedy such defect. Thus we find that they are mainly concerned with the daily pursuits of boys, at home, in the city, in the boarding-house, in the school, at church ; with their characters and temperaments, with the different types of home and circumstance ; with the work, difficulties, aims of the school-master's life. The evangelical view of duty and of authority, divine and human, colours the whole book. A large number of his pupils at Geneva were sons of exiles ; many of them intended for the ministry, not a few of them, indeed, destined in the event to become martyrs to their creed. The pupils of the Collége de la Rive were viewed as the children of the city state, and the precious seed of the future harvest of the Faith. Cordier, therefore, aimed as in his practical work as a master so in this handbook of the *Colloquies* at establishing in the young a seriousness of purpose which should colour their entire lives. We learn from the *Colloquies*, for example, how daily from eleven to twelve o'clock psalms are sung by the entire school, that public prayers in church or in school are repeated twice or perhaps three times a day, that verses of the Bible were systematically learnt and repeated, that questions were regularly put upon the subject-matter of the sermon, and that private prayer was formally insisted upon. Again, the employment of monitors, common in Paris and in many German schools such as that of Trotzendorf at Goldberg (1531) where they were regarded as the eyes of the master and were apt to have a bad reputation as mere spies, was continued by Cordier, but in a wholly new spirit. " The master, unable to supervise everything in detail, calls to his aid the eldest scholars who stand in the position of elder brothers to the rest. They are invested with their responsibility for one month, after consultation between the master and the boys themselves. It is an election as in the sight of God; the monitors are installed with prayer. They gather in the master's study when they are instructed in their solemn functions, and the name of the Saviour is invoked to inspire them with a due sense of their duty. They must show no favour nor antipathy, they must not take vengeance, nor lose self-control; they must fear no threats but fear the Lord only." (*Coll.* Bk III. 6.)

Different dialogues show the monitors at work; mingling kindness with rigidity, checking inattention at church, admonishing to study, examining requests for leave, repressing lying, supervising games, reproving loiterers, reporting boys for not speaking Latin. The master shows much confidence in the scholars, who had leave to go into the town upon parole; their word was readily taken. Cordier, in fine, respected youth, and endeavoured to train boys to become self-reliant men obeying an inner law of their own.

Apart, then, from the definite purpose of moral and religious discipline which runs through the entire book, the *Colloquies* of Cordier have no little interest to-day as a document of historical value giving us, as do also the similar dialogues of Vives, direct insight into the school life of the time. They differ from those of Erasmus in their much greater simplicity, in their absence of bitterness and controversial point. Indeed, although the atmosphere is avowedly Calvinist, the author is so free from sectarian bitterness, so full of human sympathy, that his book was largely used, with slight excisions, for two centuries even in Catholic schools. As a manual of conversation it was not intended to be learnt by heart, but to be "read and re-read as a pleasurable exercise." It was peculiarly a text-book for the Fifth Class, that is boys of ten to eleven years of age, for whom it provided appropriate material for systematic conversation in Latin.

The characters are old pupils; in many cases their actual names are retained. Conversations are framed upon such a subject as a family, in which everyone speaks Latin except the mother, and she only is permitted to converse with her boys in French at stated hours. This family is often supposed to have been the household of the Estiennes in Paris. Cordier however in this respect merely represents the usual attitude of the humanist school-masters towards the uninstructed mother. Gentle and amiable as he is, he has a considerable vocabulary of hard words for the mother. In one dialogue he exhibits maternal fondness for her child as weakness for which excuse may possibly be found by referring it to unregulated nature. In another dialogue we find him complaining that parents were restless under long continued and apparently unprofitable instruction in Latin. Burghers, in particular, see their sons drawn away from the shop by an education fitted only for priests or professional life. If, they say, it is necessary to teach Latin, let it occupy a year, and then be done with. We see others going farther than this, deciding to send their children into foreign countries to learn modern tongues. Cordier explains that international intercourse can best be carried on in Latin; there were too many vernaculars. The type of home life which appealed to Cordier is sketched in the fiftieth Colloquy of Book II.

Montane: "How old art thou?" *Eusebius:* "Thirteen, as I have heard of my mother." Montane speaks of a brother who is only five. *E.* "Doth he speak Latin already?" *M.* "Why dost thou marvel? We have always a school-master at home, both learned and diligent. He doth teach us ever to speak Latin. He uttereth nothing in French unless to make something plain. Moreover we dare not speak to my father except in Latin." *E.* "Therefore do ye never speak in French?" *M.* "Only with my mother, and at a certain hour, when she commands us to be called unto her...the servants themselves do speak to us in Latin...Thanks be to God by whose gift we have a father who hath a care to have us so diligently instructed."

Marcuardus: "As often as our father is not necessarily

busied he doth exercise us at all hours ; in the morning, before and after dinner, before supper, after supper very long, last of all, also before we go to bed." *Picus :* " In what things doth he exercise you ?" *M.* " He doth exact of us those things especially which we have learned in the school all the week. He looketh into our themes and doth ask us concerning them : he often gives us something to be written down, sometimes in Latin, sometimes in French. Sometimes also he doth propound unto us a short sentence in our mother-tongue which we may turn into Latin. Sometimes, contrarily, he doth command us to repeat some Latin sentence in French. Last of all, before meat and after we read always something out of the French Bible, and that before the whole family...I have forgotten the civility of manners concerning which he is wont to admonish us at the table." *P.* "Why doth your father take so much labour in teaching you ?" *M.* "That he may understand whether we lose our labour in the school and abuse our time." *P.* " The diligence of the man is marvellous, and so is his wisdom. Oh, how are ye bound to the heavenly Father who hath given you such a father on the earth !" (Bk II. 28.)

From Bk IV. 27 we may quote the following, characteristic of the religious difficulties of the time :

A. Methinks you are somewhat sad Gralianus, what is the matter ?

G. I think night and day of my father that is from home, and I grieve myself away for that matter.

A. How long hath he been from home ?

G. About four months.

A. Hath he writ nothing to you in the mean space ?

G. Since he went from us we have not heard one word.

A. It may be that he writ, but his letter either miscarried or was intercepted. Went he not to Paris this summer ?

G. Truly he set out then with that resolution.

A. I am confident he is safe.

*   *   *   *   *   *

But I pray you hear what is come into my mind.

G.   What is that?

A.   What if your father be sailed into England to traffique? For there is now the greatest liberty.

G.   What liberty do you mean?

A.   Of the Gospel, which is heard there and most freely.

G.   Do you say that the Gospel is now in England?

A.   That is for certain.

G.   And that idolatry is expelled?

A.   Yes.

G.   O glad tidings and pleasant to be heard!

*   *   *   *   *   *

A.   Moreover, a certain Englishman, no light person, nor one that dallieth, told my father within these few daies that he had received a letter worthy of credit thence, in which this thing was amongst the rest, that all that were driven their countrey for the name of Christ were most kindly entertained and freely welcomed in England.

G.   Why then should we doubt any more?

A.   There remains no doubt (as you hear) about that matter.

G.   It only remains that we first extol the goodness of Almighty God, with as much praise and thanksgiving as can be[1].

*   *   *   *   *   *

As to the method of using the *Colloquies* the custom was for the master to explain the selected Colloquy to the class; the boys were without difficulty brought to enter into the spirit of the scene which was one within their daily experience and directly concerned themselves.   Now and then the dialogue is rehearsed by picked boys each taking a character in turn and from it the master developed extempore conversation, exercising the class upon the subject-matter in impromptu forms. Occasion would be taken for declining or conjugating a word,

---

[1] From Hoole's version of the *Colloquia*, 1657.

or quoting a rule of syntax. The essential aim of the lesson was to show how boys could frame in the form of sound Latin their intercourse upon matters of common life. Cordier himself did not use the *Colloquia* as a memory lesson, although doubtless the ordinary master lacking the verve, freshness and versatility of the author only too often degraded the original purpose of the book.

As a school manual the *Colloquia* of Cordier had extraordinary repute. Its circulation during the last decades of the sixteenth century exceeded that of any other Latin text-book. It came into immediate use in England: an English translation by Brinsley (1614) was employed as material for exercises in Latin composition: Hoole in 1657 issued an edition with English and Latin side by side. In the preface he quotes the commendatory opinion of Reynolds the Public Orator at Oxford, that "when young students came to him and desired him to inform them what books they were best to peruse for the speedier and surer attainment of a clean Latine style or speech, he ever bade them get Corderius' *Colloquies* and be sure in reading them to make those expressions their own both for writing and for speaking, because in them they should finde Terence and Tullie's elegancies applied to their foreign talk." The book was still in use in English schools as late as the middle of the nineteenth century.

CHAPTER IX.

CARDINAL SADOLETO (1477–1547) *DE LIBERIS RECTE INSTITUENDIS.*

THE treatise of Jacopo Sadoleto, papal Secretary, bishop of Carpentras in southern France, and Cardinal, deserves attention on several grounds[1]. It was written in 1530, at a time when Italy still lay horror-stricken and inert under the memory of the Sack of Rome, her complacent light-heartedness gone never to return. Hence Sadoleto, a cultured yet devout believer, strikes a note of deep seriousness, symptoms of the temper of the counter-reformation to which he so ardently devoted himself. Then he writes as one with a definite end in view: he has in mind the youth of the higher pro-fessional class—his own—and of landed families of modest estate. He knows what is wanted from experience of society in France as well as in Italy. Again, no other humanist writer upon education has as thoroughly entered into the true spirit of Plato. The end which Sadoleto puts forth is that of a liberal training not concerned with any of the possible technical superstructures which taste or need may suggest. The impres-sion we gain from the *De Liberis recte Instituendis* is that its author knew well the class for which he was writing; that he kept within the bounds of the attainable: that he set himself to exhibit in harmonious outlines an adaptation to the modern and the Catholic world all that was best in antique

---

[1] The works of Joly (1856) and Charpenne (1855) are useful studies of Sadoleto as humanist.

education as the unwearied scholarship of the Italian Renaissance, which had already reached its zenith, had revealed it. Sadoleto himself was amongst the greater scholars of his time, surpassing most of them in insight into the significance of Greek thought.   His treatise, it may be added, forms an instructive introduction to a study of the Jesuit *Ratio*.

Jacopo Sadoleto was born in 1477; his father was a Modenese and held the Chair of Civil Law at Ferrara when Agricola was there, and was colleague of Baptista Guarino. The young Jacopo attended the courses in Letters and Philosophy, making at that time Cicero and Aristotle his chief studies.   On leaving Ferrara in 1499 he went to Rome.   A little later he became acquainted with Pietro Bembo, who was appointed along with Sadoleto, papal Secretary on the election of Leo X.   The position of papal Secretary had been for nearly a century past one of distinction in the world of learning.   It had been filled by Bruni, Poggio, Biondo, and even Valla ; it lent itself readily to ambitions worthy and unworthy, and gave opportunity for exhibiting elegant Latinity and deep erudition.   But Sadoleto had more than epistolary gifts and always showed himself an upright and disinterested man, with scant sympathy for much of the mischievous diplomacy of which he was the mouthpiece.   He became bishop of Carpentras in 1517, but saw little of his diocese until the death of his master in 1522.   Clement VII recalled him to Rome, much loth to leave his charge. His advice and his own high standard of life were alike ignored at the papal Court.   A few months before the Sack he claimed his liberty, and for some years devoted himself to philosophy and exegesis, diligently ruling his diocese, where he was greatly beloved.   Paul III recalled him once more, made him Cardinal in 1536 and gave him his whole confidence.   The recovery of the credit and the spiritual territory of the Church was henceforward the pre-occupation of the Vatican.   Sadoleto was instrumental in effecting peace (1538) between the two great Catholic monarchs, Francis and Charles. The most learned and most respected member of the Sacred College, he was still bishop of Carpentras when he died in 1547.

Sadoleto complains that public authority has no concern for education. There is infinite care for property, order, justice, yet a need as urgent is ignored and left to the caprice or neglect of fathers. "Upon education above all other things depends the moral soundness and the prosperity of the community." Imperial Rome set a better example. The absence of organised schools of satisfactory type compels him to advise an education conducted at home, where a small group of boys may be gathered from friendly houses under a tutor.

The master must be attentive not only to the greater ends but to the minor details of training. Moral education stands in relation to Letters as the aim to the instruments. "For the effect of sound learning is to fashion the self which we receive from Nature—an undeveloped, unformed personality—which thus may realise and manifest its innate distinction." Education has two sides, one which results from self-reflection, self-discipline; this is the late fruit of experience, pertaining to manhood rather than youth, which is the easy prey of various passions. The other factor is the pressure of discipline and authoritative order. Rightly applied this external control creates an inner self-mastery, which is "virtus." The two forces making for character are the knowledge and fear of God, and the influence of the home example. The father by outward demeanour, bearing, and dress satisfies a right standard of appearance. His conduct should command respect. Sadoleto praises particularly self-restraint under all circumstances; even anger, bad news, unexpected joy, should not be allowed to set a man loose from reason. Nothing is more divine than the exhibition of such perfect control. In other matters—dress for example, which should not be ostentatious, nor mean, nor neglected, and in outward gestures —he will allow externals to express his inner temper. This of course is of the essence of humanist conviction, and does not forbid that in special stress of emotion display may be appropriately allowed. The boy will thus learn to understand the two central virtues of life, the one αἰδώς, the other regard for τὸ μέσον, which are implanted in us when young by training, and enforced throughout life by watchfulness and experience. It follows therefore that the rule of the home is firm, yet orderly, quiet, dignified, without loud emphasis or harshness. A rhythmic principle pervades discipline.

The household he contemplates is one in which the earning of money is not the daily interest of the parents ; an assured but moderate income from landed estate is that which he has in mind. Luxury in furnishings, a multiplicity of works of art and ornaments, elaborate service, and table, with extravagant waste on amusement conduce to a wrong view of the business of life, and in particular to a concern for our fellow beings only in so far as they subserve our pleasures

The centre of the home is the father. The influence of womenkind upon children at home is not very good. The weak, indulgent nature which is unwilling to enforce upon boys any standard beyond that of self-gratification is the dominant fact about mothers, "fere et feminae omnes," in his experience. Like other humanists he does not perceive that the refusal to her of all share in responsible influence limited the mother's relations to her growing sons to the sphere of indulgence. He contrasts the hardy up-bringing of Cyrus with the harem-training of Cambyses and points the moral. The general home environment which is to be desired is thus set out : "The temper of the home life should be serious and strict, yet with a distinct note of refinement, and a certain open-handedness in the treatment of dependents, and courteous hospitality in intercourse with equals." Sadoleto is keenly alive to the selfishness which underlies social extravagance and display, even when it takes the more subtle form of the collector's enthusiasm for works of art.

The stage of growth in which the mother has control of the boy is soon passed. Probably by the fifth year she is deposed and the father takes full responsibility. It is his duty, not the mother's, to impart religious truth, to inculcate respect for parents and elders as did the fathers of Sparta and Rome, and that bulwark of character, self-respect, which is "the dread of ill repute." The influence of the father is built upon the son's conviction of his sincerity, his affection, and his judgment. With constant allusions to Terence, "who expresses best the image of human life as it is," as Castiglione says, Sadoleto urges the need of "gravitas" and deprecates "sodalitas," from which, as implying too much familiarity, proceeds contempt, or at least too great freedom from constraint. The end to be kept in view is that of inducing the boy to take pleasure in the type of interest that attracts his father, and to dislike what the latter distrusts. Terror of a father's power is a worthless sanction to conduct, in that it is certain to give way at a crisis. Yet though gentle the father must never be negligeable. Discretion is shown in distinguishing between a corrupt mind and the natural effervescence of youth, which indeed needs serious guidance, by reasoning rather than sheer authority. Under no circumstances may a father lay hands upon the boy, and even to lose self-control in anger is "semper indecorum." The highest motive to parental self-abnegation is the sense that life is renewed in the son, which is indeed the principle that governs the family bond. Should the father be unequal to this high duty let him efface himself and commit the boy to another. The house in which he lives is the boy's world, and the head of it stands for the supreme power which governs all things.

Like the Florentines Sadoleto holds for the family life as the centre of training. Upon school and its organisation he has nothing to say. He offers nothing new upon curriculum, and elaborates no new methods : nor has he before him a scheme which will fit all men of all countries. The essence of this ideal is the stress laid therein upon environment, upon *unconscious absorption* from sights and sounds—which he carefully differentiates — harmonious and rightly proportioned. There is an entire absence of that belief in the power of talk, of the moralising and didactic processes which were so dear to Erasmus. Education is won in early years by instrumentality of things which are not avowedly concerned with training anyone. The timbre of the voice, the gesture, the dress of those who are instinctively felt to be our examplars ; the grace and rhythmic order of daily intercourse ; the fashion of its outward frame ; the restraint which proportions the material to the spiritual in life :—these are the notes of an environment which is in itself an education. Such at least was the foundation which Sadoleto demands, in true Platonic temper.

The stage of systematic instruction is now reached. The religious concepts of the divine majesty and goodness are taught from history and enforced by example. Modesty, horror of lies, in act and word, are prime virtues. Truthfulness indeed is to be taught as both moral and intellectual, sincerity and knowledge are the opposites of lies and ignorance. Hence imitation of the unworthy, in persons or actions, is not permitted ; for it offends against Truth. Imitation of the "good" aids Truth, as tending to uplift man to the spontaneous practice of right. Play, too, must be allowed, without too much repression from the point of view of the taste of elders, for precocious austerity is not to be demanded. So far as moral bent is concerned it may be hoped that the boy needs little direct supervision, for he rejoices in the spring of a self-directed personality.

Instruction is based upon curiosity, power of application, and the instinct to excel. Sadoleto has no fear of competition, which to him is a noble motive. The child will be taught to like work, and Letters are not to be put forward as a thing abhorrent. Some boys in particular enjoy learning by heart. From the outset Latin will be taught as a necessary instrument of learning and of intercourse, for we cannot confine our reading nor our conversation to our own speech. It is assumed that communications with foreigners will be through Italian, and that the ancient literature of his own country is on the same footing as Dante. But the rudiments of Greek are to be learnt along with Latin, and it is understood that nothing but the vernacular will be taught before the stage when systematic instruction begins. To Sadoleto, as to Bembo, Latin was not a living tongue; and classical purity rather than careless familiarity was the goal of teaching.

The motive for the inclusion of Greek is, so the author reminds his readers, that the two tongues are so intertwined, and the wisdom preserved in the Latin literature is so manifestly dependent on that of the Greeks, that a knowledge of Latin alone " is a maimed and halting thing." From the beginning therefore let the boy be steeped in both.

The course of study which Sadoleto sketches is only a variation from that which the humanist practice of the past century had elaborated. Like his predecessors he builds upon the foundation of Plutarch and Quintilian, though he suffuses what he has drawn from Roman experience with a feeling for Plato unfamiliar in the earlier scholars or in German apostles of the Revival. As to grammar he deprecates with Erasmus the complexity both of accidence and syntax which some teachers have introduced. What does it concern a beginner, he asks, whether the participle is part of the verb or an independent part of speech? All that really matters is (1) parts of speech, (2) inflexions, (3) concords, (4) quantity, the last, along with orthography to be learnt by reading. Indeed grammar taught merely as such is a trying study; but as a logical summary of laws drawn from reading of authors it is not unattractive. Yet, with Melanchthon, he will have the grammar securely known within the desired range. Composition then, as a grammatical exercise, accompanies construing. Rhetoric, as an art, takes from grammar the laws of syntax, and adds to them the principles of logical and tasteful exposition, so producing prose writing both accurate and persuasive. Hence the place of Cicero as a model for imitation : though even here we lose much unless we place him side by side with Demosthenes and Isocrates. Youth, however, as Sadoleto almost alone among the later humanists perceives, is not the stage at which a critical style can be acquired. For " judicatio," the faculty of weighing and selecting in expression, is not yet possible. If the boy accumulates examples, absorbs insensibly the usage of his models, developes taste by tentative recognition of what is fine, this is all that ought to be expected of him. Amongst prose authors the Roman and Greek historians must be read "ad confirmandam prudentiam"; for " from history we may easily learn what ought to be avoided, what pursued, in the affairs of life." And this is not limited to affairs of State but to the emergencies of private station. And Sadoleto, who had no small share in administering Papal policy for fifteen eventful years, ought to know how the story of Greece and Rome helped him in advising Leo and Clement. The results certainly seem disappointing to the onlooker.

Sadoleto differs from the usual humanist teacher in postponing the poets to the prose writers. Here too Greek and Latin authors are to be read at the same time. He will not banish poets, though he agrees with Plato in excluding what is degrading. There is no attempt to define limits. Terence is allowed for his knowledge of humanity and for the sake of his colloquial Latin : Plautus also, though with more reserve. Homer is the prince of poets. Upon music he draws the distinction between trivial and unworthy melodies which lower moral sensitiveness, and that strong, sound music whose function is to refine, strengthen, and inspire what is noblest in human feeling. Strictly, it is in education a subject fit only for the preparatory stage, but one of its functions is to serve as introduction to the full understanding of poetry. The " sententiae " of vocal music (i.e. the purport of the songs) is of great significance. The Roman practice of chanting the deeds of ancestors, Vergil's praise for him who sang of the motions of celestial bodies, suggest to him that Christian lore affords wide scope for songs. The State should see that innovations in music and song are carefully guarded—in true Platonic vein. He pours scorn on the kind of cleverness which imitates the voices of animals as frivolous and unworthy of intelligent beings. Music was much cultivated in the sixteenth century, and nowhere more sedulously than in the Vatican circle under Leo X. Luther was not less open to its attraction. The Ciceronians, with their training in the rhythm of words were naturally susceptible, and both Bembo and Sadoleto agreed that nothing had more direct effect on emotions. "No soul is so strong that it can resist it, that can refuse to yield, obedient, vanquished, to its power." Yet music fills only a secondary place in education, auxiliary to and compatible with morals. As a relaxation, dancing is not prohibited to the young, but it must be limited to dignified and graceful measures. Subject to the canons in μουσική thus laid down Sadoleto allows, nay urges, the growing student to wander amongst authors, to enrich his mind and enlarge his tastes by the exercise of choice, to establish the beginnings of a critical faculty. Exclusiveness based on grounds of style alone he held to be detrimental to intelligent appraisement, which must rest on far broader standards of taste.

So far the foundations of education. He has a few words on gymnastic before treating of his main theme. He realises that Italian society of his time does not admit of the Greek standard of physical culture. The palaestra, the Olympic contest, the baths, filled a place in Greek life peculiar to the nation. But the traditional exercises of ancient Rome, ball play, running, javelin throwing, riding, he approves, indeed all sports which take youth into the open air and have as their note of excellence energy, spontaneity, rather than elaborate skill and highly specialised training.

He feels called upon to offer defence for the width of the curriculum which he is about to propose. At the stage which the pupil has now, *ex hypothesi*, attained, multiplicity of subjects is helpful to intellectual growth rather than a hindrance. It is not intended to expect a profound study of each ; but it is good that the boy should rise to a general view of accepted knowledge and seize its important features. He will thus become familiar with new regions as a traveller might, who learns enough to enable him to choose the area or soil which suits him best, intending to return and settle there as a colonist and citizen. The true method of specialisation implies three steps : first, the rapid review of the arts and disciplines approved by antique and humanist practice ; next, the co-ordination of knowledge in " philosophia"; thirdly, the selection, in light of this broad outlook on life and thought, of one special region of learning, to which the student will come with a mind better fitted to sincere enquiry than is possible to one whose range of instruction has been kept narrow from the outset : " revertetur enim ex opibus copiisque philosophiae et animo et ingenio multo paratior." We do not indeed find any precise definition of " philosophia " in Sadoleto. It is, apparently, the complex of all liberal arts : it is also " omnium scientiarum domina " ; it is something more than ethics yet not the metaphysic of scholasticism. It is the art of life as well as of wisdom ; history, morals, dialectic are its three chief constituents.

Arithmetic is a necessary acquirement; as a form of ab-stract reasoning, independent of concrete cases, it is a valuable mental training. As an aid to business, it also deserves respect, for business, in honourable hands, is not to be disdained as unworthy. But the main argument for its place in education is that it is the necessary introduction to all mathematical disciplines—music, geometry and astrology alike depend upon it. Geometry, as a subject of rigid reasoning, is a source of immediate intellectual pleasure. Sadoleto means that the direct response of the intelligence to plain logical proof has in it an accompaniment of pleasing emotion. Further, the practical use of geometry in building, sculpture, painting, fortification and other warlike arts, in navigation and geography, gives it additional attractiveness. However, it is the abstract nature of the subject that renders it worthy of such a mind, for example, as that of Archimedes. It serves as a ground-work or introduction to philosophy, in that it is a first step in the method of withdrawing our reasoning from dependence on sensible and therefore variable phenomena, and so enabling us to rise to pure generalisation. Astrology is "a subject of awe-inspiring interest," but has no relation to the interpretation of celestial phenomena as influencing human fortune. Sadoleto refers of course to astronomy, studied on Ptolemaic principles.

Philosophy thus has as its immediate preparation the study of mathematics. Sadoleto admits his dependence upon Greek thinkers, who were the greatest of all philosophers. The Romans had no aptitude for scientific speculation. "Do you think," he asks, "that there is much in the realm of philosophy which has escaped the great minds of Greece?" Though, after a long interval of darkness, we have again men who are capable of the highest levels of thought: Bembo, Aleander, Pico, in whom wisdom and eloquence (power of exposition) are conjoined. He is careful to add, that whether we go to the ancients or to the moderns, we must go to the original sources themselves, for mediaevalism has buried Greek thought under a veritable mountain of perverse comment and gloss.

The two chief factors of philosophic reading are ethics, and dialectic, to be both studied direct from Aristotle. We must remember that Sadoleto wrote at a time when the Aristotle of fact as distinct from the pseudo-Aristotle of the scholastics had become the subject of profound analytical study. For the rest of the century all political and ethical enquiries were bound to fall into forms of discussion made familiar from the *Ethics* and the *Politics*.

Philosophy, it is obvious, is the scientific exposition of the end instinctively, but confusedly, sought by the average thinking man. Its function is not only to develope and systematise the working of the intelligence, but to form the heart, govern conduct, and guide the student of it to supreme happiness. It is thus a study of much significance to the man of affairs, whilst to the enquirer in the field of learning it alone enables him to stand on sure ground.

The studies of Letters and philosophy serve the soul as steps to mount to the highest wisdom, which is the conscious unity of self and God. The great service which they render is that they turn the thoughts from things of the senses and lead the mind to reflect upon the things which are beyond the variation and imperfection of sensible phenomena. They are the rightful complement of religion and morality in that they draw out and give expression to the finer instincts, and repress lower impulses and unworthy pre-occupations.

M. Joly sums up the impression which is left by a study of Sadoleto's attempt at reaching a solution of the ideal end of education. "The aim of perfection governs the illuminated intelligence. Now all that is truly a product of intelligence may serve this end. This is true even of the technical arts in which the worker proposes as his end material welfare, or the artist strives at the imitation, the visible expression, of ideal beauty. Thus, according to the direction impressed by the individual intelligence upon the material on which it works, the soul can find its satisfaction. Hence not only pure science, Letters, and philosophy, but also art in industry may be recognised as factors in self-development, and as filling out our highest wisdom."

Yet the life of devotion to philosophy and all that such devotion implies brings man nearer to God, and herein attains its noblest function.

The aim of Sadoleto is to fashion a man fit to fill the place of the cultured citizen in a civilised and secure polity. And as he does not contemplate any exceptional position so he does not sketch out a novel or a plethoric course,—say of Miltonic proportions. Further, we gather, by negative evidence, that there was with him no sense of a reconciliation to make between the Christian and the pagan in the material of education. For an Italian humanist the question was settled. The work, indeed, was received with applause, though northern critics like Reginald Pole thought that not enough stress was laid on religion and that the claims of theology were wrongly ignored. To which Sadoleto would naturally make reply that he was drafting the lines of a liberal education upon which theology—or law or medicine—would find its due place as a technical superstructure. But as regards the religious under-lie, it is not hard to see that the very foundation of his training is compact of the ordered pieties of home. A contrast, no doubt, presents itself when we turn to the Calvinist teacher, Cordier or Knox. For Sadoleto, like Erasmus, has no overmastering conviction of sin. Man is indeed imperfect, commingled of good and evil; but under wisely planned circumstance, and with sound teaching, the youthful evil will slowly abate, and natural good slowly establish control, in so far as lofty interests find room to develope under the stimulus and example of parent and master.

CHAPTER X.

JUAN LUIS VIVES. 1492–1540.

LUIS VIVES[1], born at Valencia in Spain in 1492, has but recently gained the recognition which his place in the development of humanist education rightly merits. Less distinguished than Erasmus in the width of his outlook over both the ancient and the modern world, of smaller powers as a judge of men, more sparing of literary production, he was, on the other hand, a more thorough scholar, of more skill as a teacher, and had a stronger grasp of the educational needs of his age. In one important respect Vives was a pioneer in a new and significant region of enquiry. For he was the first humanist to submit to systematic analysis the Aristotelian psychology, and to regard the results of his study in their bearing upon instruction. In this interest in philosophy, and in his comprehensive grasp of the possible content of a curriculum which should correspond to the advance in knowledge and the needs of the new society of the northern Renaissance, Vives stands

---

[1] There is nothing substantial upon Vives in English. An edition of the *De Tradendis Disciplinis* (both parts) and of the *Exercitatio*, or Colloquies, is to be desired. A survey of the former by C. Arnaud (1887) and Thibaut's *Quid de Puellis instituendis senserit Vives* (1888) are useful to the student. H. Veil in his account of Sturm (Strassb. 1878), and Schmid, *Geschichte der Erziehung*, treat of his historical position. Mr P. S. Allen has cleared up the facts about Vives' residence in England. His psychology is fully examined by Dr Hoppe. The memoir by Namèche (1842) is of little value. The writings of Vives enumerated below, p. 183, well repay first-hand study.

forth conspicuously amongst the scholars and teachers of the century.

His life was a comparatively short one. After receiving a sound education at home, tinged with at least the rudiments of humanism, including possibly some Greek, he went to Paris in 1509. The characteristic note of Spanish humanism was the comparative smoothness with which the transition from the mediaevalism to the new learning was effected, and, further, the enthusiasm with which the claims of the mother tongue to full recognition were conceded. Spain had but lately brought to a triumphant close its secular struggle with the Infidel. Hence Christianity, nationality and the Castilian tongue were bound together by the one common sanction of victory. Vives typifies the Spanish Renaissance thus regarded. He is always a devout churchman. He was never perhaps wholly at ease outside the sphere of Spanish life and society. He has a sincere pride in his mother tongue, and affirmed and illustrated its function in education.

In the year 1512 he left Paris, with no love for dialectic, and made for Flanders. At Louvain he became actively engaged in the University. He lectured upon Vergil and Cicero, the *Historia Naturalis* of Pliny, and the geography of Pomponius Mela, an author not wholly to official taste, as we know from some sarcastic comments of Erasmus. Indeed, the University was but half-hearted in its welcome of humanism, which explained the important foundation of the Collegium Trilingue in which Erasmus and his friends were so deeply interested. It was at this stage of his career that Vives formed his personal friendship with Erasmus. In or about 1518 Vives became tutor to the youthful Cardinal William de Croy, and on his death in 1521 continued to live at Louvain, until in 1522 he came over to England for the first time; in the following year he was invited by Wolsey, then deeply concerned in his Oxford schemes, to take the University Readership in Humanity which he had just established. He was lodged in

Corpus Christi College, which had been founded some seven years before by Erasmus' friend Bishop Foxe. As a Spaniard he enjoyed the patronage of Queen Katherine, at whose command he wrote the treatise *De Institutione Feminae Christianae* (1523). His work at Oxford as Latin lecturer was marked with distinction. Vives was no doubt the best scholar in the University; he found congenial company in Claymond the President, in Thomas Lupset, and others chiefly centering in Magdalen who bore the brunt of the struggle for the new learning against the "Trojans." In 1524 Vives was in Bruges, and in June married a cousin, a Spaniard like himself, and daughter of a merchant settled there by reason of affairs. In the Michaelmas Term he was again lecturing, living still at Corpus, and in communication with the Court. He left for Bruges in the spring of 1525, and there is no evidence that he returned to Oxford. When the Divorce became the pre-occupation of public men Vives was called to the Queen's household, and taught the Princess Mary. The little manual of Latin rudiments which he drew up for her use survives. But Vives, perhaps naturally, took the Queen's side in the great controversy, became suspect of Wolsey and the King in consequence, was kept in some kind of modified restraint, then dismissed and ordered to quit the Kingdom. He lost the King's pension, and in 1529 the Queen's also. He now settled at Bruges for the remaining years of his life; writing and teaching, corresponding with men engaged in education, and though holding aloof from controversy, trying his best to make peace in the Church, from the point of view of a sincere Catholic ardently desirous of internal reform. Although probably never a man of wealth, and at times plunged, after the manner of scholars, into extreme poverty, there is around Luis Vives an undefined air of social and personal distinction.

His experiences were gained in the society of the governing rank, to which by birth he belonged. In Flanders his associates and pupils were always of the Spanish ruling class, in

England his home was naturally the Court. The same impression is left by his school-book, the *Exercitatio*, where the allusions and illustrations are drawn from like society.

The works which chiefly concern the present study are the following: *Satellitium*, a collection of Latin maxims, *Introductio ad Sapientiam*, *De Ratione Studii*, a small abstract of accidence, and *De Institutione Feminae Christianae*. His most popular religious writing was his commentary, thoroughly evangelical in spirit, yet in learning perfectly sound, upon the *De Civitate Dei* of Augustine. *De Anima et Vita* and *In Pseudo-dialecticos* (1519) a criticism of the studies and methods of the University of Paris, are his chief philosophical works. The volume of Colloquies *Linguae Latinae Exercitatio* (1538) was compiled from normal experiences of child life as he knew it, for beginners in Latin[1].

But the great monument of his experience and wisdom as an educator is the *De Tradendis Disciplinis* (1531), the first part of which is often quoted under the separate title of *De Causis Corruptarum Artium*. This, as the title implies, is critical in substance, taking the form of an examination of the reasons for the slow progress of knowledge in an age of rapid social and political change. In the seven books which comprise this portion of the entire work Vives treats of (1) the general causes of the decay of knowledge, instancing such varied reasons as avarice, arrogance of the unlearned, unwillingness to stoop to learning, wars, loss of learned tongues, confusion of different regions of knowledge, ignorance of the real Aristotle, corruption of Universities; (2) the lack of true instruction in Latin and Greek; (3) the perversion of logic as an instrument of enquiry; (4) want of trained powers of expression; (5) ignorance of sound natural science; (6) decline of true study of moral philosophy; (7) degenerate methods of study of law. The second part treats of the aim,

---

[1] See Massebieau, *Les Colloques*, p. 158, for an account of the *Exercitatio*.

the methods, instruments, and curricula of education, viewed in light of the learning and the practical demands of the day. This comprehensive work, by far the most systematic of those produced by the Revival, is not only compiled (as is inevitable) upon the basis of Aristotle, Plutarch, and Quintilian, but also draws from the masters and writers of the fifteenth century, notably from Erasmus. But, notwithstanding this dependence, the breadth and the methodical presentation of the *De Tradendis Disciplinis* rendered it the standing authority to which authors and workers in the fields of education uniformly turned for a century or more.

Before revising the general scheme of education presented by Vives, it is convenient to summarise his attitude to psychology[1], a subject which he approached from the point of view of effectiveness in instruction. He was the first humanist to apply the method of empirical enquiry to the phenomena of cognition ; he led the way to that emancipation from the authority of Aristotle, Galen and Aquinas which characterises the philosophical thought of the seventeenth century. His interests were those of a humanist and practical teacher, and his study of psychology was rather the product and accompaniment of his educational activity than its originating impulse. Had he been less many-sided he might have achieved epoch-making results in this subject.

Hardly a single humanist of distinction, from the days of Vergerius downwards, had failed to protest against the accretions which rendered the Aristotelian dialectic worthless as an instrument of sound mental discipline. Valla, Agricola and Melanchthon had contributed to restore the simplicity of deductive logic as an aid to thought and expression. But the phenomena of mental activity lying outside the function of pure reasoning, such as sensation, memory, imagination, judgment, had received no systematic attention from scholars.

[1] The *De Anima et Vita* is the title of the work in which his psychological theory is developed.

Such enquiry, indeed, was scarcely differentiated from the traditional physiology of Galen on the one hand and the metaphysic of Aquinas on the other. The Church, in effect, held the latter as the fullest statement of orthodox speculation. Vives, however, in an imperfect and tentative way, initiated a new line of approach to psychological analysis. His method is not that of recurring to "the real Aristotle," "the true wisdom of antiquity"; but, abandoning the hope of reaching an adequate explanation of mental activity from any *à priori* starting point, whether classical or theological, he pursues an enquiry by the method of observation and analysis of actual intellectual processes. The "Soul" is not to be explained by dogmatic assertion but by noting its multiform expressions in thought, belief and action.

Now it is to be remembered that the claim to respect which we make for the work of a pioneer in any new branch of human activity rests less upon achievements definitely attained than upon the double distinction—that he has been the first to realise that *a given problem exists*, and that he has divined the *general line of method* for its solution. In the region of educational progress the truth needs perpetual recall, and our estimates of men must be based upon it. Accepting this, Vives demands high recognition for his contribution to psychological advance.

It is natural that he should lay most stress upon psychology in relation to training and instruction, specially concerning himself with the analysis of Memory, in which he formulates a doctrine of Association. Memory, he says, is the specialised faculty of the soul by which the mind retains percepts apprehended through sensation and reflection. These percepts are mental images which inscribe themselves as upon a slate and are read off by the spiritual eye. In another metaphor he describes Memory as the hand of the spiritual part of us seizing and retaining external impressions. The power of receiving, the power of recovering, and the power of reconstituting this record are the three factors of Memory. A capacity peculiar to humanity is the search for the partly defaced record. As a function of the organ of the brain, Memory has its seat in the back of the head. A dry brain is the more retentive, a moist brain the more impressionable. The excess of heat is detrimental to fixity of impression, as we see in the excitable or fevered subject. The proper adjustment of such physical conditions is a matter partly of constitution partly of health and diet.

But Vives has more to say than this, which he takes of course from the medical lore of the later empire. He passes to the conditions precedent to the right remembering of any matter. We can only retain what we attend to, and we can only attend to that which interests us. If emotion is intimately associated with the perceptive act the record is far more definite and will be longer held. This, he says, is his own experience as student and as teacher. Next, length of time occupied in receiving the impression determines the strength of its record. Vives thinks that this may explain why highly gifted minds, with the faculty of rapid apprehension of facts and ideas, may be inferior in memory power to slower and therefore of necessity more plodding types. Application of recorded matter in exercises and regular testing of it by questions are aids to security. His analysis of the forms of Forgetfulness is instructive and original. He considers it as due sometimes to physical causes, as illness, or to emotional distraction (the emotion present not being one intimately associated with the matter impressed) or to any disturbance set up by the body or the feelings. Or it is due to a complete or partial disappearance of the record, brought about of distinct purpose, as when we dismiss material as being no longer wanted or of no value— the waste substance cast aside in the selective process of study, yet possibly found to be wanted unexpectedly when no longer at hand. Or the impression was originally indefinite, due to faulty perception or illogical reflection. Or by accident one

link of association has dropped and the chain is irrecover-
able.

The exposition of Association follows.   Such associations
depend upon cause and effect; upon the relation of part and
whole; upon environment in space and time and related fact;
upon similarity of one fact to another.   Some associations are
rapid, instantaneous; yet even so links can be traced by a
searching analysis.   If two impressions be simultaneously
apprehended and recorded the emergence of the less important will revive the more important.   This, he expressly
states, is the form in which his own experience leads him to
state the law.   Recall can be facilitated by the teacher who
takes necessary pains in the arrangement of his subject-matter,
whereby the pupil's mind is hedged in as on a narrow road
and cannot stray.   Mathematical laws, rhyme, deductive sequences, and chronological order, all facilitate accurate record
of fact, and lend themselves to easy recall.   The emotion of
surprise and wonder evoked by good teaching of appropriate
subjects will be a great aid to the young learner.   Yet it must
be remembered that anything which produces excitement is
apt to militate against accuracy of percept and of the consequent image, especially if presentations follow rapidly or
confusedly.   The phenomena of unconscious acquisition and
of capricious recall, as well as of the inconsequential retention
of apparently trivial facts when serious truths are wholly forgotten, are dealt with by Vives on analysis of his own personal
experience or that of his pupils.

It is in this portion of psychological enquiry that Vives
showed his method to best advantage.   He did not establish
the doctrine of Association in the modern form which it
received from the school of empirical psychology.   But he
accepted deliberately, and tentatively applied the empirical
basis of the study of mental phenomena, and devoted himself
peculiarly to the region of memory.   If in mediaeval fashion
he clung to the mode of explaining functions by virtue of a

special *vis*, inherent in each, at the same time he broke away from that dependence of philosophical enquiry upon theological dogma which was a far more serious obstruction to scientific progress. Vives, in fact, made the first steps in modern times towards an independent science of mind ; and, a result in part of his first-hand study of Aristotle, he was brought to realise that psychology is conditioned (however imperfectly he conceived the truth is not material) by physiological factors. Vives, indeed, exemplifies the inevitable law that the man who breaks out a new road for mankind to follow carries with him into the new land something at least of the type which was his in the old home.   Scholastic philosophy was but slowly yielding ground.   Aristotle was for the first time read to find the actual meaning of the philosopher during Vives' lifetime. Preconceptions and forms of thought, imposed of necessity by his environment and his education, could not fail to colour his own enquiry, however original the method which he ultimately attained.   Thus the principles of psychology which Vives reached, and upon which he based his teaching practice, are of the new age, whilst the form in which he states his judgments are not seldom inconsistent with them.   It must be repeated that his interest in the subject was derived from his enthusiasm for all that concerned effectiveness in education.

The opening sentence of the *De Tradendis Disciplinis* gives the note of the entire work.   "Seeing that by the surpassing bounty of God we are endued with the faculty of thought and of enquiry, whereby we not only observe what lies before us, but reflect upon things past and forecast things to come, it is our rightful claim to employ these our powers in the examination of all facts and all truths, comparing and ordering them one with the other, and surveying the whole universe as it were our own domain : even though we may wander ignorantly therein and fail to view it with right apprehension."   The divine *obligation* of knowledge, the breadth of its content, the need of right method in attaining it, lie at the basis of all that Vives has to say about education. "Pietas," the word so familiar as the educational end with reformers like Melanchthon, Sturm and Comenius, is not with Vives merely a question of obedience to the law of conduct but a recognition of the sanction upon which all intellectual effort rests. In the training of the young *pietas* and *eruditio* are a consistent unity. Letters are no foe to faith, if the motive to their study is the right one. "Pietati nulla est ex se materies contraria, nulla cognitio" (p. 244), but the end of all wisdom as the uplifting and improvement of human life is always to be presupposed.. The function of teaching and of school is to train character as well as to impart knowledge. "Doctrina cui non respondet vita res est perniciosa ac turpis": this was no mere convention with Vives, whose own life was singularly free from the pettiness, jealousy, and sordid ambitions of so many men of Letters of his age.

On the earliest care of the young Vives offers advice which coincides with that of Erasmus. He perceives the law of heredity and allows full weight to it in training. He urges the weight of responsibility which lies upon both parents. School can scarcely eradicate evil impulses fostered by wicked example or gross neglect of home discipline. It is the father's duty to oversee everything that concerns his son: he will stiffen domestic control, keep in touch with all that affects the health and occupation of the boy, and above all select the teacher or tutor into whose charge he is placed. The mother may teach the letters, read aloud edifying stories, give the first grounding in morals. Such duties are a stimulus to a sensible woman to continue her own study that she may be a help to her children. Vives quotes a mother who learnt Greek and Latin, and even trained herself to rise early in order to hear her boys' home preparation. Such a woman can do more for her son's character than she suspects. This strikes a different note from that which is familiar to us in Erasmus' writings. He regarded a woman's influence as generally doubtful: though it is to be remembered that he had in mind the feeble education received by the German mother as a girl. Vives also believes women to be lacking in strength of will, and as the source of much of the lack of self-discipline shown by young men on entering manhood. He would allow a mother to flog her son, which Erasmus regards as dishonouring to both.

Vives would send the boy to school "etiam extemplo a lacte," if the school available were of a thoroughly satisfactory sort. But he did not know of any such. Home tuition for *young* boys is certainly preferable to the average school, always supposing instruction to be sound. But the advice he gives in ordinary cases is that a boy at the seventh year be sent to "gymnasium civitatis publicum," "vera et perfecta Academia"; with opportunity of attending the courses in Arts of a University where one exists. He should board with a relative or friend competent to supervise. But he objects to boarding-schools. School keeping has become a profitable undertaking, and much money is to be made out of boarders. In every city and in certain country centres there should be a public school. It is noticeable that Vives, himself a layman, seems always to prefer a lay institution to a monastic or clerical school, following Erasmus and Colet. If home tuition is necessary, there must be at least one companion brought in.

Vives deals at length with the conditions necessary to such a school as he would approve. His constructive treatment of the subject is of infinitely more value than the somewhat unreal contributions of Erasmus, and are in effect in advance even of Melanchthon's views. His judgment upon existing schools has much in common with the strictures of Erasmus or of Thomas Elyot. Anyone twenty years of age can get a licence to teach from a University, a Bishop, or other authority. Worthless young men, elderly failures in life, drunkards, even men released from prison, are in charge of schools. Assistants are very often graduates in Arts, working for degrees in Law or Theology, and wholly indifferent to their nominal duties. The profession as such hardly exists: to be a master is a stepping stone to something else.   Hence the low stipends paid to men who are not in earnest in their career, but just passers-by. France, Germany and Italy provide him with examples of masters socially reckoned with servants, and not undeservedly; ignorant men, and therefore cruel disciplinarians, a source of life-long mischief to their charges.   A boy of good bringing-up degenerates under such influences: he goes home rough, heavy, uninterested, a shock to his parents.   Vives makes no reference to the famous schools of Deventer or Liège, or to certain episcopal schools in France where conditions of boarding seem to have been quite satisfactory.

Coming to the positive conditions which Vives requires, he deals with site, staff, training of masters, curriculum, games and exercise.   It is especially upon the first three points that Vives is in advance of his contemporaries.   He demands an airy, wholesome site, not adjoining a manu-facturing town, nor, on the other hand, near to a Court.   The neighbourhood of a market town is desired, that food may be good and plentiful.   But he has nothing to say as to the buildings of his day-school.   That Vives was writing for the behoof of a social class other than the quasi-feudal landed order is obvious from the absence of all mention of training in arms as part of education.   Yet it is not less evident that he has in mind families raised by wealth, opportunity and culti-vation above the ranks of the lower burgher class.   Sport occupies a subordinate position, as a means to an end. But he insists that exercise should be frequent; games are to be played at least once daily, football, tennis, or runs. Long walks ought to be encouraged.   In wet weather shelter should be supplied and entertainments of an attractive sort organised for indoor occupation, such as the Latin plays generally performed in German schools of the time.

The actual development of the body for its own sake hardly seems to be an object with Vives.   There is no trace of pure asceticism. That exercise stimulates mental activity he expressly states. From the point of view of health he insists on early school. We know that both in Italy and north of the Alps school hours often began about six or seven in the morning. Four meals a day must be taken; water, very little beer, and, rarely, wine much diluted, may be drunk. Punishments must be entrusted to masters carefully chosen for their humanity. Vives does not shrink from corporal chastisement in the last resort: "eum revocet dolor cui ratio non est satis." But no serious harm must be caused.

The selection of masters is a question upon which Vives has much to say. He has dwelt upon the futility of the degree of *Artium Magister* as a qualification for teaching boys. A recognised "gradus docentis" ought to be obtainable only after probation and careful observation by a head-master and other experts. Aspirants for teaching posts ought to satisfy repeated tests carried out in actual class work under the eye of skilled masters. There was apparently a practice current in which two candidates were pitted against one another in adjoining classes, observed by a number of unskilled onlookers whose judgment was taken in selecting the better teacher. This Vives thinks wholly unreal. He desires a working school of good type to be used as a school for practice, in which "facultas et dexteritas docendi" may be tested and the title of "professores magistri" awarded. The significance of such a suggestion at that stage in educational history needs no emphasis. But the qualifications of the master on the side of attainments are of equal importance. The tract of Erasmus, *De Ratione Studii*, so profoundly respected by Melanchthon, is evidently very familiar also to Vives, who like his great predecessor will have, if he can, a man skilled in the whole circle of knowledge to fill a teaching post of responsibility. At least he will insist that such subjects as he has been able to acquire shall be thoroughly studied, soundly apprehended, and properly worked up for purposes of class-teaching. His school-master will be one who moves freely, as though at home, amidst high intellectual interests. The type of man he has in mind is further indicated by the stress which he lays upon the absence of all commercial considerations in the relation of master and pupil. Particularly does he insist that the masters shall take no business interest in the meals and lodging of the boys. The pupil should pay no fees direct to the master, whose stipend is a public charge. Such stipend should preferably not be excessive—Erasmus would have had an ironical rejoinder ready—for men drawn by pecuniary motives are not in place in education. His objection to private boarding-schools rests in part on the motive of profit which is implied. In this way the relations of the master with parent and with pupil will be more natural and sincere. Gravity without harshness, friendliness and confidence without indecorous familiarity will mark his attitude towards the boy.

In one important respect this personal relation will prove significant : viz., in enabling the master by careful observation of his pupils to determine the right planning of their respective training. Vives is not of opinion that it is a simple matter to deduce bent of mind and character from a superficial noting of youthful behaviour. His own psychology rested, indeed, on empirically acquired facts ; but he was not led astray by the readiness with which a conclusion, right or wrong, might be plausibly formed[1]. No two boys, he affirms, have received from nature precisely the same endowments, nay the same boy varies from time to time with the conditions under which his life is spent. A promising boy is seen to degenerate ; a boy of doubtful promise grows up to a sound manhood. Nothing is more useful, and nothing more difficult,

---

[1] See M. Vegius, *De Liberorum Educ.* i. 18, for the import of moral differences in children. Vergerius laid great stress on native quality : "in quas res natura proni, aptique fuerimus...in eis totos versari conveniet." Ingenium might be " plumbeum " or " ferreum " or " glebae ascriptum " : each needing appropriate care. Cp. Woodward, *Vittorino*, p. 109.

than to follow out such idiosyncrasies. Masters should confer upon these as they affect their work so gravely; and apart from informal conversations, four times in each year, at the least, serious conferences should be held upon the bent and temper of the boys under instruction.

Vives here touches in perfectly reasonable fashion upon a question which was raised by almost every humanist writer on Education. Alberti, for example, insisted that an observant father can with certainty make himself aware of the tastes, inclinations, aversions and capacity of his son. At as early an age as ten the boy's career may be forecast. But he thinks no doubt mainly of temper and bent of character rather than of special intellectual qualities. Erasmus[1] laid great stress upon the *natura specialis* which is recognisable in individuals, and which determines the type of career, and even of the particular field of study suited to each. Such recognition is possible very early in the educational course. Sturm, writing in the year of his appointment to the Strassburg School (1538), says: "industrii doctoris atque magistri est videre ad quam quisque artem accommodatam naturam habeat." The characteristics to be sought are "ardor in suscipiendo, studium in vestigando, acumen in percipiendo, et in conservando memoria." But here again these are general qualities of mind rather than special gift and bent, and imply only mental power. If we pass to a remarkable English observer of the next century, Sir Henry Wotton, Provost of Eton[2], we find that this careful estimation of youthful ability is affirmed to be the prime function of the master. "There must proceed a way how to discern the natural capacities and inclinations of children." Two methods are open by which such conclusions may be drawn: that of noting face, gesture and attitude: and that of regarding "some emergent art of mind." The eye, complexion,

---

[1] On the Erasmian psychology, see Woodward, *Erasmus*, p. 77.

[2] Wotton's *A philosophical survey of Education*.

expression, shape of head (which he prefers to be "great and round") are signs of the first kind ; waywardness, dreaminess, love of solitude, are discouraging ; alertness, self-assertion, memory, firm articulation, are amongst the promising indications. "The office of a tutor is first to know the nature of his pupil, that is to say, whereto he is most inclined," said Elyot[1] before him. But the thinker who devoted especial attention to the relation between capacity and instruction was Juan Huarte, a Spanish philosopher, who published, in 1575, a work which he called *Examen de Ingenios para las Ciencas*, translated into Italian under the title *Essamina degl' Ingegni degli Huomini acconci ad apparare qualsivoglia Scienza*, and thence into English as *The Examination of Men's Wits*.

The author, like Vives, approaches psychology from the standpoint of instruction, and his main thesis is that Nature has set up in different individuals a special genius which is peculiarly adapted to one type of study, and to that only. That there are natures to which no study at all is found congenial, he also admits. Quoting from the English version just referred to, "None hath clearly and distinctly delivered what that nature is which maketh a man able for one science and incapable of another, nor how many differences of wits there are found in mankind, nor what Arts or Sciences do answer (correspond to) each in particular nor by what tokens this may be known, which is the thing that most importeth," as he rightly observes. His positions are the following :

1. Out of several types of spiritual endowment one only is in preeminent degree allotted to any one individual. He admits that there are "dolts" who have none at all.

2. To each type of capacity there corresponds a specific region or subject of knowledge, which can be discovered and applied.

3. But there is need of further discrimination between

[1] Elyot, i. 38.

"the practick and the theoretick parts" of each subject, for "each require wits so different as if they were contraries."

4. The faculties or "wits" are (*a*) Memory, to which Latin grammar or any other language, theory of laws, divinity positive, cosmography, and arithmetic specially respond; (*b*) Understanding or Reasoning, which is exercised fruitfully by school divinity (dogmatic), physical science, logic, ethics, and "the practick of laws," which is pleading; (*c*) Imagination, which is peculiarly called into play by all arts and sciences which consist in figure, correspondence, harmony and proportion; such are poetry, eloquence, music, and skill of preaching. Also the practice of physic, mathematics, astrology; painting, drawing, writing, reading; the government of affairs; the technical arts, and the curious power of dictating different matter to four writers at once.

It is obvious that such a supposed relation between mental quality and intellectual, aesthetic and practical activities, is not of much value for purposes of education. Huarte, however, deserves attention for the assertion of a principle which provokes him to attempt such a correlation, viz., that teaching has to take account of the psychology of the learner not less than of the logical order of the matter and the class-organisation of the school. As in Vives so in his fellow-Spaniard what most interests us is the fact of direct concern for psychological analysis as a specific aid to the right adjustment of instruction. That Huarte learned much from Vives there is ample evidence. Both agree in the importance of examinations.

So far the ideal school of Vives attracts notice from the insistence with which he calls attention to the need of fitting site and surroundings, the training of its staff, the duty of the master to adjust instruction to individual ability and bent, and the importance of systematic games.

The curriculum is discussed at length; and is arranged in the following order: linguae (which term he uses in preference to grammatica), logic, physica, prima philosophia or metaphysic, dialectica inventrix, rhetoric, mathematics.   Such a course covers the period from the seventh year to manhood. It is to be regarded as preparatory to professional training. Without examining it in detail certain points suggest themselves for consideration as illustrating the principles involved.

In the first place, Vives differs fundamentally from Erasmus or Sturm in respect of the function and worth of the vernacular tongues.   He had been brought up as all Spanish humanists to be proud of his Castilian ; he cherished it in his new home amongst the Spanish colony of Bruges.   He spoke Flemish, and French, and no doubt English.   " It is the duty of the parent and of the master to take pains that children speak their mother tongue correctly."   The master ought to be competent in the vernacular of his pupils or he will fail to teach adequately the learned tongues by its means.   A rightly educated man will never neglect the study of his national speech, but will do his utmost to foster it and to enrich it. Vives then taught Latin through the vernacular.

Yet he reminds his readers that the variety of tongues is the result of sin, viz., the arrogance of man at Babel : a perfect state implies one race, one nation, and one speech.   But facts and realities are against the attempt to assume such conditions. Hence the further need of a universal language.   Intercourse between foreign peoples, the common Faith, works of permanent and universal interest, demand such a tongue, and by its history, its structure, and its relation to its great Romance offshoots Latin is clearly indicated as the symbol of human solidarity.   Vives follows Valla in insisting upon the abandonment of mediaeval concepts of grammar, and mediaeval vocabulary, which destroyed Latin as a standard tongue.   Logicians had dwelt upon "causae," whereas eloquence only regarded "usus."   It was of no importance to ask "*why* the fifth declension is limited to feminine nouns," or why the absolute case is in Latin always the ablative : to know the fact is enough. Hence he denounces, in Erasmus' vein, the old dialectic grammars, and urges Despauterius or Melanchthon. Latin is not touched until the boy reaches the seventh year. Rules are to be learnt, but there must be no superstition about completeness and rigid accuracy. At first the child is not required to do more than show a teachable and attentive mind, but after a short experience of school he must begin to speak Latin. To this end Vives, like Erasmus and Cordier, wrote appropriate aids in the form of Colloquies. Upon this method of teaching Latin something has been said above. Apart from his practice of utilising the vernacular in the process of teaching, Vives followed Erasmus in his view of the function of grammar, and its relation to construing and composition. Accidence and syntax should be taught at each stage only so far as they were needed. It may be doubted whether Vives added anything to the stock of knowledge on grammatical usage. Certainly upon Greek he is avowedly content to follow Lascaris and Gaza.

As to the authors to be read, he deprecates the use of Excerpta, which were common in schools as cheap text-books. The full sense and dignity of an author is lost, and, as the study of Aristotle through extract and abridgment had proved, the gravest errors in interpretation were apt to ensue. Boys will naturally prefer the poets, amongst whom Vives like Erasmus recommends Lucan as the author to follow the "delectus" and the easy prose writer which the pupil begins with. It is to be borne in mind that Vives like many humanists, and notably John Milton, regards the classical writers as the source of wisdom rather than as mere examples of style. The authors specifically set down (*Op.* VI. 341) for boys up to sixteen, are the following: Caesar, the *Letters* of Cicero, Terence, the *Eclogues*, *Georgics* and *Aeneid* (in that order), select *Odes* of Horace, Prudentius, Bapt. Mantuanus; Livy, Valerius Maximus, and finally Cicero's *Speeches*: in Greek, without which Latin language and culture are barely intelligible, Aesop, Isocrates, Lucian, S. Chrysostom, Demosthenes, Homer, scenes (not whole plays) from Euripides and Aristophanes (Sophocles and Aeschylus are not included), Hesiod, Xenophon and Thucydides. Private reading will cover a wider field. The scope of such reading is enlarged with boys of sixteen. "Poetry is not the food but the spice of life," he remarks with emphasis.

He ridiculed excessive veneration for Cicero, as on other grounds for Plato or Aristotle. He could not admit that antiquity produced a type of mind of a different order from that which the modern world could show. Antiquity presents subsequent ages with examples of men passionately devoted to truth, and laborious in pursuing it. But in reverencing their spirit it is not necessary to affirm that they had attained final truth in all subjects of enquiry. The classics were to be studied that in due course they might be if possible surpassed. In reading histories he urges not Livy or Plutarch only, but Froissart, Comines, Monstrelet and the Spaniard Valera. "A general outline of Universal History down to our own day is desirable." As Elyot also advised, this should be preceded or accompanied by a course of geography. But he goes on to ask what elements in history are of chief importance? "Wars? No: for these are largely mere brigandage, and should be treated as such." As facts they are to be noted, but merit no special study. The pupil should deal chiefly with civil history, with events and characters "worthy of commendation." Yet few historians give right prominence to this aspect of their subject. It is but poor instruction which bids the pupil learn by heart details of less worthy actions yet ignores those which spring from wise policy. He advises the reading of Xenophon, Herodotus, Thucydides, Livy, Tacitus and Plutarch. No moderns equal these great writers, all of whom rise from narrative of incident to noble and eloquent "sententiae," and are thereby specially valuable for purposes of education. Vives no doubt has an eye to edification in his claim for the place of history ; but he regarded political lessons to be drawn from it as suitable only for a more advanced stage, when a young man took up the study as a technical preparation for public service. Yet even regarded as a school subject, he takes a position upon the treatment of history which is different from that propounded by any humanist before him : he is more akin to Montaigne than to Erasmus.

Such an attitude towards the past relieves Vives of anxiety as to the moral dangers of a study of ancient literature and society. He is able to take the historical standpoint. The admission of Christian Fathers and of Scripture as school texts is due to his breadth of view. They too are part of the world's inheritance. But as to excluding on religious grounds the fine flower of antique wisdom he is obdurate : the suggestion is intolerable, as though one should refuse to grow wheat for the poppies amongst it.

Although Vives gives rhetoric a later place in his curriculum, it is convenient to note it in connection with "linguae." The mediaevalist viewed rhetoric on one side as related to grammar and on the other to logic. "Inventio," the ordering of matter in logical shape for exposition, was a branch of dialectic, whilst "elocutio," style, or expression, was a province of grammar. The aim of the "grammaticus" was to give facility in "sermo simpliciter congruus" for common use, and the teacher of rhetoric facility in "sermo figurativus" (or "ornatus") for learned or literary purposes. Rhetoric thus aimed at effect through aesthetic and emotional impulse as well as by rigid reasoning. The superstitious deference paid to Cicero and Quintilian by many humanists has been dwelt upon. Vives, however, protests against it. He is with Erasmus in deriding the "imitatorum servum pecus," and refers to the arguments of the *Ciceronianus* as "well known to every reader." Budaeus, we may be reminded, held the same view. Style follows subject, and is only to be pronounced perfect when it is rightly adjusted to the matter, to the speaker, and to the audience.

In the teaching of rhetoric he takes the point of view that the master's duty is to put the scholar in the right path, and not to bring him to the goal. Nature (i.e. taste and capacity) and practice will complete what the teacher begins. Without them the task is not worth attempting. "But in my day everything is expected from the teacher, who is in turn nothing but a conduit from the ancient authorities." Hence the master will not concern himself primarily with "elegantiae," drawn from Cicero and tacked on to any kind of matter. "Elegans" is "purus," "nitidus," "aptus"; "sooner would I state truth in blunt, untrimmed fashion than say a mere nothing in tricky finery of speech."

Yet the study of models is a necessity, and he instances a method of *vera imitatio.* "To imitate Cicero is to put yourself into Cicero's place. His purpose is to convince, say, the senate. His procedure is perfectly clear. He makes himself master of his facts, historical or contemporary ; he has analysed the motives of the characters concerned, and handles them with ease : fact and motive are shown in their obvious connection, all with masterly skill. Follow Cicero, therefore, through one of his speeches : take up his theme, and try to work it out in your own way. Then examine closely Cicero's own method— his handling of material, the "inventio," order, and construction of argument. Next notice the function of "exordium," his opening argument, the kind of "nexus" he employs, his applications of general principles, and so on. In this way you become acquainted with Ciceronian rhetoric, not by directly copying him but by entering into his spirit."

Such imitation is to develope our own individuality, not to destroy it. Perhaps Vives was thinking, though he does not say so, of rhetoric in the vernacular as a product of the training in the classical style. The space which Vives gives to advice on instruction in the art of composing Latin epistles shows the importance of this form of composition to men engaged in public service, the career to which his pupils mostly looked forward.

Upon logic he takes the position of Agricola and Melanchthon. He added nothing to logical doctrine, but regarded

the subject as a discipline for the young.   It is curious that
Vives failed to perceive the objection which Bacon later on
brought against the inclusion of logic in the curriculum of
children as a premature study.   But it should be remembered
that the humanist school was without the other chief instrument of exact thinking, a systematic mathematical course.
Yet the task of purifying logic was no light one.   The old
trick of the schools, of throwing all knowledge into dilemmas
for the sake of disputation, died hard.   Boys left school, he
affirmed, conceited, argumentative, loud and self-assertive;
proud to be smart and ingenious, cavilling and contradictory,
rather than well-informed.   Sir Thomas More knew little
boys so steeped in logical rudiments that they were ever
controverting what they heard just because they could not
help it.

     After dialectic comes the knowledge of Nature, " physica,"
which stands for the scientific learning of the time : "The
origin and nature of plants and animals and the causes of
phenomena, whether terrestrial, celestial, aetherial ; in field, on
mountain, or in forest."   But such Nature-knowledge was as
yet unorganised ; on the one hand Vives holds that Aristotle
is still the one authoritative source of scientific truth : on the
other he admits that the best book is Nature herself.   In
the contemplation of Nature the learner must employ his daily
leisure and his holidays.   What is thus observed will be
amplified, verified and reduced to generalisation by the aid of
the great enquirers of antiquity : Pliny, Columella, Varro,
Aristotle and Theophrastus.   The difficulty was obviously twofold : first, methods of observation were not yet formulated ; and
next, the literature of scientific "eruditio" was wholly unsuitable
to school purposes.   There were manuals in mathematics, mostly
crabbed abridgments worthless for teaching, or enormous folios
like the Euclid of 1482 and L. de Borgo's still more cumber-
some work on arithmetic and algebra.   Vives sees no need
for more than a limited knowledge of arithmetic, geometry,

astronomy and music: to go beyond this may even be dangerous, as mathematical abstractions "withdraw the mind from practical concerns of life, and render it less fit to face concrete and mundane realities." Faber, Sacrobosco (Holywood of Halifax, an astronomer) and Purbachius may possibly be made intelligible to boys. Most mediaeval books on the subject were overlaid by gloss upon gloss, and modern productions were not compiled for beginners.

On all these grounds Vives was minded to turn the entire subject out of the school, until scientific enquirers had so far grappled with the different branches of their subject as to be able to present authoritative results in a form at once certain and intelligible, fit for the untrained intellect.

The dilemma which confronted Vives illustrates the principle that the school can only incorporate a subject in the curriculum when its exponents have attained conclusions definite and secure, capable of systematic verification, and admitting of illustration by such apparatus, literary or other, as can be utilised under the conditions of class teaching. If it be alleged against the humanist educator that he made no adequate recognition of the claims of science the answer is as simple as it is final, that men of science had as yet provided no organised material which lent itself to the instruction of the young. But in Vives at least "physica" had a sympathetic supporter, foiled in his aim by the imperfections of the subject as then developed.

To the humanist, as has been already made clear, the end of all study is the higher well-being of man. "This must be the first rule of any study of Nature in school: not to push research into causes and principles, which are beyond our reach, but to order all our enquiry with reference to the practical needs of life, to some definite advantage of mind or body, or to the end of personal piety." Abstract contemplation of Nature, tending to absorption in metaphysical subtleties, such as delighted the schoolmen, Vives regards as a grave danger to wholesome intellectual life. He was aware that the mediaeval "physicus" had destroyed all reality in the study of "res." He was more ignorant than a blacksmith or farm labourer as regards actual objects lying under his eye, and spent himself in arguing interminably about properties which do not exist at all. The curse of *à priori* method which the humanists lived to eradicate in the interests of human progress brooded especially over science as it stood in the opening years of the Cinquecento when astronomy had not shaken itself free from astrology, nor chemistry from alchemy. He himself wrote a small manual, *De prima Philosophia*, for the use of elder boys. It is definitely planned on a Christian basis. Ignoring wholly the controversy of Nominalist and Realist he expounds simple notions "de Deo," "de Materia et Forma," upon the origin of Ideas from sense impressions, "de Tempore," "de Substantia," "de Accidente"; perfectly plain in language, and though in no sense a contribution to abstract truth, it is yet well suited as an introduction for young minds to philosophic thinking, and the understanding of terms.

Such an education Vives regards as the preparation for the studies of manhood, which are naturally the technical and professional subjects of law, medicine, architecture, theology, political science, war. Like Vittorino he contemplates a full course of liberal training as attainable without attendance at a university, in which, as Vives knew, purely humanist studies often occupied a subordinate place. The recent establishment of the Collegium Trilingue at Louvain, under the influence of Erasmus and Vives himself, was a protest against the hostility of the great professional interests to classical studies.

So far for the education of the boy; but Vives has something definite and instructive to say respecting the training of the girl[1]. He was, it will be remembered, for four or five years

---

[1] The work *De Institutione Feminae Christianae*, dedicated to Queen Katherine (1523), should be compared with the tract of Erasmus on the same subject. See Woodward, *Erasmus*, p. 148.

tutor to Mary, the daughter of Henry VIII ; her husband Philip, as a young man, was one of Vives' patrons.   The ideal set out by Vives, whilst it falls short of the great Italian models of womanly distinction, the Duchess Elisabetta of Urbino or the Marchioness Isabella of Mantua, marks a striking advance upon the concept of a girl's training recognised in countries north of the Alps.

The mediaeval judgment upon the education of women which survived in German, French, and English society down to the Reformation was the natural outcome of the subordination of women in feudal communities.   Here and there a writer like Vincent de Beauvais or Christina à Pisanis, an Italian, pleads that "artes et literae" are not rightly forbidden to women.   But the influence of territorial and, still more, of ecclesiastical authority was against all pleas for the enlargement of woman's life.   Domestic duties were hers by nature and by prescription ; training for these covered reading, writing, "computatio," with the rudiments of medical and surgical lore so far as to qualify her to nurse in sickness or injury.   Other necessary acquirements were needlework, spinning, and the like ; the accomplishments, music, astrology, and, less commonly, French and Provençal.   Religion was, ostensibly at least, a subject of prime importance.

Lionardo Bruni, the contemporary of Guarino, was the first to advocate that the treasures of ancient literature should not only be thrown open to a woman but should form an integral part of her education.   Vittorino was perhaps the first school-master to carry into practice the doctrine of the educational equality of the sexes.   By the student of educational opinion the tract of Bruni should be carefully read and its significance appraised.   In Italy, as Vives undoubtedly knew, the social status of women underwent a striking change during the Quattrocento.   The new place which she gradually came to occupy in society rendered necessary a wholly different training and a much wider and more thorough instruction than was permitted to her sisters in northern Europe.   In Florence or Ferrara the individuality of a woman was regarded as not less worthy of respect, and not less capable of cultivation, than the personality of her husband or brother.   It was not that women in virtue of their education forced their claims to a new social recognition but (in accord with the universal law of educational advance) the freer, worthier, status of women compelled a higher type of training to correspond to it.   Thus the new frame and content of education only touched women in so far as they belonged to the class in which their social equality with men was duly accepted.   Now this was never a large class.   It had no existence at all, as will be seen in a later chapter, in Naples or Palermo, nor in Venice, any more than in Paris, or in the Rhineland.   Even in communities which express the very spirit of the Renaissance, classical education was the fortune of women only of the governing class.   The Florentine banker or merchant of distinction accorded equality to women whilst the burgher of middle rank did not, just because in the former case society was more advanced and demanded far higher qualities of literary knowledge and the arts of conversation in the woman called to take her place in it.   Even so it was not until 1480 or thereabouts that the ideal of graceful and intelligent intercourse attained its development, reaching its fine flower of perfection, as in the Court of Urbino, in the twenty years preceding the Sack of Rome (1527).   But the burgher class in Italy, so far as evidence is available, did not modify the training of the girl to accord with the education which the Renaissance had moulded for boys.

The examples of cultivated women of northern lands who are so often quoted—the same names perpetually recur—the daughters of Thomas More, and of Pirckheimer of Nuremberg, Lady Jane Grey, the ladies Cooke and others, were undoubtedly far rarer phenomena than learned women were in Italy.   So that we may affirm that whilst the classical revival determined the education—in a large degree—of the boy of the upper and the well-to-do middle class, only in the upper class, and not by any means uniformly there, was the education of the girl moulded by the same influence. This statement holds true of all countries north of the Alps, at the period (1520-1540) when Renaissance influences began to penetrate English and French society.

Schools for girls there were during the fifteenth century in France, in considerable numbers, where girls could receive such education as social opinion demanded, namely in reading, writing, number, and religion. Such schools were partly under ecclesiastical and partly under civic or corporate direction. Yet the intelligence of a woman was not taken seriously. Erasmus regarded women as generally weak, unstable, irritable and frivolous. But he recognised that their education and their usual interests were unfavourable to moral and intellectual force. Hence the grounds of his appeal for a worthier training on lines similar to those laid down a hundred years before by the Tuscan Bruni. It is precisely on the same grounds that Vives thinks it essential in the interests of the community that the problem of the training of girls must be attacked.

A woman, he urges, needs "to be fortified by the aid of wise philosophy," for she is weak. She is frivolous ; therefore she must be filled with serious interests. Moral dignity is the glory of the woman ; if ignorance were the best means of securing this, then should we welcome ignorance for her. But is this true? Ignorance, by common experience, is no safe-guard against vice. On the other hand, true learning affords both example and stimulus for finer moral purpose. If mental cultivation is dangerous we ought to do all that we can to destroy our own intelligence, and to reduce ourselves to the level of the unreasoning brute creation and so banish the risks which beset folk who think! He sums up his position : so many women are difficult, morose, fond of dress, absorbed in trifles, arrogant in success, abject in misfortune—in a word, unbearable—and why ? Because of their lack of sound interests such as learning will afford. Never, he affirms, has he known a well educated woman fail to command respect; whereas evil disposition, in his experience, goes hand in hand with ignorance. Hence it is equitable in the interests of the woman herself, and of the community, that she should enjoy like opportunity with men of acquiring knowledge.

Yet the proportion to be observed amongst the various elements of instruction is not the same in the case of the two sexes. For example natural philosophy ("naturae cognitio," as set out above), mathematics, history, except so far as it supplies illustrations of good and evil, and political reasoning are properly omitted. With these he expressly includes rhetoric, as the art of ornate speech, for a woman's duty is mainly to keep silence. The temper of the devout churchman, imbued with the instinct of Spanish seclusion where women are concerned, finds expression here. It is the opposite of the doctrine of the high Renaissance in Italy.

In her education vernacular speech, taught with care, holds the leading place. Then follows Latin. He prefers, if such may be found, a woman teacher. Poetry, the usual reading for beginners, he allows, with careful supervision. No modern romances are to be allowed; *Amadis de Gaul, Lancelotte*, like Boccaccio or Poggio, are forbidden: "feminae non minus aversandi sunt quam vipera et scorpio." Naturally, therefore, he finds Fathers and the Christian poets of the fifth and sixth centuries more profitable reading. But Plato, Plutarch, Cicero and Seneca are prescribed, for "all these have written upon self-control." "Women specially need this lesson of philosophy." Next come books upon the bringing up of children, and household management, such as the *Cyropaedeia*. Lastly, the Bible. Nature study is admissible as a preparation for the woman's function as nurse in sickness: for home duties generally must take precedence over Letters. Skill in cookery, he thinks, is a gift not far removed from moral excellence. " Why," he asks, " is there so much indifference to home ties in these days?" speaking of what he knows of Bruges or Louvain. "This I take to be the real cause—the idleness of wives and mothers, and their carelessness in the art of cookery which induces in husband and son a positive repulsion for the entertainment they find at home, and drives them to seek more attractive fare elsewhere." It is instructive to contrast with this insistence upon common-place duties the indifference to the arts of music, painting, or dancing in Vives' concept of a girl's education.

The general end of a girl's training, therefore, is the preparation of the devout, high-principled lady, the affectionate wife and mother, the equable, intelligent companion, and above all the skilled mistress of the house, marked by serious interests on the leisure side of life. It is an ideal not unlike that worked out by Thomas More in the case of his own daughters, and is suggested by the conditions of the higher society of the governing class in the Spanish community of Flanders as Vives knew it. He is, indeed, typical of the somewhat severe, almost puritanic, cast of Spanish feeling which manifests itself in the writings of the first stage of the Renaissance in the peninsula. It is an ideal of woman's life far less gracious, far more circumscribed, than that of the notable society of contemporary Italy. But it corresponded more nearly, no doubt, to the standards acceptable in the lands where his lot was cast, where the field of activity open to women took a more sober hue than that which characterised the brilliant Courts of the south.

Vives never failed to admit his debt to Agricola and in especial to Erasmus in all that concerned learning and education; "discipulus, filius, Erasmi" is his own expression. It is not difficult to trace the parallel between the two men. Both held by the unity of the Church, both desired reform from within, upon lines made clear by sound learning and unbiassed historical enquiry into Christian origins. There is in all that Vives writes a strong Evangelical vein, which reminds us of

Agricola's later days, but which is a marked feature in Spanish religious writings before the Reformation. Hence we may say that his aim was to inculcate the union of pure learning with a rightly developed and well informed conscience. In this respect he is akin to English humanists of the serious sort like Ascham, Sir John Cheke, or Sir Thomas Hoby.

In comparing Vives more closely with Erasmus the identity of the point of view may be recognised in these respects: the stress laid upon the earliest stage of education, the home, parents, nurses, tutor, companions; the need of a serious change in the education of girls; the choice of masters, their attainments, pay and status; his hatred of scholastic methods and books; the contempt for Ciceronians. Vives, on the other hand, was in advance of Erasmus, in the care which he takes in considering site and equipment of the school, the training of the master, and the important place of games; his keen interest in psychology, his desire to widen the curriculum by the inclusion of modern knowledge, and his respect for vernacular languages as instruments of teaching. Moreover, Vives refused to follow Erasmus in the virulence of his invective against the ignorance of the monks and the clergy, and the sarcastic spirit which he delighted to impart to discussion. Yet we are not to ignore the fact that as a figure in the history of learning, an influence upon intellectual progress, Erasmus belongs indeed to a rank to which Vives could make no claim. None the less Vives deserves more attention than he has yet received as a force in educational advance, if only that such men as Ignatius Loyola, Nausea and Sturm, drew from him the inspiration of their own work which in differing ways gave an impulse so significant to the art and the ideals of education.

CHAPTER XI.

MELANCHTHON, PRECEPTOR OF GERMANY.
1497–1560.

PHILIP SCHWARZERD, known in the history of learning and
of the Reformation by the Graecised form of his name Philip
Melanchthon[1] was born at Bretten in the Palatinate in 1497.
He was fortunate in his home ; his father was a substantial
burgher of good repute and of notable intelligence.   His family
came into closer touch with learning than was usual with the
ordinary well-to-do burgher of the time.   Johann Reuchlin
was Philip Melanchthon's uncle, and took no little interest
in the boy, whose diligence and zeal he early recognised.
Melanchthon was taught at home by a private tutor, who was
scholar enough to give him a thorough grounding in Latin,
and a sincere taste for language.   Melanchthon cherished the
memory of this early training, and in later years realised to the
full the exceptional opportunities which his home life had
afforded to him.   When he had passed his tenth birthday, his
father being now dead, he was sent to the Latin school at

---

[1] The references to Melanchthon's works are quoted from the *Corpus
Reformatorum* of Bretschneider.   The two works upon Melanchthon's
educational activity of chief use to the student are Hartfelder's *Mel. als
Praeceptor Germaniae*, and his *Melanchth. Paedagogica*.   For all that
concerns German humanism Paulsen's *Geschichte des gelehrten Unterrichts*
should be referred to.   There is nothing in English of any importance
upon this aspect of Melanchthon.   Geiger and Schmid have already been
mentioned.

Pforzheim, Reuchlin's native town, which was held to be the best town school in south-west Germany. Reuchlin now gave Melanchthon a Greek grammar and vocabulary, whereupon Melanchthon prepared for him a recitation from a Latin comedy of Reuchlin's own composition. At twelve the boy spoke Latin with fluency and was rapidly mastering the Greek grammar. In 1509 he went to Heidelberg, which was intimately associated with the beginnings of the German Renaissance. The names of Agricola and Dalberg, of Spangel, Geiler, Wimpheling and Reuchlin himself are all connected with this brilliant but short period of " illumination." Dalberg's house, indeed, as for England that of Sir Thomas More at Chelsea, had been for twenty years a centre of all that was finest in the early days of German humanism. Yet since the death of Dalberg, in 1503, Heidelberg had illustrated once more the dependence of humanism, as a permanent force in the universities, upon the existence of endowed Chairs in Classical Letters, whereby continuity of teaching could be secured. Without such recognised status the teaching of the humanities, whether in the Rhineland, in Paris, in Oxford, or in Louvain, was imperilled by the competition of professional subjects, with their vast endowments and consequently cheap, if not free, instruction. Melanchthon, therefore, found humanist interests on the wane at Heidelberg. But he became, young as he was, the centre of the new generation of scholars who looked forward with Agricola as their inspiration to a new Germany which should dispute with Italy the place of leader in the " Republic of Letters." At Heidelberg he devoted himself mainly to the study of Greek, in which he was already recognised as a youth of great promise. From the authorised teachers of the university, however, Melanchthon protests that he learnt little or nothing, and that he was thrown upon his own resources. Such criticism has from time to time been made by other scholars, but in Melanchthon's case it was undoubtedly true that he was compelled to rely upon private teachers and his own extraordinary industry for his insight into Greek literature. In no university north of the Alps were the historians and dramatists the subject of systematic instruction. His own words are : " cum adolescentibus nihil publice traderetur praeter illam garrulam Dialecticam et particulam Physices." After taking his degree of bachelor in 1511 he passed to Tübingen, where he became magister in 1514. His capacity for reading seems to have been even at this time remarkable, and with it he possessed peculiar dialectical power. He was acquainted with the Italian humanists, amongst whom he regarded Poliziano as the Latinist of first distinction. The six years that he spent at Tübingen (1512–1518) were the truly formative years of his life. Not only did he master the text of Vergil, of Homer, of Terence, of Hesiod, give lectures in Cicero, Livy and Demosthenes, but he devoted himself to a first-hand study of Aristotle, of which he planned an edition specially devised for use in German universities. He spent much time upon mathematics, astronomy and physics, and read the classical books upon medicine, and worked for some months upon Roman Law. Already before he had reached his twentieth year, he was interesting himself in ecclesiastical controversy, and was prepared to go forward in Church reform with the keenest supporters of Erasmus or Hutten.

The humanism of Melanchthon was of the earnest, national and ethical type which we associate with the Teutonic Renaissance. It had less of the Petrarchian spirit than that of Agricola, and his affinities are rather with Colet, Reuchlin, and Erasmus, than with Bembo or Castiglione. None the less in Melanchthon the humanist was never lost in the theologian. He believed sincerely in the efficacy of Letters as a force making for progress, and in particular held antiquity to be the fountain head of wisdom both secular and religious. To apply this wisdom to the training of the young generation of German-speaking folk and to the national form of the Christian faith was the twofold aspect of his life's aim.

When in 1518 the Electoral Prince of Saxony asked Reuchlin to find for him a young scholar willing to come to Wittenberg to teach Greek in the university there was not much doubt amongst scholars as to the choice which should be made.   Melanchthon was invited and accepted the post. In the autumn of that year he delivered his inaugural address, *De Corrigendis adolescentium Studiis*, a manifesto on behalf of university reform in Germany.   " All the students of theology at Wittenberg are clamouring to learn Greek," writes Luther, of the effect of this address, and henceforth a disciple of Melanchthon was one to whom Greek was the indispensable key to all sound knowledge.

The influence of Luther, whose personality dominated Wittenberg, was speedily felt by the young professor.   He had not been at Wittenberg a year before he had prepared to enter the faculty of theology, in which he became bachelor in September, 1519.   Yet, it is to be noted that, like Erasmus, Melanchthon was drawn to theology from the point of view of its historical aspects.   Scholarship as applied to the study of origins is his point of contact with the Lutheran movement. It was a sore disappointment to Erasmus that Melanchthon should have abandoned the method of reform from within the Church and lent his hand to the creation of national barriers in religion.   And strong as was the influence of Luther in determining his career Melanchthon was too profoundly conscious of his debt to Erasmus the scholar to forget the peculiar contribution which he was fitted to afford in the crisis of the history of his nation.   To reconcile Protestantism and humanism, to adapt antique learning to modern life, to harmonise historic continuity with national self-dependence, was a no less integral task than the purification of religion in the re-creation of Teutonic culture.   In the present chapter Melanchthon will be regarded under these two aspects : first as " Praeceptor Germaniae," as he was called, the organiser and reformer of German schools; and, secondly, as the most complete type of the reconciliation of humanism with Protestant and Germanic consciousness.

Within fifteen years of his appointment at Wittenberg Melanchthon had become recognised as the supreme authority in Protestant Germany upon the organisation of universities and high schools, and had put into operation schemes for the remodelling of ancient universities (Wittenberg, Tübingen and others) and the foundation of modern ones (Marburg, Königsberg, etc.), which expressed at once the Germanic, humanist, and Protestant ideals of the new age. Further, Melanchthon as adviser to cities and to princes had set forth detailed plans for the establishment of new schools (such as Nuremberg and Magdeburg) and the reorganisation of many others. He devoted special pains to the development and inspection of humanist schools in Saxony under the direction of the Electoral Prince. And he maintained in his own house at Wittenberg a private school, preparatory to the courses in the faculty, in which we may recognise certain important principles of his doctrine of instruction. The work that Melanchthon did in North Germany was accomplished on not dissimilar lines by Sturm and Oecolampadius on the Upper Rhine, by Zwingli at Zürich, and by Calvin and Cordier in western Switzerland.

Apart from the especial note of Melanchthon's foundations, namely the intimate association of evangelical religion with classical teaching, his peculiar service to education lay in the impulse which he gave to systematic organisation of school instruction, which should correspond with the logical relations of the subjects themselves. The mediaeval schools were in Germany slowly and imperfectly incorporating certain elements of the humanist curriculum without a radical modification of traditional methods. Neither books, nor assistant masters, nor processes of teaching were in harmony with the possibly enthusiastic aim of a head-master lately fired by a zeal for the new learning. Moreover the proper relation of grammar to composition and to construing was rarely understood. Authors were read for their contents before adequate vocabulary or knowledge of syntax had been acquired. *A priori* modes of studying "physica" and scholastic logic wasted valuable years. The connection between the Trivial, or Latin, school and the university was but confusedly understood, and the entire place of Latin and Greek viewed as language and as literature in a German university was wholly undetermined. It was the work of Melanchthon in the north and of Sturm in the south to co-ordinate education, as it was the achievement of Luther to provide its national stimulus.

Melanchthon, in a word, supplied to the German Renaissance what Erasmus or Agricola lacked, namely a genius for system. It was his function to give practical application of educational theory and ideal as Erasmus had indicated it in his works and correspondence.

He was himself profoundly dissatisfied with education as he found it at the outset of his active career as a reformer of schools. He was aware of Wimpheling's proposals for a high school at Strassburg (1501), the aim of which was to provide an organisation intermediate between the Latin schools and the universities[1]. He was intimate with the men

---

[1] Wimpheling published in this year a tract to which he gave the title *Germania*, a patriotic appeal for aid to learning. The second chapter is addressed to the Council of Strassburg, pressing the establishment of a "Stadtgymnasium." Such a High School would confine its curriculum to Latin orators, moralists and historians, the study of whom bears directly not only upon training for Holy Orders but upon that of the burgher, municipal councillor or knight. For boys who may be too young for knightly exercises, for commerce or the civil service, a course of preparation could be thus provided in the elements of the art of administration of the city or of the conduct of the home, say from Aegidius Columna; and training in morals from P. P. Vergerius *De Ingenuis Moribus*. As they grow older they will learn the principles of the virtuous life from Seneca and Cicero, the science of war from Vegetius, campaigning from Fronto, the art of building from Vitruvius, of agriculture from Varro. "This, and more than this, can be taught in a special gymnasium to be erected in the

who were identified with high school education at Münster, Alkmaar, Liège and Deventer—typical schools of the early Renaissance in Germany and the Low Countries—in all of which Greek found a place, and Roman literature was seriously studied. Melanchthon himself had not suffered from the lack of a school of this type, only because he was of exceptional ability and intellectual ambition. He was quite right in perceiving that for the average boy of thirteen university life was profoundly unsuitable, and that for lack of grounding as well as lack of discipline years so spent were apt to be largely wasted.

Melanchthon has left under the title *De Miseriis Paedagogorum* a lively picture of actual instruction in the less distinguished schools of the period. It is not the complaint of a disappointed or unsuccessful master, nor is it the expression of the contempt of the man of letters for the teacher of rudiments such as inspired, for example, Petrarch's sarcastic warnings against the school-master's destiny. Rather it is the sorrowful admission of the failure of fine ideals when method and organisation are lacking wherewith to apply them. The boy comes to the Latin school hopelessly ill-prepared. The master complains that the pupil remembers nothing. To simplify his subject he talks himself hoarse and finds that the boy has gone to sleep. Endless time is occupied upon the bare rudiments of grammar; then the master attempts conversation, only to find that the boy has no vocabulary, cannot pronounce simple words, and knows no inflections. Written exercises are only to be got by persistent worrying, and there are boys from whom you can scarcely extract one short Latin letter in the term. What with correcting grammatical mistakes,

city of Strassburg at no great expense of time or money, so that children may be attracted to the town rather than drawn from it to some more famous seat of education. Your city will thus become an object of envy throughout Germany, and might indeed claim to be the very crown of the Empire."

clearing up meaningless phrases, straightening out the style, adding illustrations, etc., the master's patience is sorely tried. "Nothing can succeed in life without some touch of enthusiasm, but the pupils I am thinking of are impervious both to praise and to blame, and never show a spark of eagerness to excel." Such intellectual temper begets the moral faults which are akin to it, and which need eradication by flogging. Who can deny that the master's is a poor career? But at least the payment is poor to match. Like Erasmus, Melanchthon sets himself to raise the school-master and the status of his function.

Melanchthon's "schola privata," which he set up in his own house at Wittenberg within a few years of his arrival, deserves attention as an attempt to remedy the defects to which he alludes in the tract above quoted. He carried on the experiment for not less than ten years, limiting his pupils to a number which admitted of direct personal instruction. His object was to provide thorough preparatory training for boys who were to pass on to a high school or the faculty of arts in a university. Hence the school was of the nature of a model Latin, or trivial, school[1], in respect at least of the standards of instruction given. The grounding in Latin was the main purpose of the teaching given. No specific courses were provided in religion, mathematics or "physica." These were taught through the instrument of Latin and from Latin authors. The rudiments of Greek, however, were taught, and this constitutes a distinction from the practice of the trivial school. Text-books were written by Melanchthon himself, containing selections from prayers, extracts from the New Testament, etc. Prose and verse composition were taught: Latin was spoken and Latin plays in abridged shape were performed, partly as relaxation, but mainly as an aid to conversational Latin. Melanchthon wrote prologues defending the practice, and offering moral interpretations of the scenes selected. He preferred Terence

[1] The best authority on the school foundations, German and Dutch, is J. Müller's *Schulordnungen* (1885).

for the purpose, but included Seneca and at least one play of Euripides. Amongst the pupils there was a system of promotion and of competition, and the discipline was apparently of a thoroughly human sort. The pupils were all boarders, drawn from various German towns by the educational repute of Wittenberg.

A more fully developed type of trivial school as Melanchthon conceived it is exhibited in the school of Eisleben, founded in 1525 by Count Mansfeld. The school may be described as the first distinctive product of the Protestant-humanist influences of Wittenberg, which was near enough geographically to affect the opinion of the ruling family. The programme of the new foundation has always been ascribed to Melanchthon, whose fundamental principles it well expresses. The aim of the school is affirmed to be the inculcation of true religion and sound learning (which are further identified with "bonae literae"), whereby youth may be trained to become competent teachers of the evangelical faith and useful citizens. There is a note of opposition to the Anabaptist fanaticism which was as hostile to humanism as the most obscurantist orders.

The organisation is that of the ordinary Latin school with the important addition, as in Melanchthon's "schola privata," of a higher section of the upper class in which Greek was taught. The school was divided into three classes to provide for the gradation of capacity and the due testing of progress, so that solid foundations may be laid before the superstructure is added. The first class, the "Classis Elementariorum," receives the admissions who come without any previous school experience. They read *Vulgati Libelli*, written as reading books, such probably as the *Enchiridion elementorum puerilium* written by Melanchthon in 1524, imparting through the vernacular the rudiments of Latin. Such a manual would contain short sentences, prayers, psalms, etc., in Latin and in German. Extracts from a similar book used in Nuremberg after the date of Melanchthon's school activity there will be found in the present volume. The class then passed to Aesop's fables, the *Disticha Catonis*, and the *Paedologia* of Mosellanus, dialogues written for school boys by a contemporary of Melanchthon. The boys were required to learn these by heart, and by aid of explanations from the master made them the basis of Latin conversation. In the first class the method of Latin teaching was to be imitative and empirical. Grammar was taught only in so far as was necessary to enable the simple sentence to be construed and composed. There was much learning by heart of sentence forms and of vocabulary, but the principle which underlay the teaching of Latin rudiments was obviously identical with that of the so-called natural methods of teaching a modern language in our own day. Melanchthon himself was distrustful of the linguistic training which was attained by a method in which grammar took a subordinate place, and he insisted that a boy should be transferred from the first class to the second so soon as the master perceived that he was ripe for a more rigorous type of instruction. Indeed it may be said at once that Melanchthon represents a definite reaction against what he regarded as the superficial methods of Latin instruction which had been introduced into the newer schools by teachers whose own scholarship was not very secure. For himself he did not believe that the practice which obtained in the teaching of Greek, namely to treat grammar lightly and to go direct to authors for the sake of content, before a sound mastery of syntax had been reached, was permissible in the teaching of Latin. It is significant—but generally ignored—that it was necessary in the period of the high Renaissance to raise a protest against indifference to grammar in classical teaching.

Hence the second class at Eisleben was concerned almost exclusively with the thorough acquisition of Latin grammar, the " programme " recording grave warnings against attempting to learn Latin in any other way. With the grammar were read Terence, Vergil and the *Bucolica* of Baptista Mantuanus.

But these authors are to be read primarily, if not exclusively, as illustrations of grammatical rule, and as aids to a poetic vocabulary. Rules come first and illustrations afterwards. Teaching is invariably deductive, and the methods which we find approved by Erasmus, Vives and Cordier are not followed by Melanchthon. Composition of simple narrative, of letters, and short pieces of verse was required, apparently not from vernacular originals, but upon themes propounded by the master.

A boy entering the third class would be thoroughly steeped in accidence, syntax, and prosody. He is thus prepared to attack the rudiments of logic (regarded as an aid to consecutive thinking after the manner of Rudolph Agricola), and with it the principles of rhetoric. The *De Conscribendis Epistolis* of Erasmus, and a translation of Aphthonius[1], a Greek rhetorician, were used as text-books, conversation and correspondence in Latin being now required at a high standard of excellence. In construing, the historical writers, especially Livy and Sallust, were to be read for their content; amongst the poets Vergil, Horace and Ovid; with select orations and moral treatises of Cicero. It is clear from certain allusions that this class at least (and probably the two below) was rarely taught as a whole upon a uniform class method. Boys were grouped according to ability and special aptitudes, and work both as preparation and with the master was largely individual. This indeed it may be affirmed was almost the invariable practice in classical schools in Germany and in England during the century. It is, however, expressly prescribed that twice a week there shall be two lessons (e.g. upon a play of Plautus, or a book of Cicero's *Letters*) given to the entire class.

Such portion of the third class as is well advanced in Latin and shows signs of peculiar capacity is set to learn Greek. The *Dragmata Graecae Literaturae* of Oecolampadius is the

---

[1] No doubt that by R. Agricola of the *Progymnasmata*.

first text-book. Lucian, Hesiod and Homer are mentioned as the authors to be next read ; the absence of prose writers is to be remarked. Care is to be taken to lighten the task of Greek study by careful regard for sound method ; but we notice the entire lack of insistence upon that syntactical knowledge which was held essential in the case of Latin. We may assume that a thorough drill in the principles of Latin speech was found sufficient to the student of Greek, who apparently was not required to prepare exercises in composition. A few boys are to be encouraged to begin Hebrew.

In this class also mathematics and "totus orbis artium" were to be introduced. But in view of the limitations of the human intellect such subjects were to be delayed until a satisfactory mastery of language had been attained. For the languages (Greek and Latin) are the one avenue to "cognitio rerum"; supposing language to have been accurately known, there is promise that mathematics may be effectively attacked. The explanation of this lies partly in the fact that mathematical books in the German vernacular did not exist. One hour daily was given to music and singing.

But the curriculum, however carefully devised, can only secure right training if with instruction be conjoined exhortation to, and exercises in, personal religion, "even as Jehovah required that the children shall be taught the fear of the Lord (Deut. vi. 7)." Therefore let Sundays be given to this great duty. Then the head-master shall before the whole school expound a gospel, an epistle or a chapter of *Proverbs*, with simplicity and without controversy, to the end that children may gain a knowledge of true and sincere religion, may distinguish it from its counterfeit and may be won to a life of obedience and uprightness. To further this knowledge of divine things, the boy shall be required to learn by heart the Lord's Prayer, the Apostles' Creed and the Commandments, with approved portions of Scripture which shall be repeated every Sunday.

In October, 1524, Melanchthon was invited on grounds of his expert knowledge and his scholarly renown to undertake the foundation and direction of a new high school at Nuremberg. Although he declined the invitation to become the first head-master he busied himself with some enthusiasm in planning the general lines of organisation, advising upon the appointment of teachers and the details of the curriculum. The "Ordnung," or Scheme, is characteristically Melanchthon's; and on the opening day, May 23rd, 1526, Melanchthon came down to deliver the inaugural "declamatio in laudem novae scholae."

For more than thirty years Nuremberg had concerned itself with higher education. The importance of the city lay in its commercial and industrial activities; it was characterised by a sincere feeling for art, but it was without a high school or university. No town north of the Alps so much resembled Florence in the distinction of its civic life and in the breadth of interests which marked its leading citizens.

In the year 1496 the council agreed to engage a humanist to teach the youth of the city, but the first choice of master for the proposed "schola poetica," as it was termed, was apparently unfortunate. Heinrich Grüninger, although a thorough humanist and acquainted with the schools of Italy, failed to attract pupils or at any rate to retain them. The new school was in 1509 merged into, or united with, two existing schools of grammar (or in modern terms, lower secondary schools) connected with the churches of St Sebald and St Lorenz. Two classes were added to the usual curriculum in which "the new grammar and poetry, or 'ars oratoria,' shall be taught." The visitation of the city schools was entrusted to a board of inspectors, the president of which was Pirckheimer, a pronounced humanist. By 1511 it could be reported that "the study of sound (i.e. literary) Latin has begun. Boys begin to understand the works of antiquity, to compose in verse and in prose, and to speak Latin correctly. We are now reading

Vergil and Sallust and have taken first steps in syntax and etymology." To resume the abortive attempt to erect a higher school, to which such schools as those of St Sebald and St Lorenz should serve as the preparatory grade, was the purpose of the Ordnung for the new Obere Schule of 1526.

Melanchthon in his inaugural address sets out his view of the educational system suited to a large city, regarded from the standpoint of the evangelical humanist. "The purpose of Providence that children should be brought up to be virtuous and religious is evident to all, but the obligation is not limited to the children of this or that individual citizen, it extends to the entire youth of the state whose training demands corporate provision. For the ultimate end which confronts us is not private virtue alone but the interest of the public weal. The truths of religion and moral duty cannot be rightly perceived except by minds soundly prepared by a training based upon the practice of past ages. The school which we are now about to open will provide liberal disciplines upon which the professional arts of medicine, law and preaching must rest.

"Upon the parents therefore and upon the community falls the common obligation of the education of the youth of your city. In the first place they must take care that religion be rightly taught, and this implies as a necessary condition sound instruction in Letters. In the next place social security and respect for the laws demand like training. The civic council of Nuremberg has had regard to both in their new foundation. Grammar schools already exist for teaching the elements of Latin, and will be modified to serve for the preparatory training of pupils destined to pass to the high school. The distinction between the two grades of school has been determined in order that pupils shall not pass to more advanced subjects until they are fit for them. A secure mastery of grammar, and that alone, qualifies the pupil for conversation, construing and composition in the Latin tongue. The Latin school, however, will not ignore approved authors amongst whom Erasmus (the

Colloquies), Terence, Plautus, and the easier parts of Vergil will find place. In these schools also music will be taught daily and the rudiments of faith and religion will occupy one day in every week.

"The high school itself is organised by classes for the due ordering of studies. The lowest class, into which pass the boys who come up from the Latin school, is in charge of the master (with title of 'Professor') of rhetoric and dialectic. His text-books will be the *De Copia* of Erasmus, an oration of Cicero, used as illustration of rhetorical and dialectical methods, and, at a later stage, portions of Quintilian. This class will also be exercised in disputations, in order to apply the rules of logical argument[1]. The second class will be under the Latin master who will be chiefly concerned with reading poetical authors and in teaching verse composition, in which subject he must be strong. The third class will devote itself to mathematics. The fourth, or senior class will be under the master of Greek." Melanchthon adds a few words upon composition, which apparently does not include exercises in Greek, for he specifies practice in the *De Officiis* of Cicero, in Livy, and other Latin historians; he requires exercises to be prepared weekly; and insists that verse composition is essential to attainment of a proper appreciation of a prose style.

Melanchthon is eloquent in commending the zeal of Nuremberg for the cause of learning. Bishops are no longer on the side of Letters; princes are not always enlightened patrons, but Nuremberg reminds him of Florence, which welcomed Greek exiles as honoured guests. Nuremberg will prove to be the northern counterpart of the city on the Arno as the protector of the humanities, and stand forth as the model to all German states.

The Obere Schule, however, had but a short-lived

---

[1] The master will, for example, take a question from history, Was Brutus right or wrong in murdering Caesar? or, Was Manlius right or wrong in slaying his son for accepting the challenge of the Samnite chief?

success. The numbers remained small. Melanchthon had dwelt upon the enterprise of the wealthy capital of south German commerce, but herein lay the root of failure, for it was soon found that the right equipment for a young man of business was not attained when he could write passable verses, or speak correct Latin, under the guidance of a distinguished humanist. The wealthy citizen, therefore, after the first year or two, continued to send his boy to Switzerland[1] or England, to Venice or Bruges, to learn the great commercial languages. He at least had no intention of bringing up his son to starve on the stipend of a scholar.

The failure of the rigidly humanist schools, except those organised on a large scale and in important centres such as Vienna, Strassburg, Bordeaux, or Louvain, is not difficult to understand. The average burgher could not afford a humanist education which could only be effectively gained by ten years' schooling. The business man put his son to trade at 14; only exceptional children capable of the professions were kept longer at school. Hence we see a tendency to provide technical instruction, e.g. in proposals like those of Wimpheling above referred to (on p. 218), or in Humphrey Gilbert's *Academy*; the same attitude of doubt is revealed in Mulcaster's protest against too much higher education, and in the criticism which Montaigne makes against the unpractical nature of the education of his day. The chief products of the Protestant-humanist school were the school-master, the civil servant and the preacher. It is the common complaint of the time that men of parts drifted for a time into the work of teaching without any sense of vocation and quitted the work on the first opportunity. The truth seems to be that western Europe outside Italy was not yet rich enough to afford the luxury of learned leisure except to a very limited class. For whatever reason, the

[1] Compare Cordier's complaint that boys were sent abroad to learn foreign languages instead of being kept longer at the classical school.

Nuremberg school failed to strike root, to the sore disappointment of its sponsors throughout Germany.

But of more importance in the development of German humanism was the contribution which Melanchthon made to the reform and extension of the university system. Amongst the instances of his direct influence in the reform of learning the transformation of Wittenberg into a Protestant-humanist university is the most noteworthy. But, elsewhere, his inspiration and advice moulded the activities of those engaged in the work of humanist advance, for example in Heidelberg and Tübingen, which were outside the immediate range of the Wittenberg influence. At least three of the more prominent Protestant universities of Germany were founded upon lines laid down by Melanchthon within his own lifetime. Marburg, Königsberg and Jena, are monuments to that reconciliation of evangelical faith with classical erudition which was the prime achievement of his genius. The significance of this statement is readily perceived by any one who reflects upon the place which the universities have filled in the national life of Germany for the past four centuries. It alone serves to explain and to justify Melanchthon's claim to the title of "Praeceptor Germaniae."

No humanist was a more unsparing critic of the mediaeval universities than Melanchthon. But it is necessary to utter a warning against an easy acceptance of the attitude of the scholars of the Revival towards the studies and methods of the great Studia Generalia of the Middle Age. We must distinguish amongst the opponents of these strongholds of scholasticism those scholars whose attack was primarily inspired by Reformation zeal, such as Melanchthon or Calvin, and those actuated by passion for liberal learning, of whom Agricola and Budaeus are the type. It is probably true to say that neither class made an unbiassed effort to appreciate the system which they denounced. On two points, in especial, it is obvious that the humanists failed to understand the problem of the relation of learning to life as it presented itself to the mediaeval mind. The first is that, amidst all their verbiage and intellectual confusions, the scholastics were engaged in the endeavour to attain a logical exposition of universal truth. No phenomena, therefore, were alien from their enquiry. In the next place, the particular object of humanist satire, namely scholastic Latin, had its obvious defence, as Paulsen has well pointed out. The current Latin of the fourteenth and fifteenth centuries as spoken by clerks and in the universities was independent of classical sanction. It was not of Augustan purity and did not aim at any such standard. For mediaeval Latin was a living language, elastic, assimilative, progressive. Vocabulary, therefore, was bound to expand with new needs ; sentence structure to adapt itself to modern modes of thought and expression. " Hence the daily life of the educated German in his civic or monastic environment, borrowed little enough from Cicero, who indeed had nothing to contribute to supply the wants of the Thomist commentator, the clerk to the chancery, or the King's secretary. 'Cicero,' says the humanist, 'would have made nothing out of your Latin'; 'but,' is the reply, 'we are not writing for or talking to Cicero, but our own colleagues and contemporaries'; and they might well have added that classical Latin is singularly imperfect as a philosophical medium compared with its mediaeval development[1]." Nor, as regards the worth of mediaeval grammars, were the humanists wholly competent judges. That syntax is the expression of dialectic truth was ignored by them. Although for purposes of teaching, particularly of teaching the young, usage is the indispensable basis, nothing is gained by refusing to admit that grammar, as an analytical study, is a defensible subject of enquiry. Hardly a humanist but girds at Alexander de Villa Dei and his *Doctrinale*, but the great Latin grammarians of the eighteenth century were frankly indebted to him in establishing the principles of Latin syntax.

[1] Paulsen, *Geschichte*, i. 42.

Yet whilst admitting the perverseness of humanist criticism in certain important directions we may frankly allow that the new age demanded a recasting of the relative values of knowledge. The world had become keenly alive to the worth of classical antiquity as a factor making for progress. The universities, broadly regarded, could find no place for the new interests which were stirring in the minds of thinking men. And further, they seemed incapable of reforming their methods of teaching, or adapting their organisation to changing conditions. The force whereby they were brought unwillingly into line with the needs of the modern world was never generated from within, but with hardly an exception was applied from without. In Italy it is generally true to say that princes, patrons and scholars acted independently of the great university interests. In France nothing less than the direct intervention of the King was of avail to break down the exclusiveness of the university of Paris. In Germany, the prince also was in nearly every case the instrument by means of which the expansion of the concept of higher learning was actually attained.

It is hardly worth while to attach great importance to an early diatribe of Melanchthon against the universities as he knew them, for the *Oratio adversus Thomam Placentinum* was but a Protestant controversial tract of no critical value. Yet we may notice that in so far as its author denounces the methods of dialectic, metaphysic, canon law and scholastic theology, he is at one with Valla, Agricola and Erasmus. At the same time it is obvious from other sources that Melanchthon recognised the existence of humanist influences in Heidelberg, Erfurt and Tübingen[1], long before the old disciplines had begun to crumble under Lutheran attack or Erasmian satire. Reference

---

[1] For example, Freiburg and Basel both founded Chairs for " Poetry " between 1470 and 1474. Tübingen in 1481 offered a stipendium for "ars oratoria."

may be made to the chapter on Rudolph Agricola for allusions to humanist influences at Heidelberg.

Melanchthon was called to the university of Wittenberg in 1518. It was a new foundation dating only from 1502, and from its birth had granted a certain recognition to humanism and the "poets," though without subordinating in any way the claims of scholastic philosophy and theology. The new learning and the old, the liberal arts and the professional subjects, subsisted side by side at Wittenberg without avowed antagonisms, such as marked the reception of humanist ideas at Heidelberg, Leipzig, or Oxford. The endowment of a Greek Chair for Melanchthon gave the classical studies a more definite status. A Chair of Hebrew being also set up, Wittenberg was on the eve of the Reformation a *collegium trilingue*, and therefore an adequate school for the Teutonic student of the humanities. Melanchthon's influence was promptly felt in the expansion of the humanist teaching power of the university. In 1522 Camerarius was summoned to lecture upon Quintilian. Courses were given upon the *Natural History* of Pliny. Teachers in mathematics were engaged, and, on strictly humanist lines, the teaching of medicine was ordered to be based upon the study of Galen and Hippocrates. It need not be said that in the region of theology, Luther's influence had displaced the scholastics in favour of Augustine and the Old and New Testaments. Canon law ceased to be read. In a word the subjects of university study were without exception reorganised on humanist principles with a thoroughness that would have satisfied Lorenzo Valla himself. These changes indicate sufficiently the spirit in which Melanchthon attacked the problem of adapting the universities to the needs of modern learning and of the reformed faith. It is enough to grasp the spirit of Melanchthonian reform to perceive the immense change which was effected thereby in German learning. At Wittenberg the influence of the prince counted for much, and the fortunes of Melanchthon's schemes depended upon the readiness of the Electoral Prince of Saxony to find money or to appreciate the value of this or that subject of instruction. Not until 1536 did Melanchthon see his ideal expressed in university statutes, but from that date forward the humanist and Protestant character of the university was finally determined[1].

The faculty of law included four endowed professors ; that of medicine, three ; the philosophical faculty, i.e. the enlarged school of liberal arts, contained ten independent teachers : one each in Hebrew, Greek, classical poetry, grammar (specifically required to lecture upon Terence), senior and junior mathematics, logic, rhetoric, physics, and ethics. Declamation and disputation are expressly required in classical subjects. It is to be noted that Melanchthon, like Vives, attached high importance to the use of disputations, regarding them as a necessary safeguard against mechanical absorption of the teacher's thought or erudition. He goes so far as to say that a university without a carefully organised system of disputations is unworthy of the name of "schola." As the practice of Latin speech died down during the sixteenth century—an inevitable result of a religion which appealed to its believers through the vernacular, and of the development of nationalities—the declamation gave place to narrative or critical composition. Except for the purposes of public display the declamation gave place in university and school to the essay in Latin, and, by a natural process, later, in the vernacular. The Latin essay long continued to be the crucial test of promotion in the German school.

[1] The evangelical note of the Melanchthonian reform is typically expressed in the following passage from the *Ordnung* of the University of Wittenberg of 1546: "We (the Professors) must remember the nature of the Society of which we form part, not a Platonic Academy, but the Church of God, within which we are called to the work of training youth. How great then the sin, if by our actions the holy Temple be defiled!" Cf. *Mel. als Praeceptor Ger.* p. 477.

The importance of the professional subjects of law, theology, and medicine is expressed in the comparatively high stipends paid to the theological, legal, and medical professors, as compared with those paid to teachers in arts.   At the same time Melanchthon himself exceptionally received as high a stipend as was paid to any teacher in Europe.

It is possible to describe the course followed by a student entering the university of Wittenberg (and what follows will apply to the other universities of the same type) when he applied for his matriculation.   If he were unable to read, speak, and write Latin with some facility he would be required to attend preparatory courses or to "put on a coach."   At this stage he would also attend elementary courses in logic and rhetoric.   Attendance at public worship and at specified examinations in religion was obligatory under pain of expulsion. Upon entering the faculty of philosophy as a matriculated student, he would take up courses in logic, rhetoric, and poetry, reading Cicero, Quintilian, and certain Latin poets. In addition to these literary subjects the elements of mathematics and physics were studied.   The degree of bachelor could now be taken.   In order to qualify for the degree of master Greek grammar and certain authors were necessary, with special study of the *Physica* and *Ethics* of Aristotle in the original, mathematics and astronomy also being read in Euclid and Ptolemy.   Such a linguistic-philosophical course was the indispensable preliminary to the professional degrees.

In addition to the reorganisation of Leipzig and Tübingen upon similar lines, Melanchthon's influence was evoked in the foundation of new universities at Marburg, Königsberg, and Jena.

The influence of the prince in humanist reform has already been alluded to.   The instance of Budé in his relation to Francis I may be here recalled.   As in France, so in Germany, humanism gained access to the university through the favour of the Court.   Melanchthon, following the approved example of the Italian scholars, wrote the inevitable tract *De Institutione Principis*. It is inferior in Latinity and perhaps also in general scope to the corresponding tracts of Æneas Sylvius and Lionardo Bruni. A full classical course is propounded indeed, but we notice the absence of a perception of the finer graces of antiquity as they were manifested, for example, in the practice and ideals of Vittorino or in Castiglione's *Book of the Courtier*. Probably Melanchthon was aware that the German prince, as he knew him, had but moderate affinity with the peculiar distinction which the Italian called *virtù*. His world was that of Dürer, not that of Raphael, of the Elbe, not of the Arno. But, as we should expect, there is an inner seriousness in the advice that he gives to the prince which we miss in the essay of Æneas Sylvius.

The function of secular authority both within the church and within the university was immensely enlarged by the Reformation. The freedom of the mediaeval university, its autonomy in the midst of the ecclesiastical or the feudal power, was a guarantee of its intellectual independence. The universities had in a real sense constituted a federal republic of learning. Erasmus feared as a result of the reform that learning would become sectional and dependent. In so far as national universities became restricted by creed or race Erasmus was proved right in his forecast. Another result of the Reform was the predominance of the theological end in the new or the reorganised university. The Protestant prince inevitably regarded his own creed as, in one aspect of it, a bulwark of his State. Learning, therefore, once identified with Protestantism, shared the risks which attached to dependence upon the civil power. In the history of Protestant Germany, however, the authority of the secular arm has, on the whole, been consistent with intellectual freedom. The dominant position of the German universities in the learning of the sixteenth and seventeenth centuries was due to the combination of princely support, of Protestant seriousness, and humanist methods. In the bringing about of this union no factor was more effective than the personality and genius of Melanchthon.

It remains to enquire in what respects the position of Melanchthon in regard to the *content* of humanist instruction differed from that occupied by his great predecessors. Speaking generally, it may be said that upon the relative educational value of the classical writers he follows the humanist tradition, though, as we should expect from the rapid advance of criticism, he carries his analysis further than did Agricola and his contemporaries. Melanchthon views the great authors upon their triple aspect as masters of language, as exponents of knowledge, and as fountains of moral wisdom. In this he does not differ from the pioneers of humanism, except in so far as he discriminates clearly between these several functions in assessing the educational worth of individual writers. It is instructive to examine his attitude towards Homer and towards Terence respectively, viewed from this standpoint.

Homer excites in Melanchthon a veneration which is only less fervent than that which he owes to the Hebrew poetry. "Primum quidem sic statuo nullum unquam scriptum, inde usque a primum condito orbe, ulla in lingua aut natione, ab ullo ingenio humano, editum esse, sacra ubique excipio, in quo vel doctrinae tantum sit vel elegantiae vel suavitatis[1]." This is his affirmation after long years spent in the interests of evangelical education. Homer is the pre-eminent poet of the ages. His treasures can never be wholly explored by one intelligence. His poetic charm is only equalled by his profound insight into character and motive. "Humanitatis morum nullus eo melior magister[2]." The common duties of private station, as well as the most exacting needs of sovereignty, are enforced and illustrated in the *Iliad* and the *Odyssey*. The obligations of family life, constancy, piety, courage, devotion—these are the theme of the poet when he sings the fortunes of Odysseus.

[1] *C. R.* xi. 407.   [2] *C. R.* xi. 403.

Melanchthon is not affected by Plato's criticism of the treatment which gods and heroes undergo in the Homeric poems. Homer is true to nature, and to Greek nature above all[1]. If his own countrymen failed sometimes, as in Plato's case, to understand him, that has been the lot of most men of outstanding genius. But let all who desire to know the best read and re-read their Homer. "For he enriches the human spirit—the highest, the immortal, element in man— with treasures noble, priceless, and eternal." Homer then is to be studied for the "elegantia" and "suavitas" of his diction, for the "doctrina" and "eruditio" which his narratives contain, and for his didactic worth in the region of conduct.

Yet a further question must be asked. How far did Melanchthon feel the actual charm of the *Iliad* and the *Odyssey* as poetry, as literature? It is evident that he responded to the rhythm, the majestic roll, of the Homeric hexameter; as an artist in words he perceives the fitness of epithet, of figure, simile, and the like. But Melanchthon will not have a Greek writer read for "pleasure": the ethical significance of the content is that which matters. Hartfelder appositely quotes from Melanchthon's comment on the *Odyssey* in illustration. The ideal of the poet is the "vir prudentissimus et constantissimus: quam sancte enim ille parentes colit ac veneratur! quanto amore natum, quanto coniugem amplectitur, a quo nec consuetudine dearum immortalium avelli se patitur." Then, "a modern reader, as he lays down his Homer instinctively says, 'how fine it all is'! the scholar of Melanchthon's day was not less touched by human feeling than we, yet all he thinks of is, 'how edifying[2]'!" It is the problem that confronts us in Erasmus, and in all northern

---

[1] *C. R.* xi. 410. Speaking of Homer and his disciple Vergil he says: "descripserunt enim tales heroas quales fuerunt, nempe qui et humanis casibus obnoxii essent et iis moverentur."

[2] *Mel. als Praeceptor Ger.* p. 396.

scholars of the Revival, excepting always Agricola ; erudite men of learning though they were, had they more than an inkling of the true Greek spirit?   Nay, had they even, a very few instances apart, a living sense that what they spent their lives in reading, analysing, and interpreting was first and foremost *literature* ?   It is pertinent to such a question to remember that the German humanist put Aristotle before Plato, Euripides before Sophocles : that he ignored Æschylus whilst he prized Hesiod, that he showed no true appreciation of Vergil, that he treated Cicero as a philosopher.   This is not inconsistent with the fact that Melanchthon and his circle realised the rhythm and majesty, the logical precision, the figurative quality, the descriptive capacity of Greek and Latin speech, as language ; but their aesthetic perception stops there, or if it goes farther, it is dependent upon the conscious assent of the ethical self. Upon the Roman Comedy, to take a typical illustration from Latin literature, Melanchthon takes the usual standpoint of the serious humanist.   Like Vittorino he thinks Plautus only to be used with discrimination both on linguistic and on ethical grounds.   The *Aulularia* and *Trinummus* he will allow, and certain scenes from other plays.   But Terence[1] he regards with the whole-hearted approval which we have noted in Guarino and Erasmus, and which was shared also by Luther. Melanchthon was no doubt influenced here, as so often in his educational judgments, by the pronouncements of Erasmus, who placed Terence at the head of Roman authors suited for the instruction of youth.   His utility as a training in spoken Latin, the light that the comedies throw upon Roman life and manners, satisfy Melanchthon's demands respecting two of the conditions—*elegantia* and *eruditio*—needful in every classical writer chosen for educational use.   But above all he is in

[1] " Conducunt etiam comoediae ad emendate loquendum et ad parandum uberiorem dicendi facultatem.   Nam in hoc uno autore videre est mirabilem copiam in aliqua re explicanda, item diligentem dispositionem argumentorum "; &c.   *C. R.* xix. 692.

accord with every humanist in prizing Terence as a gallery of moral example. " Habet is multa egregia exempla civilium morum et humanorum casuum, unde judicium certum peti potest de rebus humanis. Nam qui diligenter expenderit hos casus, et personarum officia et consilia, de rebus humanis prudentius et ipse judicare discet." He is the more to be commended for school use that the standpoint of the author is always that of a wholesome morality : and that every play points some appropriate lesson. Melanchthon is at pains to bring out in each case the edification which he desires to be impressed on the young learner[1].

The lines of appreciation which we trace in Melanchthon's treatment of Homer and Terence as school authors are typical of those which he observes in weighing classical literature generally. In such a writer as Pliny he dwells naturally more upon his importance for "cognitio rerum," just as in Demosthenes "eloquentia" is the chief note. But the triple qualification of style, matter, and edification is to be demanded in the case of every writer. Hence Melanchthon is averse, like Erasmus, to the use of the Christian poets, which Colet and others were apt to prefer.

This same combination of form and content is characteristic of true eloquence. The function of Latin composition in German humanism is well exemplified in Melanchthon. The ideal of the Orator as the completely educated man has been set out in the previous chapters treating of Palmieri and of Erasmus. But the Reformer had before him the serious aim of religious persuasion and of civic duty. It is impossible to keep out of sight the relation of thorough training in Latin rhetoric so ardently inculcated by the great Protestant masters, of whom Melanchthon, Sturm and Cordier are the types, to

---

[1] He thinks of Greek Tragedy chiefly as a means to moral edification, somewhat in the Aristotelian vein. To read a play for pleasure merely is to treat great things with lack of due seriousness. Cf. Hartfelder, *op. cit.* p. 395.

vernacular eloquence in pulpit and council. The English humanists like the Italian made no concealment of it, as we see in Elyot[1] or Hoby, and in Palmieri. But Melanchthon dwells exclusively upon "eloquentia" as aptitude in Latin, and as a master of Latin rhetoric therefore we must consider him.

In the perfect "orator" Quintilian and Cicero had postulated a union of integrity, erudition, and eloquence. No modern student of antiquity dreamt of realising the standard of perfection as reached in Homeric, Attic, or Roman rhetorical eminence. Melanchthon meant by it first, the intimate combination of thought with expression, next, the moulding of such expression to the artistic shape in which it carries conviction and arouses appropriate emotional impulse. The relation between logic and style as Agricola conceived it has been touched upon. Melanchthon accepted that standpoint with complete assent. The power of speaking clearly and in logical sequence upon a subject is evidence of full apprehension of it; indeed there is, if we could reach it, an ideal mode of stating truths, wherein the correspondence is so delicately adjusted that language and thought have become a compact whole. We perhaps are ready to allow this in the supreme heights of poetry, but to Melanchthon, passionately eager to shake off the baffling confusions of scholastic thought, and to force to modern use the precision of the elaborate and logical Latin tongue, the inter-action of thinking and of expression appeared to defy analysis. Hence, as has often been pointed out, the fundamental error of the humanist rhetorician. A training in

---

[1] The preface to his little work, *The Knowledge that maketh a Wise Man* (1533), should be noted. The following from the *Governour* shows his position: "Undoubtedly very (i.e. true) eloquence is in every tongue where any matter or act done or to be done is expressed in words clean, propise, ornate and comely: whereof sentences be so aptly compact that they by a virtue inexplicable do draw unto them the minds and consent of the hearers, they being therewith either persuaded, moved, or to delectation induced." i. 116–7.

speech was equivalent to a training in thought. The study of language created a right aptitude for thought : a historian destitute of style was no historian : "eruditio" without "elegantia" was mere selfish complacency of wisdom, morally bad rather than helpful to man. The two ends therefore of all education were inseparable : "scientia judicandi de rebus humanis" and "facultas dicendi." Thus "eruditio" itself became too often mere definition of words, as we see from Erasmus, and even from Vives ; "res humanae" are all to be observed in their rhetorical dress, and "res naturae," which lack adequate literary form are useless for education. Indeed Melanchthon would have said that "elegantia" is of the essence of exact statement : the harmony of truth and expression is no superfluous or accidental quality but partakes of the nature of necessity.

Hence the importance of Latin writing, the only available instrument of thought common to the educated world. Melanchthon was right in holding that composition in a learned tongue involves a far more intimate analysis of the concepts to be expressed than does passable construing. Probably there is no exercise so well fitted to afford practice in logical thinking. But viewed apart from copious reading of antique authors "eloquentia" may be an empty thing. Here he comes back to Quintilian. Constant study of the great classics must go hand in hand with composition. "Eloquentium scriptorum lectio," for purposes of content even more than for style, can alone give matter, and train judgment, and without these there can be no "eloquentia." The empty oration of Ciceronian form so dear to the Italian humanist has no attraction for Melanchthon. Yet he is sensitive to the music of fine Latin oratory ; in words worthy of Agricola he affirms : "neque musica dulcior aut jucundior auribus aut mente percipi ulla potest quam aequabilis oratio, constans bonis verbis ac sententiis. Quare si quem nulla voluptate talis oratio afficit is longe a natura hominis degeneravit." The insistent advice that all boys should practise verse composition, as a necessary exercise in the enrichment of prose by figure, simile, metaphor and rhythmic phrase, is associated with his aesthetic perception of style. Grammar is indeed the foundation of all eloquence, but not the edifice itself. Merely *accurate* speech may fail entirely to win assent or to provoke emotion ; it lacks therefore the essential note of "eloquentia."

As regards mathematics and natural science, Melanchthon was the first educator of the Renaissance to demand their systematic treatment in the university and the gymnasium. Wimpheling in his famous appeal to the Council of Strassburg made no allusion to mathematics ; Agricola had desired geography and natural history to be taught from Aristotle and Theophrastus. Luther in 1524 declared in his famous appeal : "I speak for myself, but if I had children of my own I would have them learn not only languages and history, but singing and instrumental music, and a full course of mathematics as well." But printers of mathematical books were few, and those chiefly in Venetia. Alansee in Vienna (1518–1530) produced others for German use. Mathematical instruments were made in Italy, but after 1490 these became cheaper as they were turned out in Ulm, Vienna, Basel and Nuremberg. Meantime practical or commercial arithmetic had made great advances in Florence, Genoa and Venice ; as also in the Hansa towns and in south Germany. But no humanist ever regarded this as a liberal subject. Private schools supplied the industrial need in the subjects of writing and computation, but formed no part of educational organisation as understood by scholars. Exchanges, averages, percentages, and trade tables, astronomical tables for navigation, were taught as purely technical matters : and were treated in vernacular manuals[1].

The year in which Melanchthon was engaged upon the organisation of the Nuremberg school (1525) was marked by the appearance of Albert Dürer's manual of applied geometry

---

[1] See Günther, *Gesch. d. Mathem. Unterrichts.*

in German[1], by the introduction of mathematics into the scheme of the elementary (as distinct from the Latin) school, and by the definite allotment to a senior class in the Obere Schule of Nuremberg of a professor of mathematics at Melanchthon's instance. He himself delivered an address (1536) upon the history of mathematics in antiquity; and edited the famous *De Sphaera* of the Englishman Sacrobosco (Holywood), and the arithmetic of Peuerbach. Upon astronomy and physics he showed much activity in the university. He made no original contribution to these sciences, nor to the methods of teaching them. Probably he never accepted Copernicus, but he was broad enough to urge the claims of those who did. As a true humanist he believed that the ancients had not been surpassed by modern enquirers. Euclid and Ptolemy, Aristotle, Pliny, and Pomponius Mela were his authorities. The method of study was still "verbal" and not "real"; and the aim which inspires a teacher of to-day—the inculcation of precision in reasoning—he would attain rather by language and by dialectic. Probably Vives was the only humanist who weighed consistently the claims of this field of knowledge—so soon to become of absorbing interest—to a definite place in education. And as we shall see he found himself confronted by an obstacle which he could not surmount. Neither mathematics, nor, in still greater degree, natural studies had attained organic scientific exposition such as might render simplification for purposes of instruction possible to the teacher of the young.

It is not necessary to pursue the enquiry upon Melanchthon's attitude to other subjects, history for example, or religion[2]. He adopted the ordinary humanist view of the former. As to the latter, given the change of faith, he has a peculiar likeness to

---

[1] The title is *Die Underweysung der Messung mit dem Zirkel und Richtscheyd*. The first Arithmetic printed in England is Tunstall's which appeared only in 1522.

[2] Compare the attitude of Vives towards "real" subjects, supra, p. 202.

Vittorino in the earnestness of moral purpose and the over-whelming sense of the place of religion in personal life. In another aspect he had something in common with the Jesuits, who learnt much from Melanchthon; in especial holding that the world was to be won to the truth by right instruction.

And as the Jesuit determined the form which that instruc-tion was to take for the Catholic nations, so Melanchthon, with Luther and Sturm, fixed the liberal education on humanist principles for Teutonic Europe.

Before Melanchthon's death (1560) it was becoming evident to observant minds that the social demand for the product of the humanist school whether in England, Germany or France, was after all a limited one. Melanchthon and Sturm planned their instruction to meet the needs of Protestant Germans for an educated ministry, for the school, and for a capable civil service. They had hoped to instil also a passion for learning independent of professional demands. But, north of the Alps at least, the man of business, the small land-owner, the doctor and the lawyer found nothing, or very little, in humanist studies which came into real contact with their work or their leisure. Two careers attracted the bulk of those who passed through the grammar school and the university—that of the ministry and that of the school-master. But Mulcaster's complaint that there was in his time a serious excess of educated unemployed, Humphrey Gilbert's suggestions[1], Montaigne's criticism of the results of the high school training of his day, the failure of the Nuremberg school, which caused such bitter disappointment to all humanists in Germany, and Cordier's admission that men of business withdrew their sons from classical instruction to send them to learn modern languages abroad—point to the conclusion that humanist activities had not solved entirely the problem of organising education for the new age. The difficulties were inherent in the nature of the conditions of

[1] See infra, p. 302.

the time. Vernaculars were unfixed, science hardly existent, national literatures in Germany, France and England were but at the birth, and in any case unsuitable as instruments of teaching the young; the one definite, elaborated body of knowledge available to the school-master was the language and civilisation of antiquity, limited sections of mathematics, scripture, and the formularies of religion. Educational systems can only be built upon the foundation of accepted social ideals, and the curriculum must of necessity be the adaptation to instruction of subject-matter already established and systematised by expert enquirers—scholars, mathematicians, men of science. Before the seventeenth century no appropriate body of knowledge existed except that embraced within the field of classical antiquity.

CHAPTER XII.

THE DOCTRINE OF COURTESY.

IL CORTEGIANO, 1528.

As in instruction so also in manners Italy led the way for the modern world. The New Age demanded a re-fashioning of the ideal of behaviour to correspond to the revolution in learning and to the new adjustments in moral standards and social order. A changed perception of "the things that matter" in life brought with it a corresponding change in the idea of the personality through which such fresh truths find expression[1].

The Middle Age acknowledged two specific types of education: that of the knight and that of the clerk, whether lawyer or ecclesiastic. Both types of training were professional; the first indeed was more than that for it was limited to a caste,

---

[1] The literature upon manners as the counterpart of intellectual distinction has not been properly worked. Professor Raleigh's preface to the "Tudor Translations" edition of Hoby's *Courtier* serves as an admirable introduction. Einstein's *Italian Renaissance in England* has an excellent chapter on the subject. Burckhardt is, as usual, fertile in suggestion upon manners in Italian society. *Il Galateo* (1558) is more trivial in subject and in treatment but had far wider circulation than the *Courtier* and re-appears in England under different titles, "Refined Courtier" and the like, until well into the eighteenth century. Count Annibale Romei's *Courtier's Academy* (1597) is an English version of his *Discorsi...tra Dame e Cavaglieri* (1586), treating of the same questions as those raised in *Il Cortegiano*, though in a dreary style. The bibliographical list at the end of this volume contains the titles of certain of the more widely read works of this class.

that of the lords of the soil. Each was the counterpart
of the root-idea of mediaeval society—organisation by rank,
class, and corporate unit. With the advent of a new concept—
the express creation of Italy, or, at least, her rediscovery—
of man as a layman, neither soldier nor clerk, of man as
an individual, not a nameless fraction of a group, personality
became the conscious goal of development. The intrusion of
ancient culture into the line of Italian progress at the end
of the fourteenth century had certain indirect effects in moulding the ideal of personality. Antiquity revealed types of
excellence unfamiliar, yet full of attraction, to that energetic yet
receptive age. Such were the cultured democratic statesman,
the orator, the learned adviser, the provincial governor, the
patriotic captain sprung from the people—men belonging to
no privileged class, citizens to begin with, and ending as
citizens. But although these were new types to the Italian,
they were the product of political conditions analogous to
those he knew, or of the very soil and race he claimed as
his own. Again, acquaintance with the great civilisations of
Greece and Rome, and the employment of such knowledge as
the prime instrument of instruction, led inevitably to a desire
for a standard of outward life and of manners which should
correspond to the spiritual wisdom absorbed. Hence the invariable conjunction of "artes et mores," "lettere e costumi,"
the visible sign of which is manifested in the man himself.
Every humanist, whether school-master, man of letters, or man
of affairs, uses antiquity in both these ways : the individual
type is appealed to as a model for the imitation of Italian
youth : the noble—idealised, no doubt—culture of Athens or
Augustan Rome becomes a spur to the attainment of a grace
and dignity worthy of a man called to the work of reproducing
it for his own age. Again, there was a further influence making
for new standards of manners in the marked growth of the
commercial city, where distinction sprang from merit in council
or trade. The characteristic of Florence, Genoa, or Venice

was the identity of the noble with the civic element. The Florentine man of family was a banker or trader, the patrician of Venice was a merchant-venturer. Such communities naturally created their own ideal of excellence, and of the manner by which it was made manifest. The "vita civile" of Florence or Siena was something wholly different from the obscure subordinate society of the burgher town of East Anglia or the Rhineland. It had the mark of *virtù*, the assured consciousness of its own worthiness, and indeed of its superiority to the undeveloped, semi-feudal communities of the south. It was, however, in some two or three of the smaller autonomous city states under a prince, a Gonzaga, d'Este, and above all a Montefeltro, that a reconciliation of the old type with the new—the knightly with the civic and the scholarly—produced an ideal of personality, of the complete man of modern society, which stands for the final and harmonious picture of personality as the Renaissance had fashioned it. It has been already pointed out that at the Court of Mantua Vittorino da Feltre threw himself into the task of grafting upon the knightly training characteristic of the governing class the letters and the grace of the antique culture. Federigo di Montefeltro, later the great Duke of Urbino, was a typical pupil of the Zoyosa. His career shows how in superimposing classical instruction upon a military ideal he had transformed the latter, and created a third product, new to Europe—the man of arms whose deeper passion was for art and letters, whose personality was determined by the latter and not by the former. Yet Vittorino had pupils of a different kind, whose career was to be that of civil professions; and for these too he held up the same ideal of manners and highbred courtesy. Such were not the special privilege of the well-born, but the fitting garment of that inward civility of the mind, the "ingenui mores," which is the product of humanist studies. It is indeed the text of the treatise of Vergerius ; it was a large part of the educational aim of Erasmus, of Colet, of Cordier, to inspire a personality in which knowledge and taste, character and courtesy should be but its related aspects. And the higher education of western Europe has never been consciously blind to this high precedent. In reading such works as those of Palmieri, of Alberti, and of Francesco Patrizi, the same insistence upon the conjunction of the outward and inward appears. The prime virtues of the community, "temperantia" and "prudentia," which it is one of the chief ends of classical instruction to enforce, shade off imperceptibly from high moral impulse to the bearing and gesture becoming to the citizen of no mean city. That moral worth and uncouthness are compatible was not readily intelligible to the man of the Renaissance. So Palmieri, treating of the virtue of "temperantia" in the state, after dealing with the example of the ancients in obeying the laws and the constituted authorities, in cultivating amity within the city, passes on without break to another integral factor of the "ordered life." "Here it is fitting to speak of what becomes a citizen in his personal carriage, in movement or in repose. Every motion or attitude of the body which is out of harmony with the grace and freedom of natural activity must be avoided; our gestures not seldom reveal our motives, good or evil; we speak of the haughty or the respectful look; our features may reveal contemplation or pain, suspicion or superciliousness; the voice often corresponds to fair or subtle intention, to folly or craft. Think how much is revealed through the hands; they help out expression, they are a language in themselves. They dismiss or summon, show joy or grief, call for silence or speech; threaten or implore; are brave or alarmed; assert, deny, argue, count, accept, reject. And right training should imply always that the hands be used with grace conforming to our intention. So let them give the impression of firmness of will; never have them drooping, nerveless, idle like a woman's, but always ready to obey at once the thoughts or emotions which they are so apt at expressing.

"In walking, again, how easy to indicate a pompous mind

by a pretentious gait, as though you were at the head of a procession. What a revelation of conceit is the trick of shaking out one's cloak, and swelling one's figure as though to imply that the pavement had no room for more than one of your port. If you walk too fast you may raise suspicion that you are not a very serious person." Thus a man's carriage should reveal orderliness and modesty, which are the outward marks of "temperantia"; such will consort with his rightful dignity and manifest his true distinction. Let all be natural, unaffected, and appropriate. To such proper bearing will correspond the dress we wear. Graceful dress will, first of all, be well-fitting and suitable to the figure; it will, next, be of fine quality, both in style and material suited to the Town; yet in the third place, there will be nothing feminine in its elaborateness, nothing to suggest deep concern for fashion. Its purpose will be, in a word, to set off with becoming taste the virile and distinguished personality of the wearer. The fundamental principle involved in all this must be left to be expressed in Palmieri's own words, "Nulla altro e Temperantia che ordine debito di quello che per ogni tempo a ciascuno maggiormente si conviene." Personality is one complex of morals, intelligence, emotions, and activity. In each aspect the individual obeys one and the same law of harmony, of proportion. The citizen who has drunk at the fount of ancient wisdom will so manifest "humanitas" that all who see him will recognise the *virtù* which makes him what he is.

It is perhaps now possible to understand how the Italian humanist—though in a very real sense every Italian was φύσει humanist—paid so high regard to that which a superficial analysis styles the mere externals of personality. It is necessary to realise the humanist conviction when approaching the subject of this chapter, to which what has so far been said is intended as an introduction, *Il Cortegiano*, or the *Book of the Courtier*, of Baldasarre Castiglione.

A few words only are needed to place the *Courtier* in

its historical setting. Castiglione was born on December 6th, 1478, near Mantua, of a family of some distinction. His mother was a Gonzaga, related to the reigning house, and therefore to the great Duchess Elisabetta of Urbino, and to her successor in that title, the Duchess Leonora. Castiglione was a welcome visitor to the Castello at Mantua, where he gained his first experience of a Renaissance Court of the first order. It has not been sufficiently recognised that Castiglione had in the Gonzaga household under its distinguished Marchioness, Isabella d'Este[1], the example of a learned and refined Court hardly inferior to that which he was later to know at Urbino. His education covered the full range of humanist learning in Greek, Latin, and Italian, in the arts, and, as became his station, in military exercises. Part of his later youth was spent at Milan. On attaining manhood he entered (November, 1499) the service of the Marquis of Mantua, who had perforce come to an understanding with Louis XIII, the conqueror of Milan, and who in 1503 accepted, following the tradition of his House, the position of Condottiere, or Captain-General, of the French forces fighting the Spaniards for the Kingdom of Naples. Thither Castiglione accompanied him, but in September, 1504, the young officer entered the service of Guidobaldo di Montefeltro, Duke of Urbino, thereby offending his powerful patron, the lord of Mantua. His position in the Ducal Court he retained under Guidobaldo and his successor, Francesco della Rovere, until 1516, when Leo X deposed the Duke, and annexed for a time the little state to the patrimony of St Peter. During these twelve years Castiglione was employed on various missions for which the charm of his personality singularly fitted him. He came to London in 1506 to carry home the insignia of the Garter conferred upon Guidobaldo by Henry VII; he visited at

---

[1] Mrs Ady's *Isabella d'Este* gives a vivid account of the Mantuan Court in its great days. Her book is built upon material gathered by the industry of many years of MM. Luzio and Renier.

Ferrara in the great days of that most brilliant Court, where he met Lucretia Borgia, the young wife of the heir apparent, Alfonso, and made friends with Duke Ercole, the same who had shown regard for Rudolph Agricola nearly thirty years before. His home for twelve years was the palace at Urbino, perhaps the most striking of the many notable palaces of the Italian Renaissance, built by Federigo, Vittorino's pupil, some thirty years before, piled high upon the steeps which overhang the little town. Not in size and situation only, but in the dignity of its proportions, the beauty of its detail, its harmonious adaptation of the neo-classic style, the home of the Montefeltri was indeed a lordly pleasure-house. Not less was it conspicuous for the men and women who gathered there. Urbino lay far from the main routes of communication, where the middle Apennines begin to fall away to the Adriatic. The town and territory which formed the little state were highly prosperous and their population devoted to the ruling house, in whose dignity they proudly shared. Duke Guidobaldo was, though a young man, in weak health and devoted to the humanities rather than to arms. His wife, the distinguished Elisabetta Gonzaga, sister to the Marquis of Mantua, was recognised by all who knew her as one of the most brilliant women of her time, and at the period when Castiglione entered upon service there, was the centre of the most cultivated Court in Italy, not excepting that of Ferrara. The picture of it lives in the pages of Castiglione's book, in which, with all due allowance to its literary form, we recognise a true description of the life of courtly leisure and recreation as the Duchess fashioned it. Castiglione, after more warlike experiences, represented, under Julius II, the Duke Francesco at the Vatican, but was wholly unable to stay the grasping hand of Leo X, who in 1516 annexed Urbino to the papal dominion. Reconciled to the Gonzagas, Castiglione held the Mantuan legation in Rome ; in 1524 Clement VII sent him to Spain as Nuncio at the Court of Charles V. The Sack of Rome was a grievous blow to his self-respect, as he had failed to interpret the drift of events to his master. He died at Toledo in 1529. "We have lost," said Charles V, when the news reached him, "the finest gentleman of our time."

Il Cortegiano was composed as a record of those most happy years of his vexed life when he realised for a space his heart's desire in the companionship of the notable group which Duke Guidobaldo and his Duchess brought together at Urbino. The sketch of the ideal Courtier was thrown down in a few days in or about 1508, and was laid aside, taken up again and finished in parts, until it reached well-nigh its final form in 1516, the year when the heavy hand of Leo X closed upon the little state. Though known to many people in manuscript the book was only given to the house of Aldus to print in 1528, when it speedily became one of the best read works in Europe. It appeared in Spanish dress in 1540; Sir Thomas Hoby published it in English as *The Courtyer* in 1561; it was translated into French by at least two hands in or before 1538; and it was put into Latin. It has been with just discernment claimed for Castiglione's work "that if one (book) rather than another, is to be taken for an abstract or epitome of the chief moral and social ideas of the age, that one must be the *Courtier*[1]."

The characteristic art, after all, of the Italian Renaissance was the art of speech. "Il bel parlare," "il parlar gentil," was the necessary qualification of distinction in society; oratorical grace often determined success in politics or diplomacy; the man of letters must declaim or recite as well as compose. The "conto," the short story, witty or romantic, the eclogue, pedantic, but classically correct, were the staple of an evening's entertainment. The development, under the compelling precedent of Plato and Cicero, of the Dialogue was perhaps the peculiar vogue of the mid and latter Renaissance. With Palmieri and Alberti the dialogue was nothing more than a matter of form,

[1] Prof. Raleigh, *op. cit.*

the thesis of the chief character is just punctuated by notes of assent. Castiglione, however, in shaping his argument by the way of dialogue, presents a genuine discussion, in which divergent views are left unreconciled, and thus implies actual debate and long pondering upon the conclusions he sustains. For four evenings in the withdrawing room the imagined argument ran on the subject propounded by one of the Court and accepted by the Duchess, namely, " to shape in woordes a good Courtyer, specifying all suche condicions and particuler qualities as of necessity must be in hym that deserveth this name." It was feigned that the company by whom this high debate was shared included men and women of notable fame in letters, politics, and society, such as Giuliano de' Medici, Pietro Bembo, Bernardo di Bibbiena, Cesare Gonzaga, the Contessa Emilia Pia, and many others, all of whom, it should be remembered, Castiglione had helped to entertain at the Palace at one time or another. Upon Ludovico da Canossa and Giuliano de' Medici falls the main task of depicting the perfect Courtier, amid many gracious digressions, which yet are elaborations of a special argument upon the main theme. The famous monologue of Bembo upon Ideal Love stands out as the most exquisite expression of philosophic thought which the Renaissance has given us.

The Courtier was nothing less than the ideal personality as the Renaissance conceived it. In the sixteenth century the Court stood for the central impulse and acknowledged standard of every higher activity of the community. It is not merely a question of Italy, it was true of France, of England, of Spain, of the Palatinate, and of Saxony. Governance, enterprise, arts, and letters found their common interaction within the circle of high society. A secretary of State, a soldier of fortune, a scholar, a poet or artist, a great noble, an adventurous sailor, are, or may be, all of them members of the Court, or look to it for encouragement, interest, and approval. The implications of the word in later days were no doubt often true then also ;

but they were then the recognised degradation of the ideal. For Castiglione has stated the function of his Courtier in unmistakable words : " So to direct and persuade his Prince to good and dissuade him from evil, that his lord may understand good and ill, and love the one and hate the other, is the true fruit of the art of the courtier." Again " by means of his accomplishments...the Courtier may easily and ought to gain his good will...and if he is such as has been described, will be able ever artfully to disclose to him the truth of all things." Thus it will happen that " little by little he will instil into him the chief virtues, exciting him by the examples of great characters of old, using his personal gifts to win his prince to take pleasure in his society and to have confidence in his good will and his judgment. It is his chief business to understand the nature and the disposition of his lord, as Aristotle, a courtier, had perfect knowledge of the mind of Alexander, and so discreetly adapted his discipline to it that the young prince loved and honoured him beyond his own father. Thus did Plato with Dion of Syracuse." But, as the philosopher failed to win the despot from tyranny, and so left him, in the same way, " if it be our Courtier's hap to serve a prince without the sense of right and wrong, so soon as he discovers his principles his business must be to quit his service and avoid that anxiety which a good man must feel when a bad man is his master." The true motive of the Courtier is to serve the Prince in all ways which may redound to his honour and interest, therefore it concerns his honour not to comply with commands which are unworthy of both of them ; especially seeing that the Courtier's customary employ is the transaction of most weighty affairs.

It will be seen that we have but to put "country" for "prince" to have the identical gospel of service which inspired Sir Thomas Elyot, and which in its most rigid form in modern Europe was seen in the training of the patrician youth of Venice.

The obvious criticism was that the Courtier towers high above the Prince in all but fortune, for in him are all the excellences. As Burckhardt has said, the Courtier fills the scene, the Prince and the Court being created only to find him a stage for the exhibition of his *virtù*. So the Duchess truly remarks that such a Courtier would himself be the perfect Prince. At least he deserves a higher title than that of Courtier. All of which does but indicate that the form and setting are immaterial to the truth of the conception, which is to set forth the figure of the "complete gentleman," in surroundings which permit of the consistent development in one individual of every distinction which the Renaissance held to mark the ideal personality. It is this idealisation which renders the *Courtier* so convincing a work to the student of humanism, and which during its own century gave it so far-reaching an influence. For one of its readers who had to do with courts twenty were of private station. But everyone, who by education and tastes had understanding of what was written, could find in it that which appealed to and lifted higher his own strivings for a life inwardly and outwardly fuller and more worthy.

At the outset it is disputed whether to be well-born is a necessity to the Courtier; and it is agreed that, though personal gifts are the essential condition, yet, to secure everything which may favour his influence, honourable birth is not to be underrated. Experience, it is argued, shows us many a youth of position and opportunity who has proved himself of no esteem: while not a few of lowly origin have attained the highest *virtù*. But the Prince should regard the popular feeling which assures to a young man of family freedom from carping envy and gives him instinctive courage to treat on equal terms those associated with him in the Prince's service. Moreover, such origin "inflames and encourages to virtue as well with the fear of reproach as with the hope of glory." Yet no such consideration may override the importance of right training in youth and of personal gifts of temperament and of appearance.

He must be possessed of skill in arms, which he will exercise with vigour, bravery, and grace. He is by preference not a professed soldier, with all the limitations which belong to the fighting career. For instance, he will rarely talk of war; he is no braggart, especially before ladies; though he will always show himself with the foremost against the enemy, accepting opportunity of personal risk, and manifesting prowess in skill and courage. But any trick of ostentation is unworthy of him; his is the assured distinction of one worthy of his powers, and superior to all self-advertisement. In sports and exercises he will be guided by the same principle. They are the recreation, the tests of vitality and alertness, of a man devoted to higher interests. What he does he does with the skill and the distinction which belong to his position. He is no professional expert, and certain forms of sport tumbling and strange gymnastic feats, for instance, he will leave aside as ungraceful and therefore unworthy. "Grace" is to be early acquired, and nothing may be affected which conveys a sense of unnatural effort or involves uncouth attitude. Hunting—he will of course be a perfect horseman—swimming, tennis, tilting, cudgel, and spear play, leaping, casting the stone are commended. Cesare Borgia had only a few years before brought into Italy the Spanish taste for fighting the bull, and had himself felled a bull with a fatal blow of his right fist before the Roman populace. Yet the Courtier will be unwilling to try his strength in public with those of meaner condition. If he practise dancing before company he will be careful to preserve a proper dignity and to avoid movements which are not consistent with natural grace and freedom. He is not a dancing master to jump in the air and make lightnings with his feet. Castiglione doubts whether chess is rightly called a recreation; it takes too much time, concentration, and practice. The Courtier will perform all exercises with that "sprezzatura," that air of perfect ease, of " taking it in the stride," that will mask his excellence in all regards.

In conversation, more particularly, there will be no affectation, yet the dignity of his words and gesture, of the contribution which he makes to debate, will be felt by all. For he " will discover in everything a certain negligence to conceal his art withal, and to appear that whatsoever he saith or doth comes from him naturally and easily and as it were without attending to it." The consciousness of *virtù* may not be paraded. Care taken to speak in a clear yet musical voice, not too soft nor too shrill like a woman's, to adjust personal gesture to the significance of the argument, to know how to listen, how to make retort, is of the essence of good manners. A pedantic adherence to the Tuscan standard of correctness will be avoided ; obsolete words, even though approved by the usage of Boccaccio or Petrarch, are wisely dropped ; whilst new words, from ancient and foreign sources, will be welcomed if they have made good their footing. " I would not have him scruple to invent new words or to express them in new modes and figures, using Latin as their source." The enrichment and refinement of the ver-nacular was the pre-occupation of the Italian humanist of the time, as it was of broad-minded scholars in England, France, or Spain, during the age immediately following. It would be folly, adds Castiglione, to love ancient speech for no other reason but to speak as people did formerly and not as they do at present : and this applies not to Latin only but to the Italian of the Trecento which some Florentine purists would impose as a quasi-dead tongue over the living thought of Italy.

In general, the Courtier will be superior to the habit of flattery. He will, no doubt, in matters of slight concern accept his Prince's opinion. But he will be no back-biter ; not contentious, importunate, or too fond of forcing his opinion. " I would not have him a great talker." The art of telling stories, the true secret of wit, and the permissible limits of humour, irony, and banter are dealt with at much length, with many delightful illustrations. But it is decided that the Courtier should not carry wit to the point of ill-nature; that mimicry is a dangerous adjunct to conversation, that laughter should be well under control, and that under all temptations the Courtier should remember the due adjustment of his topics or argument to the company.

The Courtier will have an alert, receptive, and well balanced intelligence; the integrity of his disposition will help to direct him to what is worthy. "Now the French set a wrong standard in their choice of interests for the Courtier. They have a mean opinion of all qualifications but that of arms, esteeming the title of clerk to be a signal mark of reproach. But if the young heir (Francis I) comes to the throne in due course the glory of arms will be eclipsed by that of learning." Again, antiquity gives us infinite examples of the combination of merit in arms and Letters in men of distinction: and no one can doubt that Letters add dignity to human life. "In Letters I would have the Courtier to be more than moderately instructed, especially in what they style polite literature, and to understand not only the Latin tongue but the Greek." "Let him be much conversant in the Poets, in Orators, in Historians. Let him practise in writing Prose and Verse, especially in the vulgar tongue." Facility in verse has its social uses, and aids us to a criterion of the poems of others. Once more, the Courtier will be diffident rather than forward in displaying his knowledge: and should, in especial, disdain flattery of his own productions. Rather let him use his learning to the formation of a sound judgment in Letters and in life. It is essential that he disclaim the authority of a professed grammarian. Bembo appropriately questions whether Letters rather than arms have not the prior claim to regard, the mind being superior to the body; but it is preferred that the man of arms be also a man of learning, and that the adjustment of the two conditions is essential to the complete Courtier.

The place of Music is easily determined : it is a diversion. Taste for music and skill in execution secure for a man of affairs relief from labour and ease for a distempered mind. The ancients support the claim. Alexander was notably sensitive to music : Socrates learnt it late in life : Plato and Aristotle include it in the ideal education. Lycurgus and Cheiron can be quoted. "Whosoever has no relish for music one may justly conclude that he is composed of spirits which are at discord with one another. Consider, I pray you, what mighty influence it has when it prevailed over a fish to convey a man through the dangers of a tempestuous ocean." Our Courtier may sing at sight, and if possible accompany his voice with the viola, or the lute. But he should abstain from skill upon wind instruments ; they are ungraceful things, and render the executant somewhat ridiculous. As in other subjects he will know instinctively when music which may perhaps suit his mood is, for the moment, out of place.

Drawing, painting, and sculpture, although some regard these as professional occupations and little suited to a gentleman, are yet necessary parts of a true education. The Greeks considered them parts of a liberal training ; and they have the practical advantage of enabling the Courtier to draw maps for use in war, or in travel, to the right understanding of the lie of a country, its weak and strong places, castles, forts. And further, such practical knowledge will train taste in the judging and the enjoyment of things of beauty whether natural or of man's art. Yet more than this, the author in a fine passage views the art from the peak of high humanist enthusiasm. "And in verye deed," to quote Hoby's translation, "who-so esteameth not this arte, is (to my seemyng) farre wyde from all reason ; for so-muche-as the engine of the worlde that we beholde with a large sky, so bright with shining sterres, and in the middes, the earth environd with the Seas, severed in partes with Hylles, Dales and Rivers, and so decked with suche diverse Trees, beawtifull floures and herbes, a man may saye it to be a noble and a great peincting, drawen with the hands of nature and of God : the whych whoso can follow, in myne opinion he is woorthye much commendacion" (p. 92).

In regard to Dress there are no constraining rules. It is desirable to conform to the mode, not to attract attention by mere externals. But if it be insisted that the mode is now so varied, and that the Italians are prone to take their fashions where they find them to their taste, then every one is at liberty to follow what he pleases. This, however, is worthy of assent : that the Courtier's dress be one which conduces to his self-respect, that it comply with the lines of his figure, and be of becoming dignity. For ordinary apparel black is to be favoured, and next to that some dark colour. On gala days he will be suitably magnificent. Yet always the dress will be in accord with the true nature of the wearer, as he judges of it. A courtier will be always elegant, of modest exactness. Anything light or feminine will provoke untrue deductions as to his taste and seriousness.

There is obviously room for divergence in the relative weight which different communities might ascribe to certain of the constituent factors of this ideal personality. At Florence, for example, the function of arms would be rated less highly, that of Letters and of civil ability being preferred to it. The requirement of good birth might, on the Arno, imply not merely descent from, but active participation in, a commercial house. It is instructive therefore to turn to another interesting discussion of the qualities that are demanded in the ideal gentleman. Count Annibale Romei places the figures of his dialogue at Ferrara, in the reign of Duke Alfonso II (1585). The seven days' discourses treat "of Beautie, of Humane Love, of Honour, of combate and single Fight, of Nobilitie, of Riches, and of precedence of Letters or Armes," each, as the Elizabethan translator says, "grounded on the firme foundations of Aristotelian and Platonical discipline and yet accompanied with a lively touch and feeling of these times."

As a book it is not to be compared with *Il Cortegiano*. It is overweighted with its philosophy, and is destitute of all true literary art. But *The Courtiers Academie*, as Keper's title has it, touches upon some three or four points which are pertinent to the present argument. Romei admits that nobility is a gift of nature and not of birth or royal caprice. Yet he cannot allow the term to one who looks back upon less than three generations of distinguished fore-bears. Riches are a condition of such nobility ; " for without them virtue can hardly appear," nor can the poor man show " magnificent actions." But riches are but means to such conditions as themselves imply nobility. The case of Venice is quoted : and it is allowed that wealth rightly acquired and exercised in due service of the State is a patent of distinction. Yet no one, however noble by riches or descent, can be called *gentle*, " which hath a far more restrained significance than this word *noble*," unless he have notable virtue.

The question of the precedence of Letters or arms is argued from the *Ethics* and *Metaphysics*. For "those who busy their minds in contemplation, addict themselves to the study of good Letters, and are than all others by God better beloved, because they adorn that part of the mind which hath greatest similitude to things divine." But the activity of the soldier is "most principally exercised by bodily force"; and has therefore "its necessary imperfection." The conclusion is thus stated : "We do determine that *Civil honour* which is the reward of excellent and heroical actions ought more specially to be yielded to men of martial profession, and that *veneration*, proper to things divine, befitteth the wise and learned…that warriors be esteemed honourable and doctors reverend."

There is evidence of the influence of Venice and the peculiar conditions of its polity in Romei's dialogue. If the Roman ideal education was that of the Orator, that of the Renaissance city-state the Courtier, that of Tudor England the Governor, undoubtedly that of Venice was the Secretary.

The end of the practical training of the patrician youth of the Republic was the civil, judicial or diplomatic service. No community attached so great importance to the liberal education of the scions of its ruling class as Venice, and careful training in classics, mathematics, and the arts of drawing was incumbent on all who were looking to official service. The Venetian state demanded work of all its governing citizens. In 1470 the Republic established a Ginnasio or high school, to serve as preparatory stage to the state university of Padua. The entire educational machinery of the Republic was centred in a Government Board, the Riformatori dell' Università, by whom professors were appointed, libraries and museums controlled, and schools established. The highest names in Venetian history are found amongst its librarians and professors, teachers and literary men. The place taken by arms at Urbino belongs at Venice to the naval service, but distinction gained at sea was subordinate to that gained in the superior duty of the civil and diplomatic officers. Hence arises another ideal of training to set side by side with that of Urbino, an ideal which accepted commerce as the necessary condition of society, with public duty, distinction in art and letters, and a wide outlook over the field of foreign politics, as the factors of the "complete life." The peculiar privilege accorded to promising young patricians of being present at discussions of the Consiglio dei Savi, where they joined in arguments upon public affairs, had access to Relazioni of Ambassadors, and to other State documents and archives, is remarkable proof of the dignity of the Secretarial offices for which such young men were destined.

Reviewing together the various presentations which the Renaissance offers us of the ideal personality fitted to the finest demands of the community, it is not difficult to perceive three salient characteristics. The first is that quality termed by Aristotle μεγαλοψυχία, which corresponds to the higher aspect of the Italian *virtù*. "We shall find," says Aristotle in the fourth book of the *Ethics* "that the *high-minded* man is he who, being truly worthy of great things, holds himself thus worthy....For he who holds himself worthy of less than his merits is small-minded, the more so the greater his true excellence." This consciousness of distinction inevitably seeks recognition, and this recognition is honour. Next stands the quality, developed especially in the Venice of the high Renaissance but typical also of the life of Medicean Rome and Florence and of the more cultivated minor Courts, which the humanist also found in Aristotle, μεγαλοπρέπεια. "A poor man can never display *magnificence*; to attempt such a display contradicts that *fitness* which virtue of necessity involves." "The magnificent man spends his wealth in accord with that principle of fine proportion in things which underlies all virtue." "Above all, he will never ignore the fitness of expense to its special object." "Whatever he undertakes he will carry through with the magnificence that becomes it." "His expenditure ought to be made in the public interest and not in his own."

In the third place, yet more consistent with the Greek spirit, is the note which is struck by Palmieri and Alberti as sharply as by Castiglione, that of harmony and proportion in the whole personality. The character and actions of the complete personality are always in perfect mutual relation. The excellences which make him what he is so regulate his life that there is no discord between "virtù" and "onestà," or, as we might put it, between person, intelligence and conduct. "Prudentia" (the φρόνησις of Aristotle), the higher practical wisdom of life, is that which best covers his active qualities. But beyond that—and herein the Courtier of Urbino stands out in supreme distinction—the perfect gentleman of the Renaissance, winning the heights of Platonic thought as the culmination of his wisdom, finds his highest satisfaction in ideal love, attaining therein to a complete reconciliation of earthly and divine beauty where neither moth nor rust doth corrupt. Without such an outlook upon the realm of contemplation and inner self-realisation the ideal of the Courtier would have proved, after all, but a maimed presentation of the loftiest thought of humanism. Of such a Courtier indeed we may well feel with Giuliano, "mai non fu, ne forse può essere"; "such a Courtier as neaver was, nor I beleave ever shall be," as Hoby puts it. Yet to some such ideal as this all humanist training aspired, and to consider duly the many-sided nature therein set forth will help us to realise how hopelessly astray are those who think that humanism stands for absorption in dead problems, and the education which it evolved for things of the letter, for imitation and pedantry.

It was inevitable that the argument at Urbino should take within its range the correspondent functions and excellences of the Lady of Court. Indeed it is obvious that the Courtier is framed in large part to hold his place in a society which postulates the presence of women of distinction akin to his own. Like him she should be nobly born, of attractive presence, with ease and grace of bearing. Such indeed are essential qualities. Prudence, discretion, real kindliness of disposition, "onestà," in the fullest sense, are all marks of a perfect Lady of Court, who will also avoid the contentious spirit, envy, backbiting, and the habit of listening to reflections upon other women. Her gifts will be specially shown in practical ability in household management, in bringing up children, in directing the social life of home, and in taking her part in conversation with wittiness and intelligent interest. She will be ashamed of all that is merely trivial in intercourse, yet without conceit of her superior powers. Dress, naturally, is of more concern to her than to the Courtier, yet like him she will find the safest rule in the law of appropriateness to her own personality. In respect of exercises she will not join in hunting parties, though she will enjoy riding. Dancing comes by nature but will be practised with great diligence to enhance graceful carriage. In music, singing and some instrumental skill are approved, but wind instruments are forbidden. She will watch, and learn to understand, the masculine sports, that she may judge of skill, and be able to speak on them with intelligence in conversation.

In matters of learning she will be versed in Letters, in which we are to include both the ancient tongues, and Italian literature. Painting is added. She will possess all the personal virtues requisite to procure full esteem, by which she will be fit for high responsibility. For it may hap that a woman be called to govern cities, and though that puts an extreme case it may be well argued that a woman's mind is more acute, and better adapted to fine thinking than a man's. "Indeed," said Giuliano, "I affirm that whatever men can know and understand, the same can women also; and where the intellect of one can penetrate there also can the other." This declaration gave rise to one of the usual digressions upon the respective natures of man and woman. But the accepted opinion was that woman had an equally honourable, though different, responsibility with man in the ordering of the complex life of the age.

It is in place to refer to certain other books dating from the first half of the sixteenth century treating of the claims of women to status and education, whereby they may be rendered worthy of high responsibility. Three may be mentioned. *De Nobilitate et Praecellentia Feminei Sexus, ad Margaretam Austriacorum et Burgundionum Principem* (1529), by Henricus Cornelius Agrippa, a scholar born at Cologne in 1486, but of Italian training. It was translated into English in 1542. Agrippa advocates the equality or even superiority of women. The work was made large use of by L. Domenichi, *Nobilità della Donna*, written about 1544. The two, however, found their way into English society chiefly through Bercher's *Nobylytye of Wymen*, written about 1552[1]. "My purpose shall consist in this, to shew the same learning to be in women that

---

[1] Printed for the Roxburghe Club, 1904, from edition of 1559.

is in man, the same fortitude, the same magnanimity," etc. As regards their capacity for Letters he quotes, in usual humanist mode, Aspasia, Hortensia, Cornelia; Cassandra Fedele, the distinguished Venetian lady, "had that understanding in liberal sciences that Angelus Politianus had who writeth her praise. The Lady Margarita Valesia, queen of Navarre, hath the same understanding of Latin and Greek that other her countrymen have." The Marchioness of Pescara (Vittoria Colonna) and others are quoted: "then I think you have heard of Thomas More who had three daughters that speak well Latin, Greek and Hebrew." In the next generation Margaret Roper's three daughters, the Princesses Mary and Elizabeth, Jane Howard—"both Greek and Latin is vulgar to her," and her composition in verse is most notable—the daughters of the Earl of Arundel, of the Duke of Somerset, of Henry Grey, and of Sir A. Cooke exhibit the powers of a woman's intellect when the opportunity of sound learning is afforded them. One of the characters—for the book is in dialogue form, as usual—Countess Elsi says: "I have noted in some (women) learning, in some temperance, in some liberality," and so forth of the accepted virtues, "and I have compared them with men that have been endowed with like gifts and I have found them equal or superior." An important argument is then brought forward. "The manner of life is a great help to matters of mind....The bringing up and training of women's life is so strait and kept as in a prison, that all good inclination which they have of nature is utterly quenched. We see that by practice men of small hope come to good proficiency so that I may affirm the cause of women's weakness in handling of matters to proceed of the custom that men hath appointed in the manner of their life, for if they have any weak spirit, if they have any mutability or any such thing, it cometh of the diverse unkindnesses that they find of men."

It has been seen in previous chapters that humanist teachers and writers of the fifteenth century were alone in advocating the higher education of women. It became usual in Italy to encourage the daughters of the great families to attend the lessons of the private masters who were in the service of citizens of position. But it is to be noted that the doctrine of joint or uniform education was by no means universally held. Naples and the south like Venice in the north held views as to the place of women in society which can only be described as oriental. It is for example impossible to find any references to the social influence of the wives of patrician families in the Venice of the sixteenth century. Only one Venetian lady is noted as erudite, Cassandra Fedele, and even the Veronese Nogarola daughters had been regarded unfavourably because they wrote Latin epistles to Guarino.

It is of course obvious that the question of girls' education is determined by accepted opinion of the status of women in contemporary society. In the fifteenth and sixteenth centuries, as in the eighteenth, teachers gave such education to girls as social sentiment allowed ; very often that meant none at all. In Medicean Florence the standard was probably a fairly high one ; and the example of great families, Gonzagas and d'Estes, would no doubt react similarly in and around Mantua and Ferrara. But the number of girls who received other than a domestic education was always very small indeed. The great burgher class and the country-dwellers stood on the old lines of training. The mother was the educator ; the circle of family duties and the diligent observance of religion afforded all that was needed. This was even Alberti's view, and it represented the traditional Florentine ideal. If we are to seek authoritative light upon the practice of girl's education we must look for it in Dominici's *Cura della Famiglia*, and not in Bruni's tract. In Venice in particular the humanist doctrine of equality of opportunity in the education of boys and girls never had an advocate. The narrowest conception of the Greek gynaeceum dominated patrician conviction on the subject of women. A girl's education naturally corresponded. She probably learnt nothing outside the routine of home duties, she took no exercise, was only seen out of doors at church, had no friends outside her family, was allowed to read nothing, to see nothing except from the loggia of the palazzo, never travelled; her one duty was to await marriage. Nowhere in Christian Europe outside Palermo was the activity of women more rigidly circumscribed than in the Venice of this period. In the same way in England, France, or Germany, advance in girls' education could only come from an enlarged view of what society demanded from or permitted to women. But wherever the sincere spirit of humanism penetrated, there was, latent or active, a force which made for the widening of women's interests, and in proportion as one or the other grade of society received this spirit so did women's claims to opportunity gain recognition.

CHAPTER XIII.

THE RENAISSANCE AND EDUCATION IN ENGLAND.

I.

THOMAS ELYOT AND *THE BOKE NAMED THE GOVERNOUR*, 1531.

In treating of the new education evolved in Italy as the inevitable outcome of Revival, illustration was drawn from the opinion of a prominent man of affairs, the Florentine Palmieri. So in tracing the spread of humanist conviction in England it is desirable to turn from the scholar and the school to learn how training in the liberal studies was, a century later, viewed by a typical public official of the new age, Sir Thomas Elyot.

Thomas Elyot was born about 1490, the son of a Wiltshire gentleman of cultivated interests, who had been brought up to the law. Richard Elyot held an appointment in his native county as Crown Receiver, was made Sergeant-at-Law, and, in 1509, Judge of Assize. During the boyhood of his son, Richard Elyot seems to have been chiefly resident in London where he became intimate with the famous group which gathered round Thomas More in his house at Chelsea. Thomas Elyot on attaining manhood was an eager student of the humanities, widely interpreted, and though sent to neither of the universities came under the stimulus, and, indeed, the direct instruction, of Linacre, certainly the best Greek scholar in London. In 1511 his father obtained for young Elyot the post of Clerk of Assize, and his career was now determined.

By Wolsey's appointment he became Clerk to the Privy Council. Five years later he is found on friendly terms with Thomas Cromwell, and he was knighted in 1530. In 1531 he published *The Governor*. His father had been dead for some years, and he had married a lady of property, and of tastes like his own, shortly after. His official work left sufficient leisure for a most extensive course of reading both in classical and Italian literature, whilst his circle of learned acquaintances, which included everyone of distinction who came to England from the Continent, stimulated his scholarly interests. In 1531 Elyot left England upon his first diplomatic mission to the Imperial Court. After his return he resumed literary production which chiefly occupied him for the three or four subsequent years. He accompanied Cromwell on his first visitation of religious houses, but went on a further mission to the Emperor in 1536 or 1537, and his remaining years were mainly devoted to authorship and translation. He died at about the age of 56 in March, 1546.

The following list of works written by Elyot will show his keen humanist interests. The *Book of the Governor*, written in 1530–1, was published in 1531 as the outcome of his studies, and of careful observation of the needs of the public life of his time. He dedicated it to the King. The argument of this work is set out in the present chapter. In 1533 he issued a small volume upon "the knowledge which maketh a man wise," a dialogue, and soon afterwards he was engaged on the preparation of a *Latin-English Dictionary*, which "shall not only serve for children, but also shall be commodious" to professional men. This was the first dictionary of its kind published in England, supplementing rather than superseding the short vocabularies prepared for beginners and used in grammar schools. It includes classical words and technical terms of law, medicine, and divinity; it appealed to a wide circle of readers, and formed the basis of subsequent compilations. Elyot had collated with much industry the various "compendia" and "thesauri" (such as Barret's *Alvearie* or *Triple Dictionary*), both of humanist and of classical origin, aiming at the production of a systematic dictionary on the alphabetic plan for the use of English students and men of the learned callings.

The Defence of Good Women (1534) is interesting from the claim in true humanist spirit for the wise training of women in Letters and moral philosophy. Special mention must be made of Elyot's translations from the Greek: *The Image of Governance*, the *Education or bringing up of Children*, and another piece of Plutarch; the *Doctrinal of Princes* "made by that noble Oratour Isocrates," addressed to King Nicoles (1534); the latter of which is an experiment to discover "if our English tongue might receive the quick and proper sentences pronounced by the Greeks"; in other words, an attempt to impart the quality of the Greek style to the English stock. In the *Governor* Elyot had set himself to enlarge the English vocabulary from classical sources; "to augment our English tongue whereby men should as well express more abundantly the thing that they conceived in their hearts, as also interpret out of Greek, Latin and other tongues into English."

There is evidence enough to prove the sincerity and breadth of Elyot's classical reading. He had a first-hand knowledge of Plato, Aristotle, Cicero, Quintilian, and Plutarch. He meets the on-coming tide of the Renaissance with rejoicing, and as a closer acquaintance with his most characteristic book reveals, he is at one with Matteo Palmieri in his larger outlook upon a world inspired and ennobled by the atmosphere of the great past. Like the greater Italians of the Quattrocento he soars above the pedantries and imitations which encumbered the Revival. He is a man of the world, the modern, eager world of Tudor England, claiming for its service the highest thought of antiquity. Elyot dedicated the *Governor* to the King as the first-fruits of his reading. Its object was to instruct men in such virtues as shall be expedient for them, which shall have "authority in a weal public." It is hardly a political treatise; it makes no attempt to set out the methods of government. It is not a sketch of a perfect state, Elyot has always England and Englishmen in his mind; but he undoubtedly has a forward look. He realised, as the need of an age marked by a revolution in political organisation and administration, a sounder concept of training for the sons of the governing class. The ideal of service of the state, lay and civil, was a new one in England, and Elyot saw that it would surely claim its place beside the older ideals of service through arms or "clerkship," and ultimately surpass them in importance, as the ecclesiastical and feudal territorial privileges yielded to the authority of the King's Court.

Italy alone offered examples of such political conditions, the subordination of landed right to new powers, civic, industrial and personal; it was natural, therefore, that from Italy too should come the literary presentation of the modern community, and of the education which should fit its citizens or princes for their share in it. Elyot had read deeply the politico-social writings of the Quattrocento. The *Governor* is clearly suggested by them, and without Palmieri and Patrizi, Æneas Sylvius and Pontano, the book would not have been possible. It is important to name the works which may be properly regarded as the modern sources upon which he relied: the *Vita Civile* of Matteo Palmieri; the treatise *De Regno et Regis Institutione* (1435–1440; printed 1529), and the *De Republica* of Francesco Patrizi, the Sienese (1494); the tracts of Æneas Sylvius, afterwards Pope Pius II, on Education (1451); the *De Principe* of Pontano; to which must be added the histories and political treatises of Macchiavelli and Guicciardini, the *Cortegiano*, published 1528, the *De Liberis Instituendis* of Erasmus (1529), and his *De Principis Institutione* (1516). But it is certain that Elyot, whose indebtedness to these writers it is easy to trace, had read widely in the neo-Latin literature of Italy, particularly in its bearing upon the preparation of youth to fulfil the higher calls of citizenship and public service.   He had from such reading and from experience realised the need of liberal training for all who aspired to share, in whatever capacity, in the administration of affairs.   "Governors" included all lay officers, paid or unpaid, involved in executive or legislative activity: royal secretaries, judges of the King's Court, justices of the peace, sheriffs, even mayors of towns, ambassadors, members of Parliament, clerks of the Exchequer or the Chancery.   For with the revolution which was rapidly substituting what Sir Henry Maine has described as the basis of contract for that of status in English society, and especially in the public service, an entirely new concept of duty was, as Elyot clearly discerned, henceforth indispensable.   And for this the Italian political and educational literature provided him with most fruitful suggestion. Naturally, therefore, he condemns "that pestiferous opinion, that great learned men be inapt to ministration of things of weighty importance"; and, as a typical man of the Revival, he supports this judgment by the instances of Moses, of Alexander, of Scipio, Caesar, Hadrian, of Cato and Cicero, and even of Charles the Great.

He starts with the concept of the community as an unit organised in due order of capacity, functions, and skill, each factor in society existing as an element of an organic whole, obeying a law of proportion based on its relative importance to the State.   The *Republic* has obviously suggested to him this idea of a division of labour, with honour graded according to the nature of the services rendered.   That there must be one sovereign he proves from the examples of Moses and Agamemnon ; from Venice and Ferrara ; from Edgar, King of England, under whom prosperity and security notably advanced. Democratic Athens is a standing warning ; Rome also was forced to rely upon Dictators and Emperors.

In the second chapter he proposes the necessary enquiry, which was antecedent to all larger questions of the conditions of public well-being: viz., "the best form of education or bringing up of noble children from their nativity in such manner as they may be found worthy and also able to be Governors of a public weal." Elyot expressly disclaims the idea of debarring men of humble origin from affairs, but his scheme of training demanded a certain standing of wealth and refinement in the home, and parents capable of taking large views. Further, he held that integrity in administration would be better secured if the holders of office were removed by their position from the temptation of illicit gains.

When Elyot turns to the course of education which he desires to lay down he begins, like most humanists, with the stages of infancy. The nurse must be carefully sought for and her physical and moral fitness duly assured. Her one function is the nourishing of the child; all that concerns bringing up is entrusted to a governess who is in control. No men except the physician are to be allowed within the nursery. From Plutarch, Quintilian and Erasmus, whose tract on the *Duties of the Married State* was certainly familiar to Elyot, he has learnt the importance of the instinct of imitation. For good and for evil a young child learns by imitation. "And incontinent as soon as they can speak it behoveth with most pleasant allurings to instil into them sweet manners and virtuous customs," to provide right companions, and to repress flattery.

"Some old authors hold opinion that before the age of seven years a child should not be instructed in Letters; but those writers were either Greeks or Latins, among whom all doctrines and sciences were in their maternal tongues; by reason whereof they saved all that long time which at this day is spent in understanding perfectly the Greek and Latin.... Therefore that infelicity of our time and country compelleth us to encroach somewhat upon the years of children, and especially of noblemen, that they may sooner attain to wisdom and gravity than private persons, considering, as I have said, their charge and example which above all things is most to be esteemed. Notwithstanding, I would not have them enforced by violence to learn, but according to the counsel of Quintilian to be sweetly allured thereto with praises and such pretty gifts as children delight in. And their first letters to be painted or limned in a pleasant manner: wherein children of gentle courage have much delectation. And also there is no better allective to noble arts than to induce them into a contention with their inferior companions: they sometime purposely suffering the more noble children to vanquish, and, as it were, giving to them place and sovereignity, though indeed the inferior children have more learning.

"But there can be nothing more convenient than by little and little to train and exercise them in speaking of Latin: informing them to know first the names of all things that come in sight, and to name all the parts of their bodies: and giving them somewhat that they covet or desire, in most gentle manner to teach them to ask it again in Latin....And, as touching grammar, there is at this day better introductions and more facile than ever before were made, concerning as well Greek as Latin, if they be wisely chosen.

"And it shall be no reproach to a nobleman to instruct his own children or at the least ways to examine them, by the way of dalliance or solace, considering that the Emperor Octavius Augustus disdained not to read the works of Cicero and Vergil to his children and nephews. And why should not noblemen rather so do, than teach their children how at dice and cards they may cunningly lose and consume their own treasure and substance?...But to return to my purpose, it shall be expedient that a nobleman's son in his infancy have with him continually only such as may accustom him by little and little to speak pure and elegant Latin. Semblably the nurses and other women about him, if it be possible, to do the same, or at the least way, that they speak none English but that which is clean, polite, perfectly and articulately pronounced, omitting no letter or syllable, as foolish women oftentimes do of a wantonness, whereby divers noblemen's and gentlemen's children (as I do at this day know) have attained corrupt and foul pronunciation."

"This industry used in forming little infants, who shall doubt but that they (not lacking natural wit) shall be apt to receive learning when they come to more years?...And in this wise may they be instructed without any violence or enforcing: using the more part of the time until they come to the age of seven years in such disports as do appertaine to children wherein is no resemblance or similitude of vice."

Elyot here enforces three of the more important points in the training of young children upon which Erasmus had laid stress: and no doubt the English writer had studied carefully the *De Pueris* (1529) as he planned his own work. These are (*a*) the necessity of careful attention to the habit of clear and refined speech in childhood, (*b*) the principle of instruction by methods of play in the first stages of teaching, (*c*) the value of the conversational method in learning an unknown language, in this case Latin. It is by comparing the positions advanced by Elyot with the teaching of Erasmus on early education that the statement that "Elyot interpreted Erasmus for England" carries full conviction. The same relation of the two writers is no less clear in the section which follows. "After that a child is come to seven years of age, I hold it expedient that he be taken from the company of women." This was the common opinion of the humanist, based, in the case of Elyot, upon a distrust of the companionship of serving-women, and even of the mother, seeing that the sterner side of character needs to be encouraged in the growing boy. For such reasons the most sure counsel is to withdraw him from all company of women and "to assign unto him a tutor, which should be an ancient and worshipful man," winning the boy by his gravity of temper combined with gentleness, and "such a one that the child by imitation following may grow to be excellent. And if he be also learned he is the more commendable." The essential quality of the tutor, therefore, is moral excellence. The office of a tutor, thus qualified, is, first, to know the nature of his pupil, "that is to say, whereto he is most inclined or disposed and in what thing he setteth his most delectation or appetite. If he be of nature courteous, piteous, and of a free and liberal heart, it is a principal token of grace, as it is by all Scripture determined. Then shall a wise tutor...declare to him what honour, what love, what commodity shall happen to him by these virtues. And if any be of disposition contrary, then to express the enormities of their vice, with as much detestation as may be."

Elyot adopts the Erasmian, and northern, idea of the necessity of a tutor to a well-born boy. No doubt the contrast to the Italian practice of school or joint instruction is due to the difference between the social custom of the two countries. In England and Germany the upper class was essentially a country class; in Italy the men of wealth and status craved for the society and comfort of a city. Moreover, social intercourse with equals and inferiors was in Italy a fine art, and fitness for it was to be cultivated as an educational end in itself. Hence the popularity of such a school as that of Mantua. Further, in England the passion for out-door pastimes and the quasi-feudal status of the landowner made country life the one acceptable alternative to a training at court. Later on in the century Roger Ascham could regard education from the point of view of the school. By that time the Elizabethan Court had popularised the "Town" as the centre of society; and, what is not of less importance, travelling in England was an easier matter, so that great boarding- and day-schools, such as Eton and Westminster, drew the youth of family; and others served local areas. Shrewsbury, which was Philip Sidney's school, served the Welsh March. Certain boys, no doubt, took their tutors with them to public school, and lodged with them in the town. That the actual instruction received by the method of home teaching was often better adjusted, more varied, more liberalising and more humane, than the ordinary schooling we may, with Locke, readily admit. For it was not until the following century that schools were called into existence in northern Europe to provide that combination of courtly training and liberal teaching which had been exemplified at Mantua.

Elyot regards as the test of the tutor's skill "that he suffer not the child to be fatigate with continual study or learning, wherewith the delicate and tender wit may be dulled or oppressed; but that there may be therewith interlaced and mixed some pleasant learning and exercise, as playing on instruments of music, which, moderately used, and without diminution of honour, that is to say, without wanton countenance and dissolute gesture, is not to be contemned." It is worth noting that Elyot realises better than Erasmus the effort involved in a hard literary and linguistic course for a boy, and the difficulty of retaining prolonged interest in the exclusive study of the rudiments of dead languages. It is apparently from this point of view that he includes music as a recreation and not as a systematic study. "The most noble and valiant princes of Greece often-times, to recreate their spirits and in augmenting their courage, embraced instruments musical." Achilles, Cheiron, King David are quoted in illustration. "But I would not be thought to allure noblemen to have so much delectation therein that in playing and singing only they should put their whole study and felicity, as did the Emperor Nero."... The "virtuoso" does not attract Elyot, to whom all liberal arts are but the preparation for social duty. "It were therefore better that no music were taught to a nobleman than that by the exact knowledge thereof he should have therein inordinate delight," and so be led to neglect the necessary duty he owes to the community. "King Philip, when he heard that his son Alexander did sing sweetly and properly, he rebuked him gently, saying, 'But, Alexander, be ye not ashamed that ye can sing so well and cunningly?'; whereby he meant that the open profession of that craft was but of base estimation." The use of music is for "the refreshing of wit," and as such is commendable.   The tutor will rebuke excessive devotion to it. Yet Elyot has gained from the Greeks an inkling of the higher function of rhythm.   "Yet notwithstanding he shall commend the perfect *understanding* of music, declaring how necessary it is for the better attaining of the knowledge of a public weal, which, as I have said, is made of an order of estates and degrees, and by reason thereof containeth in it a perfect harmony, which he shall afterward more perfectly understand when he shall happen to read the books of Plato and Aristotle of public weals, wherein be written divers examples of music and geometry.   In this form may a wise and circumspect tutor adapt the pleasant science of music to a necessary and laudable purpose."   This is far from definite, no doubt, but it carries us on to ground to which Erasmus was a stranger, but which is common to Alberti, Agricola, Pico and Sadoleto.

"If the child be of nature inclined (as many have been) to paint with a pen, or to form images in stone or tree, he should not be therefrom withdrawn or nature be rebuked which is to him benevolent; but, putting one to him which is in that craft wherein he delighteth most excellent, in vacant times from other more serious learning, he should be in the most pure wise instructed in painting or carving."   The claims of Fine Art rest on a more secure basis than those of musical skill. Elyot feels that he must defend his position.   Naturally he turns first to "ancient and excellent princes," Claudius, Titus, or Hadrian, who were educated in painting, drawing and sculpture.   The direct advantages to captains in the field of a knowledge of drawing are obvious; such are the devising and improving of engines of war, the making of strategical maps, the noting of tactical positions and the lines of fortification. In the planning of houses, in mensuration, in the making of charts and maps, every man of position will find the same art necessary.   Particularly, in illustration of history or travel, "I dare affirm a man shall more profit in one week by figures and charts, well and perfectly made, than he shall by the only reading or hearing the rules of that science by the space of half a year at least." Pictorial illustrations of historical narratives are of great aid to imagination. Elyot must have often had in his hands the Venetian illustrated editions of Livy, the great chronicle of Philippus Bergomensis, the Nuremberg chronicle and the Mallermi Bible, Valturius on the Art of War—the outstanding illustrated history books of his age. But such instruction is not for all. For "mine intent and meaning is only that a noble child may be induced to receive perfect instruction in these sciences." Yet although as boyhood advances literature claims all available time, yet the manual skill and artistic and musical feeling thus early encouraged will survive and become valued factors in the personality of the grown man. For the "exquisite knowledge and understanding that he hath in those sciences hath impressed in his ears and eyes an exact and perfect judgment in respect of appreciation of beauty to the use of leisure and technical application." Elyot perceives also that the arts have been unduly depreciated by Englishmen as unpractical. But he holds that much native talent has been thereby repressed to the national loss. So far the recreative Arts.

When he comes to lay down the curriculum of instruction to be followed by the tutor, Elyot requires that refined utterance and a knowledge of the parts of speech in his own language, at or before the age of seven, shall be already secured: the power of speaking Latin in actual practice is hardly to be looked for. Rapid progress may be expected if the tutor understands how to stimulate ambition and the desire to excel. The ancient world provides examples, in Aristotle, Antoninus, Trajan. Of the latter he expressly says, not knowing that the fact on which he relies is a late invention: "What caused Trajan to be so good a prince...but that he happened to have Plutarch, the noble philosopher, to be his instructor? I agree that some be good of natural inclination to goodness: but where good instruction and example is thereto added the natural goodness must therewith needs be amended and be more excellent." This doctrine, that a literary education can do all things, affirms the standing conviction of the confirmed humanist. But it must be remembered that Elyot postulated for his pupil the finest moral environment even more urgently than the skill and wisdom of the tutor. The educational process, as he states it, was continuous, insistent, and rested on the principle of imitation, example and personal stimulus and not on the imparting of knowledge.

In the tenth chapter he treats of the "order of learning apt for a gentleman" which is to be followed from the time when systematic instruction is entered upon. "I am of the opinion of Quintilian that I would have him learn Greek and Latin authors both at one time; or else begin with Greek....And if a child do begin therein at seven years of age he may continually learn Greek authors three years, and in the meantime use the Latin tongue as a familiar language: which in a nobleman's son may well come to pass, having none other persons to serve him or keeping him company but such as can speak Latin elegantly. And what doubt is there that so may he as soon speak good Latin as he may do pure French?" Not being himself a teacher he offers no advice as to choice of a Greek grammar, but "alway I would advise him not to detain the child too long in that tedious labours either in Greek or Latin grammar. For a gentle wit is therewith soon fatigate. Grammar being but an introduction to the understanding of authors, if it be made too long or exquisite (i.e. elaborate) to the learner it in a manner mortifieth his courage. And by that time he come to the most sweet and pleasant reading of old authors the sparkes of fervent desire of learning is extinct with the burden of grammar."

This passage carries us back directly to Erasmus. The dependence upon Quintilian is exactly paralleled in the *De Ratione Studii*. The conversational use of Latin, the simultaneous study of Latin and Greek, and in especial the gradual introduction of accidence and syntax, as the pupil's need develops with the reading of texts—all is Erasmian. Elyot's belief that pure Latin may be acquired in a properly ordered home reminds us of Montaigne's experience a little later: for when he went to school at Bordeaux at the age of six he could speak only Latin, his father having insisted that the servants and the very labourers on the estate should acquire a Latin vocabulary. Palmieri on the other hand, as has been said, and the Italians generally, felt the unreality of such attempts. The adjustment of grammatical teaching which Elyot advocates was the regular humanist practice—down to the latter half of the sixteenth century.

The beginnings of Greek (begun, as he says, immediately) are made through Aesop, whose *Fables* are to be read to the pupil by the tutor. Their vocabulary is instructive, the sense easily grasped, and they possess "much moral and politic wisdom." This regard for edification in choice of authors is but one aspect of the general humanist view that classical writers are to be used always for subject-matter as well as practice in the actual language. The text will be learnt by heart as an aid to vocabulary and power in sentence structure. Aesop will be followed by "quick and merry dialogues" from Lucian. Aristophanes, being in metre, may be perhaps more quickly learnt by heart, and so may be substituted for Lucian. Aristophanes at this period held the place in classical education which Euripides was to assume a couple of centuries later. The ground of choice lay no doubt in the light thrown by his comedies upon Attic life and opinion.

Homer comes next: "from whom as from a fountain proceedeth all eloquence and learning. For in his books be contained and most perfectly expressed not only the documents martial and discipline of arms, but also incomparable wisdoms and instructions for politic governance of people." Alexander the Great is referred to as an illustration of the stimulating force of a study of Homer, since therefrom "he gathered courage and strength against his enemies, wisdom and eloquence for consultations and persuasions to his people and army." There is no instruction to be compared with that which may be enforced from Homer "if he be plainly and substantially expounded and declared by the master." So far the Greek writers. The stress laid upon their content, especially their moral purport, must be carefully noticed.

In deciding upon Latin authors, Homer suggests the poet Vergil as parallel reading. The *Aeneid* will be found attractive by its theme ; and the *Eclogues* and *Georgics* hardly less so. The teacher will contrast the *Odyssey*, whose salient purpose is to commend prudence and endurance, with the feats of romance and the marvels of the *Aeneid*. The *Fasti* and *Metamorphoses* of Ovid will claim a moderate amount of time, as will the learned and sententious Horace. Associated with such construing, verse composition is to be taught, using Homer and Vergil as models, since such exercises afford "much pleasure and courage to study."

This course of reading, with work in grammar and prosody, duly adapted, is to be covered by the end of the thirteenth year. It will be noted that the authors are exclusively chosen from the poets. Elyot thinks the classical poets easier and more attractive reading than prose writers, in that they make no demand for sustained judgment or reasoning as does a political oration or historical narrative. He rightly argues that poetry is the language of childhood, both of the race and of the individual ; "poetry was the first philosophy that ever was known, and through it children have always gained their first lessons in right conduct," "learning thereby not only manners and natural affections but also the wonderful works of nature, mixing serious matter with things that are pleasant." He takes occasion to protest against the "false opinion that now reigneth" that poets are but a tissue of lies and impurity. He adds as a final qualification that it "should be remembered that I require not all these works should be *thoroughly read* of a child in this time, which were almost impossible," but the purpose of such reading is to be kept in view, viz., that " of inflaming the courage of the child to attempt the imitation of great deeds." " I only desire that they (the pupils) have in every of the said books so much instruction that they may take thereby some profit."

Elyot, it is clear, regards instruction in the classics as the teaching of literature, which will be read for enjoyment. He has the humanist view of poetry as a delight. The teacher will strive to imbue the scholar with a feeling for style and rhythm, will keep grammar at arm's length, and pursue analysis or criticism only to the point where it aids enjoyment of the text. In his view the poets thus taught are easy, in that their work is pictorial and romantic and carries its intelligible moral.

The second stage of instruction is, in its turn, almost exclusively concerned with classical prose, under the heads of oratory, history, and cosmography. As an introduction to oratory the *Topica* of Cicero, or the *De Inventione Dialectica* of Rudolph Agricola will be studied. Logic is thus, in accordance with humanist judgment, reduced to its function of aiding exposition. Beyond this, Elyot has nothing to say of the claims of logic as a subject of education, following Erasmus rather than Melanchthon, and in accord generally with the practice of English schools which relegated logic to the university.

The boy of fourteen is taken straight to the orators and the writers on rhetoric : Hermogenes, a Greek rhetorician of the second century A.D., and Quintilian—" beginning at the third Book and instructing the child diligently in that part of rhetoric, principally, which concerneth persuasion for as much as it is most apt for consultations." Elyot has in view the preparation of the pupil in the art of speaking, whether deliberative or judicial. Although he uses as illustration " a great audience," or the conduct of an embassy, none the less the argument applies to duties of a much humbler type, such as pleading before a court, or the deliverances of a local magistrate. Then "a man shall not be constrained to speak words sudden and disordered but shall bestow them aptly in their places." The treatises will be read along with select orations of Cicero, Isocrates and Demosthenes as the models of logical exposition and choice diction. But as a working manual of composition he expressly commends the *De Copia* of Erasmus, "whom all gentle wits are bound to thank and support." Beyond this no allusion is made to practice in epistolary or narrative styles, though Elyot expresses contempt for the mere skill in writing grandiose adulatory letters. The reference which Elyot makes in the quotations given above is further evidence that the ultimate aim of the rhetorical training through Greek and Latin was in reality the perfecting of a man's vernacular style. Even Erasmus, though perhaps grudgingly, would not have denied this. To the humanist Reformers in Germany the strengthening of the influence of the pulpit was a leading motive of classical education, just as the Italian of the Quattrocento— a purist here and there notwithstanding—found that in respect of precision, amplitude, and grace, his power in the Tuscan speech was deeply in debt to the discipline of Latin rhetoric.

Again, Elyot is in full accord with the higher view of "eloquentia" which the humanists, as has been shown, borrowed from Cicero and Quintilian. Rhetorical skill is only one part of true eloquence (Cicero, *De Orat.* 1. 12). "A true Oratore may not be without much better furniture: to him belongeth the explicating or unfolding of sense" (i.e. *sententiae*). His function also is to give counsel, to stir and quicken the despairing, to bridle the impulses of the rash. "He must have gotten the knowledge of all things and arts of greatest importance....In an Orator is required to be a heap of all manner of learning, the world of science, or the circle of doctrine, which is in one word of Greek 'encyclopaedia.'" They that know only the art of rhetoric should be called only rhetoricians or "artificial speakers" rather than orators; the difference is similar to that between versifier and poet. "Only to possess language is to be a popinjay"; the writing of mere elegant epistles is to utter trumpet sounds of no purpose or meaning. Skill in such an art is to be scorned. Underlying all this is the essential concept of the humanism of the best age that the ancient tongues are the key to the only sound available erudition, and that erudition is only of worth to the world when logically exhibited and expressed in language strictly apt and consonant with its purport. The truth of the intimate harmony of style and content is manifested exclusively in the great writers of antiquity, and only by such as had first mastered the secret of classic purity could a corresponding harmony be attained in modern speech. That would appear to be the relation of ancient and modern Letters as interpreted by the finer spirit of humanism whether in Italy or in England, and perhaps especially in France.

Passing next to Cosmography, Elyot urges the study of geography in its relation to history. "To prepare the child to understanding of histories, which being replenished with names of countries and towns unknown to the reader, do make the history tedious or else the less pleasant, so if they be in any wise known, it increaseth an inexplicable delectation....There is none so good learning as the demonstration of cosmography by material figures and instruments....For what pleasure is it, in one hour to behold these realms, cities, seas, rivers, and mountains that scarcely in an old man's life cannot be journeyed and pursued : what incredible delight is taken in beholding the diversities of people, beasts, fowls, fishes, trees, fruits and herbs : to know the sundry manners and conditions of people and the variety of their natures, and that in a warm study or parlour, without peril of the sea or danger of long and painful journeys....The commoditie thereof knew the great King Alexander, for he caused the countries whereunto he purposed any enterprise diligently and cunningly to be described and painted, that beholding the picture he might perceive which places are most dangerous and where he and his host might have most easy and convenable passage." On the other hand Cyrus and Crassus are instances of captains who came to destruction through ignorance of strategical geography. The authors to be read are Strabo, Solinus, "who is marvellous delectable," Pomponius Mela and Dionysius. It is to be noted that the substance of geography lies in the writers of the Imperial age, for Elyot doubts the value of contemporary or mediaeval books of travel; further, that geography claims a place in liberal education almost entirely on ground of its utility in historical reading. "Cosmography being substantially perceived it is then time to induce a child to the reading of histories." The special importance of history to princes and statesmen is proved from Isocrates, Plutarch and Cicero. Livy is chosen as preferable to Sallust for beginners, on Quintilian's advice, for from Livy, a master of the elegant, flowing style, the pupil will learn "how the most noble city of Rome, of a small and poor beginning, by prowess and virtue little by little came to the empire and dominion of all the world." Next to Livy in interest stands Xenophon, then the career of Alexander as set out by Quintus Curtius. Caesar and Sallust demand for their understanding "an exact and perfect judgment," and need very careful explanations, with much more knowledge of war and of geography on the part of the reader. But when studied from the standpoint of experience these historians are most informing, both to statesman and soldier. Elyot's view of Caesar's works is only now becoming accepted. The work on the wars in Gaul is "studiously to be read of the princes of this realm of England and their Counsellors, considering that thereof may be taken necessary instructions concerning the wars against Irishmen or Scots, who be of the same rudeness and wild disposition that the Swiss and Britons were in the time of Caesar." The rhetorical artifice of ancient historians appeals to Elyot, both as humanist and statesman. "Also there be divers orations, as well in all the books of the said authors as in the history of Cornelius Tacitus, which be very delectable and for counsel very expedient to be had in memory."

The general aim of historical reading is thus set out. "A young gentleman shall be taught to note and mark not only the order and elegance in declaration of the history, but also the occasion of the wars, the counsels and preparation on either part," forming a judgment on the military skill exhibited. Next, apart from war, he will ponder "the estate of the public weal if it be prosperous or in decay, what is the very occasion of the one or the other, the form and manner of the governance thereof, the good and evil qualities of them that be rulers, the commodities and good sequel of virtue, the discommodities and evil conclusion of vicious licence." Four points are here disclosed: the style of the historian, the lessons of the military events described, the causes of growth and decline in states, the political skill and moral worth of rulers, with the effects of these upon national well-being. The objection has to be met that history is sometimes "interlaced" with myth and false tradition. Elyot's answer is that the educational value of such aspects of the subject is different indeed but yet substantial. For as the moral import of history is one of its main claims to the teacher's regard, "true" things are not exclusively things that have actually occurred. "If by reading the sage counsel of Nestor, the subtle persuasions of Ulysses, the compendious gravity of Menelaus, the imperial majesty of Agamemnon, the prowess of Achilles, the valiant courage of Hector, we may apprehend anything whereby our wits may be amended and our personages be more apt to serve our public weal and our prince, what forceth it us though Homer write leasings?" No writers are so full of instruction as historians, their theme being, as it were, the mirror of man's life, expressing the attraction of virtue, and the deformity and loathliness of vice. History is thus a compendious record of military, political, and moral wisdom.

This is a more intelligent view of the educational view of

history than that usual even in the better schools of the Renaissance, where history was mainly confined to edifying biographies. "Surely if a nobleman do thus seriously and diligently read histories, I dare affirm there is no study or science for him of equal commodity or pleasure having regard to every time and age." It is noteworthy that here again no reference is made to mediaeval or modern history as a subject for instruction. The reasons are obvious: no vernacular writer outside of Italy had sufficient claims on score of style, or of arrangement, or of "sentence," i.e. the art of generalisation and of presenting moral conclusions. A student rightly trained in the finished literary histories could afterwards, as need arose, turn to the annalists and chronicles of his own or other countries for such moderate advantages as could be got from them. Elyot had no doubt lately read Lord Berners' preface to his version of Froissart (1523) which sets out much in the same vein the merits of historical study. "The most profytable thyng in this worlde for the instytution (i.e. training) of the humayne lyfe is historie." For through its study young men gain vast experience of affairs, be trained for governance, be stimulated to high deeds, in the field or in the council room, be put in fear of acts reprovable; nay, further, "by the benefite of historie all noble, high and virtuous actes be immortall."

The boy is now presumed to have completed his seventeenth year, and with it the second stage of his literary education, which, as Elyot expounds it, revolves round the arts of exposition and oratory in Latin, geography and history, military and political. The third stage, upon which he next enters, is occupied mainly with philosophy. "By the time that the child do come to seventeen years of age, to the intent his courage be bridled with reason, it were needful to read unto him some works of philosophy, specially that part which may inform him unto virtuous manners, which part of philosophy is called moral." The choice of the *Ethics* I and II of Aristotle, in Greek, as advised by Elyot, seems of doubtful wisdom.

Next may follow the *De Officiis* of Cicero ; then Plato, "when the judgment of a man is come to perfection." For in this philosopher and in Cicero are joined "gravity and delectation," "excellent wisdom with divine eloquence," and "every place is so infarced with profitable counsel, joined with honesty, that those three books" (no specific dialogue of Plato is indicated) "be almost sufficient to make a perfect and excellent Governor." Elyot further advises the *Proverbs* of Solomon, *Ecclesiastes*, and *Ecclesiasticus*, and all the historical books, including the Prophets, of the Old Testament. But the New Testament is to be reverently touched as a celestial jewel or relique, not to be handled by common wits or interpreted by canons of secular knowledge. The treatment of moral duties upon the authority of classical rather than New Testament writings, on the ground that the latter were within the exclusive province of the clergy, was common in humanist practice. In conclusion he expressly commends "the little book of the most excellent Doctor Erasmus" dedicated to Charles V when Prince of Castile, entitled the *Institution of a Christian Prince*, "which should be familiar to men of station as Homer was to Alexander, or Xenophon to Scipio, for there was never book written in Latin that in so little a portion contained of sentence (i.e. principles), eloquence, and virtuous exhortation, a more compendious abundance."

Elyot then propounds the fundamental principle of humanist education, illustrating it from his own profession. "I think verily if children were brought up as I have written, and continually were retained in the right study of very philosophy until they passed the age of twenty-one years and then set to the laws of this realm...undoubtedly they should become men of so excellent wisdom that throughout all the world should be found in no common weal more noble counsellors." He finds the same true of medicine, having no doubt Linacre in remembrance. The doctrine that the liberal arts underlie the higher professional disciplines was rejected by the "practical mind," and Elyot laments the habit of putting promising youths prematurely to study law or to Court service, or the life of the manor house. The second and third stages of education, covering the years from fourteen to twenty-one, he finds mostly ignored, and a small facility in reading Latin accepted as adequate proof of fitness for a career, whereas it is but a basis for the actual edifice of learning. A youth of fourteen finds law, for example, intolerable ; he throws it up, and with it all intellectual interest whatsoever. Further, it is the sore complaint that "school-masters decay," the profession of teacher passing into incompetent hands. The reason is partly, no doubt, that the pay is small, the social esteem low; but beyond these is the discouragement caused by the too early removal of promising boys into active life. "Lord God," says Elyot, "how many good and clean wits of children be now-a-days perished by ignorant school-masters !"

What Elyot required of the school-master may be gathered from this review of the curriculum he proposes. He sums up the qualifications, in a passage modelled on Quintilian, repeating in substance those laid down by Erasmus in the *De Ratione Studii.* The man of high character and wide learning, skilled in *speaking,* was the "orator"; write skilled in *teaching,* and we have the school-master as the humanist conceived him. That masters were harsh, often failed to teach anything, or, being ignorant and indifferent themselves, failed to stimulate, was Elyot's standing complaint as it was that of Erasmus. Both alike point to lack of interest in learning on the part of public opinion as the root cause of the unwillingness to pay for its teaching. The chief offenders were the country gentry who lay outside Court influences, and upon these Elyot pours out his contempt in terms identical with those used by Erasmus. Colet, perhaps first in England, realised the need of erecting teaching into a profession, but as yet the concept of an education which should dignify leisure as well as improve capacity had but begun to establish itself in a country socially and economically so backward as Britain.

Upon exercises meet for gentlemen Elyot has much to say. There is nothing original in his enumeration of games and sports which he commends, and which are without exception drawn from current English practice. But he brings them within the circle of the humanist training by his insistence on the classical precedent by which they may be supported. He begins by claiming as the general end bodily health and fitness for study. Wherefore in the education of children, specially from the age of fourteen upwards, he will have exercises carefully prescribed; such as are "apt to the furniture of a gentleman's personage, adapting his body to hardiness, strength and agility, and to help therewith himself in peril." Galen is much relied upon, but apart from him Elyot had studied, and, later on, wrote a treatise upon, the laws of health. Wrestling, a typical English sport, heads the list; running is defended from Epaminondas, or Achilles; swimming, popular with the Romans, is useful in certain dangers, as Horatius and Caesar found. Hunting is illustrated from Xenophon's *Cyropaedeia*. The Greeks—Theseus and Alexander—hunted the lion, leopard or bear; Pompey chased wild game in Africa. In England a man is content with red deer, the fox or the hare. Hawking is not one of the nobler sports, but is good for appetite. Riding "on a great horse and a rough," with or without exercises of battle-axe or lance, is a necessary accomplishment. The long-bow is most commendable of all sports, first for its utility in national defence, archery being pre-eminently an English pursuit, and secondly as pastime and solace. It "appertaineth as well to princes and noblemen as to all others, by their example, which determine to pass forth their lives in virtue and honesty." The national obligation for defence falls upon all classes alike.

It is natural that Elyot should enquire in what consists the status of that nobility to which he has repeatedly to refer.

The essence of his conclusion is that true nobility is constituted of personal merit. But, undeniably, inherited repute, title, lands, position, are accounted nobility also. Where, however, the two are united there is conspicuous distinction. Elyot (and his master Wolsey even more markedly), as an example of the new governing class, was eager to prove how right training may provide the state with trusted servants. The sentiment was an obvious one in the humanist, most of all no doubt in Italy, where personal distinction found its fullest opportunity. The "Governor" was the English aspect of the ideal Italian "Courtier." It is the motive of Erasmus' tract on the up-bringing of a Prince. This doctrine Elyot will enforce through instruction. "Let young gentlemen have oftentimes told to them how Numa Pompilius was taken from his husbandry and made king of the Romans by election of the people. What caused it, suppose you, but his wisdom and virtue, which in him were very nobility, and that nobility brought him to dignity?" Now knowledge makes men apt to virtue, as Erasmus had always urged; hence the supreme worth of knowledge to one who aspires to the truest nobility which includes birth, capacity and high character. The ideal of personality, as Elyot understands it, finds its practical expression in "Prudentia," or "Sapience," which is a mental quality, compact of "natura," "scientia" and "virtus," applied to practical affairs. Rome was built up by this quality of Sapience in her citizens. This "wisdom," as distinct from "doctrine," is the flower of true education, as Elyot sees the problem in the light of the needs of England.

Amongst minor recreations Elyot advises chess, "for therein is a right subtle engine whereby the wit is made to move sharp and remembrance quickened"; cards he barely tolerates, unless games may be devised in them of moral instruction. Dice he treats as the great peril of youth and manhood.

In an interesting chapter Elyot allows dancing to be of "excellent utility, comprehending in it wonderful figures, or, as the Greeks do call them, Ideas, of virtues and noble qualities," in particular that of prudence by which he means the "knowledge of things which ought to be desired and of them that ought to be eschewed"; "and by cause that the study of virtue is tedious for the more part to them that do flourish in young years," he expounds a method by which those who join in, or even watch, rightly ordered dancing may be aroused to the understanding and the pursuit of this notable quality of prudence. This ingenious argument turns partly upon the relation between the rhythmic and harmonious movement of the body and the law of proportion and temperance in the sphere of emotion and conduct; so far it is entirely Greek in spirit. Partly, again, the dance which he describes is by way of an allegory of the complementary qualities of man and woman, or of reverence, or of deliberation, and so on. This bears again every mark of its Italian origin. The interest of Elyot's position lies, first, in his intuition of that antique feeling for rhythm which marked Alberti or Agricola, and, next, in that new sense of personality which *Il Cortegiano*, known already to Elyot, was destined to graft upon English society at large. And in this connection it is pertinent to observe how high a place he accords to the virtue of magnanimity (the Aristotelian μεγαλοψυχία), the just consciousness of distinction, which in its form of *virtù* was the peculiar characteristic of the Italian moral type. From the Italy of the Renaissance Elyot drew also his conviction of the fitness of women for letters, and their rightful claim to real education as a preparation for worthy married life.

Like Palmieri and Erasmus, Elyot asks what it is that hinders the modern world from attaining the virtues and the learning of the ancient time. The Englishman finds the explanation primarily in the pride, avarice and negligence of parents, and secondly in the lack of masters. By pride he means the contempt for learning openly expressed by men of estate. "It is a notable reproach to be well learned"; "the name of 'clerk' is held in base estimation." Yet such scorners should remember Henry I of England, Alexander, Hadrian, or Marcus Aurelius, whom even the owner of manors might regard as not unworthy of his esteem.   This is not the answer of Palmieri; for Elyot is confronted by the special obstacle which feudal society, based on land ownership, raised in northern Europe against all ideals dissociated from arms and property.   Erasmus found the same difficulty in dealing with the landed class in Germany.   As regards avarice Elyot instances the parsimony of the gentry in paying their tutors, and their indifference to all qualifications except cheapness.   If it be the case of a new cook or falconer no trouble is too great. Negligence is that unwillingness to continue boys' education beyond the age of fourteen.   Such a state of public opinion needs radical amendment.   To effect this is the purport of *The Governor*.   For in the new age the future of English prosperity depended on the intelligence which could be brought to bear by all who were in a position of responsibility upon the social and political problems involved in the great changes in progress abroad and at home.   Elyot realised, though, of course, imperfectly, that England had entered upon a higher stage of development, that a new governing class, a lay, professional class, was being called into existence, and that for it a freshly devised equipment was essential.   That, following the example of Italy, he found in an enlightened adaptation of antique training.   So he concludes his work with a confident appeal: "Now all ye readers that desire to have your children to be governors, or in any other authority, in the public weal of your country, if ye bring them up and instruct them in such form as in this book is declared, they shall then seem to all men worthy to be in authority, honour and *noblesse*, and all that is under their governance shall prosper and come to perfection."

II.

THE INSTITUCION OF A GENTLEMAN AND QUEENE ELIZABETHES ACHADEMY.

In considering the work done by Sir Thomas Elyot in the furtherance of higher education in England we saw that, amongst the many sources of which he availed himself, were the *Vita Civile* of Palmieri and *Il Cortegiano*. Both lent themselves to his special thesis, the training of youth for service of the State. Roger Ascham published some forty years later his chief work, *The Scholemaster*, which had in effect the same object. When he wrote, the *Courtier* had been for some ten years in circulation in English dress. His judgment of Castiglione's book is well known. "To join learning with comely exercises, Conte Baldassare Castiglione, in his book *Cortegiano*, doth trimly teach: which book advisedly read and diligently followed, but one year at home in England, would do a young gentleman more good, I wist, than three years' travel abroad spent in Italy. And I marvel this book is not more read in the Court than it is, seeing that it is translated into English by a worthy gentleman (Sir Th. Hoby) who was many ways well furnished with learning, and very expert in knowledge of divers tongues" (p. 119). But although a book of too grave and lofty import for the vulgar, Protestant society as represented by such names as Cheke, Gilbert, and Sidney, was already coming to accept the *Courtier*. It is certain that ladies conned it reverently, not less than Philip Sidney, "who carried it ever in his pocket when he went abroad."

In the present chapter it is proposed to treat of three less known works which throw light upon the new educational aims which, deeply influenced by the *Courtier* and cognate books of Italian origin, manifested themselves in the latter half of the sixteenth century in England. They all present one common characteristic, that of public service as the end of gentle upbringing, whether such duties fall to the simple country gentleman, or such as pertain to high office in the royal Court. In the last quarter of the century a tendency is observed in France and Germany, even more than in this country, to the organisation of schools, or "academies," of a type to meet the needs of the landed class which the public and grammar schools failed to supply, schools in which arms, manly exercises, Latin, modern languages (French, Spanish, Italian), practical mathematics, and natural philosophy should form the curriculum. Sir Humphrey Gilbert was the first to sketch the basis of a new education upon these lines. Although it remained but a sketch it is of great interest as showing the drift of opinion. An ideal training framed to meet a similar demand is offered in Milton's *Tractate on Education*. The definition of a liberal education therein contained might well have been accepted by Castiglione. The three books referred to are the *Institution of a Gentleman* (1555) by an unknown author, addressed to Lord Fitzwater, afterwards Earl of Sussex; Sir Humphrey Gilbert's *Queen Elizabeth's Academy* (1572), and Cleveland's *Institution of a Nobleman*, published in 1607, but representing, as the author states, convictions formed from long experience.

The theme of the *Institution* (*institutio* = education) *of a Gentleman* is, shortly, that no man may be "gentle" without personal excellence. It follows naturally that such excellence is to be looked for as the fruit of proper education. Now the function of the gentleman is to lead; his excellence then will be proved by his usefulness in the particular sphere he occupies. The responsibility of the parents is thus not to their children only but to the State, for whose behoof they instruct them.

Parents have four ends to keep in view: to subordinate affection for their children to a right sense of duty towards them ; to teach them the fear of the Lord ; to insist upon filial respect ; to inculcate service as the end of their being. Self-restraint is the prime virtue in youth, in that too much liberty may bring them easily to become " vessels of vice." The writer, "laudator temporis acti," looks back upon a happier age. " To increase virtue by way of knowledge it appeareth that universities and places of study were first founded by nobility, gentle ancestors, our forefathers : whose virtue and wisdom, as they were passing great, so thought they it a meet thing to found places of learning as universities, for their children to be first brought up therein ; and thereby to be made inheritors of greater goods, that is to say riches of the mind, than either landed or worldly possessions can bring with them. To the proof thereof the manners of the Colleges in every University will bear record."

But the common attitude to the gentleman's life is now-a-days this : "What is a man if he know not how to wear his apparel after the best fashion, to keep company with gentlemen, to stake his twenty nobles at cards or dice ? If he be unwilling to do that, he is a lout or a miser, one who knows no fashion. But it becometh a gentleman, they say, to be a roysterer, which word I do not well understand unless it signify a ruffian. If a young gentleman use many vain words then they say that he can *talk well* and hath a good wit, but, if he talk wisely indeed, they say ' *the young fox preacheth.*' If he understand some-what more in learning than they do or get his living by way of writing, then in despite they call him a penman." There is overwhelming evidence that this is a fair representation of the attitude of the landed gentry towards Letters in the first half of the century.

Taking the three types of men by whom in England the term " gentle " might be claimed, he distinguishes them as those who are Gentle gentle, those Gentle ungentle, and those Ungentle gentle. The first are men well-born, gentle by position, and also gentle by personal worth. Such have a gentle heart

to match their "noble condition, and their gentle house."
Herein is the ideal distinction. " This gentleman for the
further ornature and setting forth of his person ought to be
learned, to have knowledge in tongues, and to be apt in the
feats of arms for the defence of his country...or at least he
ought to be able to give counsel or advice in matters of wars....
It behoveth, also, such a gentleman to have in him courtly
behaviour, to know how to treat and entertain men of all
degrees, and not to be ignorant how he himself ought to be
used of others. To such a gentleman, also, some knowledge
in Music, or to know the use of musical instruments, is much
commendable....And to speak in general, a right gentleman
ought to be a man fit for the wars and fit for the peace,
meet for the Court and meet for the country, so may such
a gentleman having in him such properties deserve to be called
gentle gentle, because his conditions and qualities agree with the
nobility of the house whereof he is descended." To illustrate
his case he quotes Julius Caesar, Alexander and Mithridates,
and refers the reader to all ancient histories for other examples :
by the imitating of whom a young man of family may set forth
" the perfect shape of nobility."

" Gentle ungentle is that man which is descended of noble
parentage by the which he is commonly called *Gentle*, and hath
in him such corrupt and ungentle manners as to the judgment
of all men he justly deserveth the name of ungentle." If it be
asked by whose fault a youth of station and opportunity fails to
merit the right title of gentle, the answer is that the parents
and their neglect of training is the cause. The lack of proper
discipline encourages a boy to live as he chooses, not as he
ought ; he has not learnt that distinction comes of personal
worth, not of the accident of birth. Such are "abased gentlemen." The last type is the significant one of the three, to the
defence of which the whole book leads up: the ungentle by
birth who by excellent merit attain the esteem and the title of
gentle, and hand down the same to their children. Such a one

"by his virtue, wit, policy, industry, knowledge in laws, valiance in arms, or such like honest means becometh a well beloved and high esteemed man, preferred then to great office, put in great charge and credit, even so much as he becometh a post or stay of the commonwealth. ...These gentlemen are now called upstarts." But if "upstart" in virtue of gifts of the mind, then is the term a high dignity: for no corporal gifts, such as birth, are equal to distinction of the spirit. The example of Julius Caesar, in whose learning lay the secret of his military success, is alleged in proof.

Yet the new man, if he will "gentle his condition," must be of true worth : there is a class which creeps into honour by sheer riches, or by "certain dark augmentation practices"; such are cunning attorneys, and especially such as have profited by the confiscation of abbey-lands. Many now are ranked with gentry "neither for any virtue, whereof they have small portion, nor for their valiance." Such are truly upstart, for they have risen by no merit of worthiness.

The training of the gentleman rightly so called will have for its aim the profit of the State : but this broad function admits of many degrees, and qualities fitting thereto will somewhat vary in each case. One common virtue is to be first secured : that the sense of justice be deeply instilled. A gentleman will strive to secure and to grant their rights to those weaker than himself. If he be a lawyer, he will aim at right, not profit : if a magistrate of his county, he will defend the poor. As a country squire, he will be an example of refinement and education, a student of Letters : hospitable and well acquainted with his estates. Or he may serve his country as captain in arms ; or, well-nigh the most distinguished service, in royal missions. The finest degree of learning is herein requisite ; especially the knowledge of languages. Wide reading is needful to the proper understanding of his own and other States. Courtesy, as bound up with liberal thoughts and gentleness of spirit, is part of a gentleman's nature. In the country he will follow sports as recreations from nobler exertions, taking as examples Cicero, Socrates, Scaevola. Long-bow shooting is the finest exercise, for its practice conduces to national security.

As regards dress, the gentleman will not exceed in costliness of array. Almost in the words of Castiglione, the writer speaks of a man's clothes as the index to his disposition. The Italian is the best model to follow; Cato, Sulla, Scipio are illustrations. English fashions change too often. The Frenchman delights in colours, "so many as be in the rainbow"; "he followeth chiefly the peacock." The Spaniard passeth the bounds of measure in costliness, whilst the Dutchman is less blameworthy than these, as he changeth his fashions rarely. Constant change in colour or fashion of dress betokens a wavering and uncertain temper, which is a great blemish to the honour of a gentleman.

The influence of the finer side of Italian feeling, evident throughout the book, is especially traceable in what is here said of the outer gifts of personality.

In the education of youth, the reading of histories is urged as the recreation of all leisure hours : for they "are very necessary to be read of all those which bear office and authority in the Commonwealth." It is of interest to note the stress laid by Elyot and the writer of the Tract under consideration upon the place of history in training for service. At the time when our English authors were content to handle the theme on the precedent of the humanist commonplaces of the preceding century, Francesco Patritio was compiling those *Dialoghi* upon the true nature of history which for the first time led to a scientific study of historical theory based upon the *Politics*. The author of the *Institution of a Gentleman* regards the subject from the point of view of the illustration of virtues. He has evidently read in a superficial way the popular historians, Plutarch, Herodotus, Arrian, Suetonius, and others, but he gives no light upon the manner in which ancient history (for he alludes to no other) helps "the understanding of things past and the order of things present." Cyrus who spared Croesus is an abiding example of "pity" in a ruler; Alexander of "justice"; Vespasian of "wisdom"; Titus of "gentleness"; Hadrian of "learning"; Antoninus Pius of "peacefulness." Cambyses on the other hand is a warning against drunkenness, Nero, Caligula and Commodus against other evil qualities. With all these examples before us the present age ought to be truly happy in its opportunities of upright life and national well-being: "which things are here written to the profit of young gentlemen."

The work had probably an academic origin: the writer may have been tutor to youth of family, or fellow of his College. The literary examples given in course of the book are, with exception of a quotation from Chaucer and others from Boccaccio, characteristic of the time. That the treatment owes most to Elyot, and something to *Il Cortegiano*, is obvious; the insistence on Letters as the essential basis of modern education, with skill in arms or military knowledge as accessories, where position or tastes imply the soldier's career; the full recognition of the dignity of civil and learned professions, the disregard of claims of birth apart from personal worth—all speak of the new age, with its urgent needs for capacity and training in shaping and administering the English life of the Tudors. Although the book itself is of quite secondary importance, it has interest as showing the manner in which the educational spirit of the Revival worked upon opinion in this country. It was not from a passion for learning for its own sake, nor from a wish to dignify outward life and leisure; not from a national instinct for a great past; not from a desire to reform doctrine or ceremony in religion; but first and foremost to meet a demand for better governance, to call into play, from new sources as well as from old, forces better equipped for the more complex tasks of the modern State; it was for such an end, practical, and, in a certain sense, limited, that the

Englishmen first grasped the weapons which the Renaissance held out to them from Italy.

Sir Humphrey Gilbert is best known to Englishmen as a pioneer of colonisation, one of the chief figures of that heroic age of our history whose literary monument is Hakluyt's *Voyages.* But like Raleigh and Grenville he was also of the Court, where indeed men of vigorous temper who turned their faces to the future, naturally foregathered. Gilbert was conspicuously one who held the forward look. He recognised that his lot was cast on the threshold of a "spacious time," and to fit the class he came of to new tasks was the motive of the scheme for *Queen Elizabeth's Academy*, which he put forth in or just before the year 1572.

Like Elyot and the author of the *Institution of a Gentleman*, he was impressed by the boorish indifference to worthy interests of the landed class. He would have "no gentleman within the realm but good for something, whereas now the most part of them are good for nothing." The learning and arts of Italy, the Low Countries, and France, were slow in penetrating English country society, where sport and heavy living were still the main concerns of existence. It may be noted, further, that the promoters of schemes for plantations from England were insistent upon the danger arising from a large class of unoccupied young men of family, debarred from trade, too ignorant for a profession, and unable as younger sons to find support on the land. Some consumed their portion in idleness at the University or at the Inns of Court. The more adventurous took service as soldiers of fortune under foreign sovereigns, joined Drake or Raleigh, or took to systematic piracy at sea. Gilbert aims at meeting the problem, which is not that of the training of a prince, a courtier, or a nobleman of estate, but that of rescuing sound material for the commonwealth by organising an education adapted to it.

Gilbert accepts the Platonic doctrine that education should be under the public authority in that the community has large concern therein. He holds that the Universities ought not to be burdened with the present and evil example of worthless youth; that both Oxford and Cambridge have none but a learned training to offer, and that is little to the purpose in hand. For the youth he speaks of has need of training through "matters of action meet for present practice, both of peace and war"; and specially must all teaching be through and in the English tongue. A short survey of the Academy as he develops it will show the aims he endeavours to attain.

The project is styled "The erection of an Academy in London for education of Her Majesty's wards and others the youth of nobility and gentlemen." He rehearses the need for such provision in that wards of court and younger sons generally are for lack of means poorly educated, and "become estranged from all serviceable virtues to their prince and country." They tend to drift to London having no tie to the soil; wherefore it is desirable that an academy for them be established there, to be attended by boys from twelve years of age to manhood.

The scheme of instruction, with the very suggestive reasons for the inclusion of different subjects, is set out succinctly under several heads, which it will be convenient to reproduce. The first group, grammar, and Greek and Latin, is to be taught by a master and four ushers. Hebrew has a separate teacher. Logic and rhetoric form one subject. Rhetorical exercises shall include orations in English, upon political and military subjects. The cultivation of proficiency in the vernacular is a necessity, as "the appliance (of knowledge) to use is principally in the vulgar tongue, as in preaching, in council, in parliament, in commission, and other offices of Commonweal." Even in the University of Cambridge Sir John Cheke contrived that declamation should now and again be given in English. But the main subject of discourse would seem to be concerning wars. Yet it is to be noted that the training for effectiveness in the mother tongue is to be attained through

the study of Greek, Latin and dialectic : there is no reference
to a study of the English language or prose writers. A reader
of political philosophy will treat separately of civil and of
military policy. The first will cover the history and present
condition of monarchies and republics, methods of government, of raising revenue, and of justice, illustration being
drawn from contemporary England. Gilbert, with odd incon-
sistency, reveals a profound faith in books and words, for
by these means "children shall learn more at home of the
civil policy of all foreign countries and our own than most
old men do which have travelled farthest abroad." Upon the
military side the lectures will expound the "discipline and
kinds of arms, training, and maintaining the fighting force of
the same states." In this way youth will acquire matters of
more practical worth than any "school learning can teach
them." "For such as govern commonweals ought rather to
bend themselves to the practices thereof than to be tied to
the bookish circumstances of the same."

Evidently the teaching of language is to lead as early as
possible to the study of history, politics and war. The humanist
feeling for the poets, for oratory, or for philosophy has no scope
in the Academy.

The second group includes the scientific disciplines. Readers
in Natural Philosophy and Mathematics will be charged almost
exclusively with the practical—the applied—sides of their subjects, such as embattling, fortifications, sapping and mining,
artillery and encampments. Cannon, powder and shot are
provided for use. Infantry exercises with pike, arquebus and
halbert, skirmishing, marching out, company drill are to be
practised daily. To another Reader will be committed geography (with the drawing of maps and sea charts), astronomy
and navigation. A ship fully rigged, with a practical shipwright
in charge, is to be at the disposition of the class. In the same
department is a doctor and surgeon, who shall read physic
and surgery, especially in what concerns wounds ; he shall

prescribe no medicine whatever, except he shall be able to "declare the reason philosophical of every particular ingredient" and of its operation.

Interesting is the stipulation that the natural philosopher and the physician shall "search and try out the secrets of nature as many ways as they possibly may," and report every year "without equivocations or enigmatical phrases, the methods and results of their experiments." To further enable such research the men of science shall have a "physic garden."

Under the third group are included the lecturers in law and divinity. Part of their duty will be "to set down and teach exquisitely the office of a Justice of the Peace and Sheriff," as not a few of the pupils will fill such places. But professional knowledge must be sought in the Inns of Court.

A fourth group covers the training necessary for the life of the polite world. First, French, Italian, Spanish and German are taught by separate masters. Next, music (the lute, bandora and cithern), dancing, and fencing, with the art of the dagger and of the battle-axe, have their professors. A herald of arms concerned with pedigrees and the registers of pupils, a librarian, with funds for the purchase of foreign books, and the right to a copy of every English printed book, a treasurer, and lastly, the Rector, who determines the course to be pursued by each pupil, complete the staff.

Then follow "certain orders to be observed." The Readers in Arts and Laws are bound to produce severally a new book upon their subject. The teachers of ancient and of foreign languages shall each of them publish once in three years "some translation into the English tongue of some good work." By such means "all the nations of the world shall once every six years at the furthest receive great benefit to your Highness' immortal fame." Lastly, there shall be a yearly sermon in praise of the Founder.

The advantage which shall ensue from such a foundation is chiefly this, that "whereas in the Universities men study only school learnings, in this Academy they shall study matters of action meet for present practice both of peace and war," such as foreign tongues and martial training. If they are backward, "they at least will exercise themselves in qualities meet for a gentleman." Gilbert has no doubt that such a school will bring this island into such everlasting honour that all nations of the world shall know and say, when the face of an English gentleman appeareth, that he is "either a soldier, a philosopher, or a gallant courtier." The Court of her Majesty will be filled therefrom with gallant gentlemen and men of virtue, and be a model to Europe for "chivalric policy and philosophy," to its undying fame, "there being no such riches under heaven as to be well thought of."

III.

THE INSTITUTION OF A YOUNG NOBLEMAN, 1607.

The Institution of a Young Nobleman is, like the *Book of the Governor*, under heavy debt to the Italians, as indeed was inevitable. But at the same time the book bears reference to other writers, Erasmus, Julius Caesar, Scaliger, Crinitus, and so on, and shows evidence of a reading of Montaigne, with whose opinion on the *Institution of Children* (I. xxv) Cleland is evidently in much sympathy. Castiglione and the earlier Patrizi are both mentioned. The *Courtier* of the former, indeed, supplies the basis of a large section of Cleland's work, and is to be read through by the pupil, before going to Court, either in Italian or Clerk's Latin translation. Hoby's version, oddly enough, is not referred to. The *Basilikon Doron* of James I is pressed upon the reader with a painful iteration. A puritan temper colours the work, but it is the puritanism of a scholar, widely-read if a little pedantic; and is not inconsistent with respect for courtly society and a certain strong common sense and shrewd worldly wisdom. His illustrations and precepts are, for the first time in a work of this kind, drawn primarily from the Bible ; though the classical sources are utilised in only slightly less degree.

There is, therefore, a vein of strong and earnest purpose running through the educational doctrine presented by Cleland. He is akin in spirit to Elyot and to Ascham, but his treatment is from the point of view of system much more complete and bears at every turn the mark of the working experience of a teacher of many-sided ability. It is not without significance that the *Institution* though Scottish in origin was printed at Oxford.

Cleland begins, after Elyot's manner, with the affirmation that nobility rests upon service ; that to such service British youth of station must be brought up, and that the king has need above all things of capacity. The preliminary ground may be quickly reviewed. Cleland surprises the reader by refusing a school-master, or "pedant," for a boy's tutor; he will have a man of the world, a scholar indeed, but something more. Women's influence upon boys is bad, on grounds familiar to us from Erasmus. The doctrine that bent, capacity and taste can be discerned in childhood he bluntly refutes. Only by education and experience do boys and girls find out what they really like, or are actually best fitted to do and become. Hence boys must submit to the regular discipline of Letters ; and should be compelled to learn whether inclination be disposed that way or not.

Health being presumed as the condition of all efficiency, upon mental gifts and the order of their importance in training Cleland has much to say which is in entire agreement with Montaigne's notable affirmations. First of all comes Judgment, the most valuable quality of the intellect. A tutor should pardon failure to learn lines by heart much sooner than inability to judge well of common things in daily experience. This practical wisdom was the one necessary end of all systems of education as Montaigne understood it. Next in worth stands the gift of Imagination, whereby a boy should correct his insularity, which teaches him that his own fashion or ideas are the only reasonable freightage of the human mind, and bids him ignore the greater world and its wisdom around us. Memory is the third quality, but it is wholly subordinate, and contrasted with judgment is of no credit. Better evidence cannot be had of the process by which, on both sides of the Channel, the Renaissance was shedding its bonds to verbalism, fetters, be it understood, which were the creation only of the weaker and later disciples of the great Founders.

Assuming a fundamental bent towards the elementary virtues of truth, integrity, desire to excel, Cleland lays down that humanity, in the sense of kindliness towards the weak (he expressly includes animals), indicates a spirit from which much may be looked. As to good breeding, the prime quality is naturalness, the absence of affectation in gesture, in speech, and in the intellectual temper whence these proceed. The stress that he lays upon this recalls Castiglione's dictum that ostentation and affectation never accompany *virtù*. In order to stimulate the serious view of life as the field of duty he especially urges the reading of histories to boys ; and as an object lesson in appropriate manners a visit to Court should be contrived.

Cleland now enters upon a systematic exposition of the general course of study which should, in his opinion, constitute the instruction desired in higher education. He begins with outspoken advice upon the general aim of education and the importance of right method. Once again he insists that memory is unduly prized as the faculty most to be cultivated ; and he blames both parents and school-masters for the error. He wishes "all tutors first to consider that, whatsoever thing they enterprise to teach, it be true and profitable ; to observe a good method in teaching, which is the most admirable and profitable thing in any wise man's mind and work that can be."

"Begin at facile to come unto difficult things, at simple to attain unto composed (complex) matters." "With a good *order* there should come a *plainness of words*," without which all the work of the teacher is sore hindered.

First amongst subjects of instruction is the art of speech, the mother tongue : as "the chiefest instrument of understanding," it should be well framed from the beginning, in seeing that the nurse and others pronounce their language distinctly and articulately, omitting nor changing any letter or syllable as foolish folks oftentimes do in wantonness. ...They (parents and tutors) should not suffer their pupil to rattle in the throat, nor to make any grim countenance (grimace) in his speech, lifting up or down his brows and eyelids." Reading may be taught— after Quintilian's method—by ivory tablets or other device by way of play ; and the boy should be early practised in reading aloud. In this is much art ; for he should be taught to "read with a sweet accent, not pronouncing verse as prose, or prose as verse, nor reading with a sharp shrill voice as a woman, or with a rough and husky voice as an old man doth, but with a pleasant harmony, reading at the beginning with leisure, pausing at the full periods, and taking his breath at the broken points, lifting or basing his voice as the subject requireth and the admiration or question offereth." Writing he will learn by tracing letters on " Venice " glass laid over an approved copy, which should contain some pleasant sentiment.

This attained, Latin is begun. Grammar should be at first as simple as possible, enough to enable the boy to read the *Disticha Catonis*, or the colloquies of Vives and Cordier, which should at the outset be explained by the master. Vocabulary will be acquired in this way, and, by parsing the reading-book chosen, both inflexions and simple constructions are remembered. Accurate parsing and practice in the concords are at the basis of all progress in construing and composition. " Yet many wise and learned men banish all rules from a nobleman's instruction to have him only conversant in authors....Which way is both tedious and unsure as they can testify who have experienced it." He refers to the method of rapid impression as distinct from thoroughness based on grammar and exercises. It will be remembered that Melanchthon and Sturm especially identified themselves with the accurate and solid apprehension of Latin in opposition to the plausible method of reliance upon conversation and superficial reading. Cleland continues: "others are so conceited that they have caused their sons to be brought up only in speaking of Latin with their Tutor, as we learn English, and for that cause have suffered none to speak any other thing but Latin in their hearing: who when they come to man's estate must go to school to learn their mother tongue." Undoubtedly the reference is to Montaigne's experience. This was, however, practically a unique case, in as far as concerns his inability to speak his mother tongue. The Estienne children all spoke Latin at home: and no doubt the practice was often attempted, sometimes successfully. But the evidence of the colloquies is overwhelming that so far as school-life was concerned boys slipped into the vernacular when they were out of the master's hearing. Not a few of the wiser teachers saw that compulsory conversation in Latin made for poverty of thought and slipshod style in composition. Cleland's protest marks the end of the artificial attempt to supersede the use of the vernacular by Latin in ordinary intercourse. His further advice is of not less interest. " I wish rather that parents were willing to have their sons taught by frequent usage and custom the French language, which is so pleasant, common, and spread through the whole world at this day. Childhood is the fittest time, and parents should sacrifice, as the Grecians did, to opportunity; their tongues will easily turn and apply unto the French accent, which is so difficult in man's estate." The place taken a quarter of a century before by Italian is now passing to French. It was the growing feeling of the importance of the French language combined with the development of a fine standard of society in Paris which led to the custom—against which Milton wrote in protest—of sending boys of good family from England to attend academies in France.

Following the better humanist method, Cleland would have the beginner take so much accidence as is necessary to his needs : then, progress made in construing, that he should revert to grammar, which is the "corner stone," "the sinews of the body," in relation to the humanities. "It will be painful unto the tutor, I confess, but yet profitable for his pupils." Accidence may be taken first, and the construing to accompany it be chosen from Cicero's *Letters* and the *De Amicitia* : or selections from *Epistles* or *Metamorphoses* of Ovid. The morning is the best time for syntax, to be illustrated from the reading of Cicero's *Speeches*—one or more of the *Philippics*, the *Catilines*, *Pro Archia*, or *Pro Lege Manilia*. At a different hour Terence, Vergil and Horace will be taken. Prosody will be studied with Juvenal, Persius and Plautus. In expounding an author it is wise to refrain from prolix comment ; rather show the writer to be his own interpreter, by quoting parallel passages in illustration. In composition he advises the method —a modification of Ascham's—whereby the master furnishes a translation of a passage from Cicero, which the pupil, "changing a little the tenses and moods of the verbs," puts into Latin ; the Latin then being turned into French, the two languages are learnt side by side. The French and the Latin versions are then compared with Cicero's text. The master will not be severe upon inevitable defects. Regular practice in composition upon this method will establish rules of syntax, Ciceronian usage in vocabulary and in sentence structure ; and, what is more important, will give insight into the laying out and exposition of argument, and other elements of rhetoric. Such prose composition indeed will be more than an exercise in Latin, for by its means "the young scholar shall profit in true understanding and right judgment, as he does in speaking and writing." There follows wise advice against a too rigid standard of

precision in Latin writing: the tutor should value the feeling
for Latin sentence structure more than Ciceronian precedent
for word or phrase, "commending chiefly to the pupil's
judgment the choosing of verbs and of their placing." It is
obvious that there is here one more proof of the position
already advanced in previous chapters that the humanists,
however much stress they laid upon Latin writing, recognised
that the outcome of the logical training therein involved was
the formation of a coherent and lucid vernacular style.
Cleland obviously feels that through Latin prose he is teaching
not the vocabulary and syntax only of a dead tongue but the
application of logic to expression through any language the
pupil may then or later come to employ.

Latin grammar fairly mastered, "lead your pupil into the
sweet fountain and spring of all Arts and Sciences," that is,
Greek: "and not for fashion's sake, as many do," i.e. superficially and for display; for Greek learning is "as profitable for
the understanding as the Latin tongue for speaking." Clenard's
grammar is advised, and properly taught will serve for a
repetition of the Latin grammar in "conferring the one with the
other"; the learner thus conjoining both together, as Cicero
counselled his own son and, as we have seen, many humanists
advised. The Greek Testament should be read well nigh
through, and then Isocrates and Xenophon. Greek is not to
be accounted difficult; "for the objection of the difficulty
thereof was invented by the enemy of mankind and pronounced
by his attorney Clement V at the Council of Vienne, to lock up
the sweet conduits of God's true word in the New Testament."
The main functions and knowledge of Greek is to lead the
scholar "to the spring of all sciences." The literature is to be
used as a guide to higher knowledge in arts and sciences. It is
unfortunate that this claim for Greek as the key to "eruditio" is
not more fully laid out. The argument is precisely that used
by Guarino, Agricola, Hegius or Melanchthon; but the circumstances at the end of the sixteenth century have greatly

changed. The vernaculars are reaching the status of precise literary tongues; the Greek writers are presented in Latin and mostly also in modern dress; specialists have begun to work, and the high water mark of Greek knowledge in certain important regions has already been overtaken and passed. Hence it can no longer be truly argued that the straightest avenue to mathematics or geography, to biology and physics, to medicine and divinity, lies through a first-hand knowledge of Greek. At the same time, the actual charm of Greek literature—whether oratory, philosophy or poetry—is not set out by Cleland, who belonged to a generation which, in England at least, had not attained the standpoint of aesthetic criticism of Letters. He reminds us in this of Melanchthon's attitude towards Homer, or that of Erasmus towards Greek tragedy.

The reading of Histories "should be the chiefest study of a young nobleman when he cometh to any perfection of speech and understanding." In the study of history, he is careful to explain that it is not the phrase and grammatical construction which he should chiefly learn from Titus Livius or from Plutarch. "Deeds and not words" are the prime interest in ancient historians. The characters depicted should be held up for imitation or as a warning.

In words strongly reminiscent of Montaigne, he goes on: "tutors should not so much busy their brains to cause their pupils to conceive and retain the date and day of Carthage, her ruin and destruction, as to tell them of Scipio's and Hannibal's manners and valiant exploits, in both sides, neither should they be so curious of the place where Marcellus died, as of the reason why he died there. This is the anatomy of philosophy and the study of judgment, as I have said the framing thereof should be a tutor's principal intention always." That perception of general principles, and their illustration in event and character, is the higher side of historical instruction, is the doctrine of our writer.

In historical reading, which is, to begin with at least, wholly dependent on classical sources, he indicates the *Epitome* of Florus, followed by Sallust and Caesar; then Plutarch and Livy with his "prolix orations." The humanist course is, however, by no means limited to the reading of ancient literature. The scientific disciplines have an important place, and these are no longer dependent upon the learning of antiquity. As a necessary introduction to the sciences a thorough grounding in formal logic is necessary. But the function of logic is carefully defined as that of an instrument, not of an end in itself. The use of weights is not to try whether one be heavier than another, nor of a pen to be cut to finer and finer points until it is all gone. The pen is for writing and the weight for weighing commodities. So logic should be taught plainly out of Aristotle, or through suitable abridgments; and the pupil be shown "the use thereof in all other things, applying it to divinity, laws and other faculties," "that he may in combat vanquish all heretical and erroneous opinions both in Religion and policy." A simplified logic is much wanted for teaching purposes; for time may not be spent on such refinements as "the troublesome doctrine of mixt syllogisms." Moreover the master cannot forget that rhetoric is a most important application of logic and should illustrate it accordingly.

The natural introduction to mathematics lies through arithmetic, supplementing which Euclid VII, VIII and IX will be useful. Then the pupil passes to Euclid I—VI, with suitable comments by certain English editors. The simplest exercises in geometry consist in the drawing of maps; to which is added the study of architectural forms and their treatment on paper. Astronomy follows, and with it mathematical and physical geography. "It is a great shame for a general of an army to be ignorant of the elevation of the Pole, the situation of shires and provinces, the diversities of climate, the length of days and nights, according to the parallels and meridians; not to know the temperature of the air, the quality of the earth and many such things. As for Astrology I would have it hid from a young nobleman's eyes." In descriptive geography let him use Ptolemy, Book I, Maginus, Ortelius and his maps of the Continents, which should be hung up in the school-room. Mercator's globe is of greater importance still. The essence of good method is skill in questioning, and in knowing how to use Ptolemy, the maps, and such illustrative matter as may be had from Merula's *Cosmographia*, upon manners and fashions of foreign peoples. And the tutor must bring into play his own experience, and be ever testing by improvised examples. Often a master soars far above the heads of his boys, and then is dismayed to see that he cannot find one able to say whether Ireland is in Europe, or Asia, or in Africa. There are two remarks to be made at this point. The intimate connection of mathematical teaching with geography, architecture and astronomy indicates that the subject was not pursued far on the side of pure mathematics. Algebra, for example, is not alluded to. The second is that geography is on the way to attain an independent status and that the new apparatus of chart, map and globe, the productions of the era of discovery, was rendering it thoroughly modern in its conception and scientific in its method.

Lastly, the gentleman needs some training in Law. Cleland qualifies his position by deprecating a professional knowledge of legal practice. Justinian forms the suitable discipline, as guiding to a consideration of principles. A man destined for a public career should understand how to read an Act of Parliament, or the Statutes of the realm, and know something of the customary or common law of the country, and how to interpret legal terms. He will at least be called upon to administer local justice, and act as adviser to neighbours or dependents in emergency. For such as aim at high legal dignities, of course due residence at one of the Inns of Court is essential.

After showing how learning profits a gentleman in the service of his country, whether in war or in peace; how essential to the stamp of distinction in a man of property; how helpful to a courtier, who, if he be rightly educated, "can court ladies with discretion, entertain them in wise and honest conference, and is able to win all men's favour by his meek, gentle and civil behaviour," he insists upon the high dignity of scholarship as the adornment of leisure.

Upon this subject of private reading Cleland writes pleasantly enough. "As ye are curious in choosing your armour and horses and in buying your hawks and dogs I counsel you to be as choice what books ye read....For there are some books which are only worthy to be tasted, others to be swallowed, and the best to be chewed, let down, and digested. I cannot find a fitter similitude to explain this point of reading than a man's travelling through some strange country. He breaketh his fast or dineth in some towns, passing slightly through them, in others he will lodge all night, but yet he will choose some pleasant and convenient city to learn the language in, and there have a settled stay for a time. So are some books only to be read in parts; others to be read wholly, but cursorily; and some few to be read wholly with great attention and diligence.

"First of all, the Bible stands forth eloquent beyond all, even the greatest of ancient writings, both for policy and for conduct. Amongst the Greeks, Thucydides, Herodotus, although a 'fabulous history'—an unusual criticism for the time—Xenophon, Lysias, Arrian, 'but chiefly Plutarch.' For in Plutarch pleasure is so mixed and confounded with profit that I esteem the reading of him as a paradise for a curious spirit to walk in at all time." Julius Caesar, who has the special commendation of "his Majesty's (James I) judicious judgment," Sallust, Tacitus, Suetonius, and Francesco Patrizi (presumably the elder). He then proceeds: "I would have you also to be familiar with the histories and chronicles of your own country before you read those of France, Italy, Spain and Germany especially, that you may know the life, nature, manners, and estate, both of your friends and foes which may be very profitable and pleasant to you and at all times.

"In Scotland we have few of this kind," except Hector Boetius : but he claims as the reason that "our ancestors could do better than say (write)," viz., in being so busy "in virtuous action." The *Basilikon Doron*, in a laboured panegyric, is hailed as a more than sufficient stay of the national repute. England is far richer in fine historians who, however, are not named. Sir Philip Sidney's *Arcadia*, "a history or rather poem," both for the worth of the writer and the eloquence of the English style, he particularly commends to the studious. "His wit is so excellent, his invention so rare, and elocution so ravishing." France provides my gentleman with admirable reading in Comines, Monstrelet, Serres, Montluc, and La Noue. Guicciardini, amongst Italians, has renown throughout Europe. Tasso, Boccaccio (always excepting the *Decameron*), Piccolomini, who "is admirable in the doctrine of good manners, and proper for all society," and above all "the *Courtier* of Count Baldassar Castilio is very necessary and profitable for young gentlemen abiding in the Court." The scope of historical reading, and the choice of the *Arcadia* and the *Courtier* as representative books in current literature, are significant of the broadening out of the standards of cultured country life in England.

Amongst historians, Cleland rightly prefers such as "have had least passions and partiality, and the best means to discover the truth either in being there themselves in person or having certain intelligence from them that were present.... Be not too quick of belief nor too incredulous." The puritan feeling comes to the surface in his fear of Poesy, of which he dare not counsel much reading, it is so alluring. It may then be only used as recreation. A book is to be judged by the method and order observed in the writing of it ; but all hasty and overwise criticism is to be avoided, as often ignorantly

pronounced.   In all reading the use of the commonplace book
is urged, following the ancient precept and practice of Aristotle
and Cicero.   The custom which the Italians have of holding
discourses amongst men of learning upon grave topics of
philosophy and life is much to be commended, as such tend
"to lift up imagination and by an honest emulation mount you
above yourself."

In two of his most impressive chapters (Books III and IV)
Cleland treats of the inculcation of right motives in the young
pupil.   "Duty towards God" is set out in the spirit of
uncompromising Protestantism.   In intimate relation to the
prime duty, stands the obedience owed to the King, whose
appointment is of divine ordering and whose precedence may
not be disputed by any Pope.   More flattery of the sort that
James liked is heaped upon the reigning king.   The Gunpowder
Plot, "that devilish design," gives the cue to the third field of
duty, that to one's country.   Cleland then takes up the boy's
duty to his parents, which needs no enforcement, for it rests
on Nature.   This is followed by a short chapter, delicious in
its *naïveté*, upon the pupil's duty towards his tutor, "which is
so straitly conjoined and unseparably connexed with that of
children towards their natural parents."   Classical examples
of appreciative patrons are drawn out in array, from Theseus
to Vespasian : and plain, if somewhat trite, advice is built
upon them.   "Therefore I counsel you not only to be
loving and obedient unto your tutors, but also thankful in
advancing and enriching them according to your abilities, as
Achilles did Phoenix, Alexander Aristotle."   "Whosoever
sheweth himself unthankful towards his tutor...it is no marvel
if hereafter he regardeth neither religion, faith, justice ; and
that he tread laws and all equity under foot."

The chief practical virtue is prudence, by which reason is
brought to bear upon life, whether private or public, whether
concerned with skill in affairs or rightness in personal conduct.
It is part of such wisdom that "a man accommodate himself

and frame his manners apt and meet for all honest company and society of men. The best wits are most universal and pliable to all sorts of people." This leads Cleland to speak of a gentleman's code of manners, the guiding principle of which is to be found in "magnanimity," which is, to be of "a spirit so framed to all things alike, as if he had been born only for that which he went about to do." The essence of Italian *virtù* is to characterise the English gentleman also; in which we may trace without hesitation the influence of Castiglione.

Like Palmieri, Cleland argues confidently from a young man's carriage to his temperament. "Consider with what grace and countenance ye walk, that ye go not softly tripping like a wanton maid, nor yet striding with great long paces, like kings in stage-plays. Away with all affectation" in what pertains to your manners abroad, for men observe, and not unjustly interpret the mind from the gesture of the body. Especially put away that sort of affectation which bids you overlook the salutations of those of lower station. Be not over-solemn, for you are not a Senator of Venice. "Behaviour," in a word, "is a fit and well made garment of the mind, and should have the conditions of a garment, viz. that it be made in fashion, that it be not too curious."

In the precepts for the Court, little or nothing is added to Castiglione. The true courtier, no doubt, will, thinks Cleland, in Castiglione's own vein, find himself disturbed by the elaborate ceremonial, but he may not escape it. "I confess that ye must conform yourselves somewhat unto the world, and that which is commonly used, but I wish ye performed it in such a generous and free manner that every man may know that ye can use all these vain compliments and ceremonies, but that ye will not make your judgment and your will slaves unto such vanity." Honour must be paid by a private person to those in public office, and this rests on "God's law and man's law": but punctilios are vain, and if allowable are only so with strangers.

The speech of the courtier is, as always, the true index of the man, "the shadow of the true self": let his words be few, well-weighed, erring on side of charity. His language should not be trivial, nor pedantic, full of ink horn terms, but soldier-like in terseness and perspicuity. Sound grammatical English is no less intelligible than untrimmed talk, affecting to be natural, but indicating ignorance or carelessness. Take pains to amend "an accent not tunable." In conversation a young man should be "not amazed but assured": not timid, even with the Prince; with elders grave, and with none mocking, never pointing ridicule at those absent. Again, no man of intelligence will waste his own or another's time with trivial gossip, nor will he lay down the law on a matter where he is on uncertain stand. Rather will he keep silence, especially in indiscreet or ill-natured company. To make parade of learning in unsuitable society argues conceit, just as wasteful ostentation in dress brings no one respect.

The exercises appropriate to a gentleman are such as Elyot had allowed. There is the same stress on archery and riding. But curiously, and contrary to the dominant fashion, Cleland forbids fencing. Yet the passion for swordsmanship was at its height at the close of the sixteenth century, and Italian masters in London were in high demand. His reason is that quarrels were more easily provoked from consciousness of skill in defending honour. Hawking, tennis, which he regrets to see becoming a veritable passion, dancing, for the good grace it gives in carriage of the body, but not to be pursued to the pitch of the dancing master's agility—such are allowable as necessary for recreation and health, but they are not the serious business of life. Chess is too trying; dice and all gambling are wicked; but cards are allowed by the example of the King. Music has ancient authority, but it is disgrace to a gentleman to play such instruments as are used by those who have to get their living by skill upon them. People too much "given to play upon musical instruments are fantastic and full of humours." Cleland says nothing of painting, and we may assume that he was something lacking in respect of the artistic temperament, which he no doubt distrusted.

Upon travel, we gather from the *Institution* that the dangers realised by Ascham, amongst others, as attending a sojourn abroad were less acutely felt. " Travelling hath ever been esteemed and used as the principal and best means whereby a young nobleman, or any other, may profit his prince, his country, and himself. It is the true science of policy and the good school of all government." " My counsel is that ye travel for the perfecting of your knowledge," the tour thus following the completion of the general education previously laid down. " My first advice is that you take your tutor with you ": for Agamemnon did not cross the Aegean without Nestor, Ulysses had Pallas at his side, and Alexander, Aristotle. The tour to be described will cost £200 for a party of four. The chief end in travelling is to perfect " prudence " ; hence the first quality necessary to success is willingness to observe and listen, with a mind free from home prejudices. Let the traveller always write up his impressions day by day.

A gentleman will not hold himself aloof in insular conceit from strangers, yet he will not be prone to over much confidence.

Following Ulysses, let him chiefly observe *Cities*, their strength, wealth, importance ; their schools and universities, buildings and monuments ; and their general lie and situation, in which, especially, "your mathematics shall stand you in great stead ": their manners, which means their government, dynasty, royal family, trade, warlike forces, nobility, and trading class, the temper and force of the population. How much more worthy are such enquiries than to ask the height of one steeple above another, or the weight of this bell or that. To study these grave questions will hinder from wasting time and money in dissipation, or from the temptation "to swagger and fight all the night long in Padua."

"Travelling is a lively history." A young man sets out, let us suppose, from Scotland. First, he should see Great Britain —Oxford, its Colleges and famous Library, Cambridge, Westminster, the Court. Crossing to Calais he visits Amiens, Paris, where he salutes His Majesty's Ambassador, Orleans, Poitiers, Gascony, and so to Provence. Ascending the Rhone he will reach Lyons, by which time he will have a store of observation upon the Parlements and the laws of France. From Chambery he will pass to Geneva, drawn thither by the fame of Calvin, as we may safely conclude, and then cross the Alps to Turin. In Italy he will see Florence, Rome and Venice, though he is warned that Italy has its sore dangers to the soul. If the traveller could find means of reaching Constantinople he should make an effort, for the novelty of the scene. Returning by the Brenner he will stay at Trent, find his way through Hungary to Poland, then homewards by the Rhineland, where his drinking capacity will be bravely tested. Flanders, Holland and Denmark will complete the tour. For an extension of the journey into Spain the author absolutely declines responsibility. "For there the best-natured nobleman of this land shall be corrupted; blasphemy, and contempt of all nobleness and religion are so ordinary and usual....Therefore come home where ye may serve God aright." It was much the same tour that Coryat describes with such verve, dating from the year following the issue of *The Institution of a Young Nobleman*.

In his country home the young laird will now find himself fully equipped for a life of public usefulness, of private responsibility, of leisure. The State may claim him for higher service, for which also he is duly fitted. Travel will have broadened the mind and set it free from the restraint of ignorant prejudice. For "this should be one of your best lessons which you have learned in travelling, to judge and esteem of a man by his wit, discourses, and integrity of life, and not by his habit, the form of his hat, or the fashion of his breeches."

CHRONOLOGICAL TABLE.

1374　Death of Petrarch.　Birth of Guarino da Verona.
1378　Birth of Vittorino da Feltre.
1386　University of Heidelberg founded.
1392　University of Erfurt founded.　Conversino teaches Latin at Padua.
1396　Invitation from the Florentine Studium to Chrysoloras. Vittorino goes to Padua.
1400　Chrysoloras removes to Pavia.
1403　Guarino goes to Constantinople.
1404　The tract of Dominici, *Regola del Governo di Cura Familiare.* Vergerius, *De Ingenuis Moribus.*
1405　Padua absorbed into the Venetian State.
1407　G. Barzizza professes Latin at Padua.
1408　Return of Guarino : he teaches Greek at Florence.
1414　Guarino quits Florence for Venice.
1415　Vittorino goes to Venice.　Death of Manuel Chrysoloras at Constance.
1416　Discovery of the complete text of Quintilian, *De Institutione Oratoria.*
1417　L. Valla teaches Greek at Florence.
1422　Vittorino succeeds Barzizza as Professor of Latin at Padua. Birth of Frederick of Urbino.　Discovery of complete text of Cicero, *De Oratore.*
1423　Vittorino invited to Mantua.　Aurispa returns from Constantinople.
1429　Guarino invited to Ferrara.
1433　L. B. Alberti composes the *Cura della Famiglia.*
1434　Return of Cosimo de' Medici to Florence.
1435　Matteo Palmieri composes *La Vita Civile.*
1444　The *Elegantiae* of L. Valla first circulated.　Birth of R. Agricola.

1445 The Greek grammar of Theodore Gaza circulated.
1446 Death of Vittorino da Feltre.
1447 Nicholas V, Pope.
1449 William Gray returns to England from Ferrara.
1450 Aeneas Sylvius : *De Liberorum Educatione.*
1453 Capture of Constantinople.
1455 Issue of first book printed with movable types, *Biblia Latina*, at Mainz.
1457 Death of L. Valla.
1459 B. Guarino : *De Ordine docendi.*
1460 Death of Guarino da Verona.
1465 First Italian press, at Subiaco.
1466 Birth of Erasmus.
1467 First Roman Press.
1468 *Edd. Princ.* of Cicero, *De Oratore*, of Vergil, Livy, etc.
1469 First Venetian Press. Agricola goes to Pavia.
1470 First Press set up in Paris.
1471 Sixtus IV founds a museum of antiquities on the Capitol.
1474 First Spanish Press.
1475 Agricola at Ferrara. Erasmus goes to Deventer school.
1476 First Greek Press set up, at Milan.
1477 Caxton sets up his press at Westminster.
1481 Death of F. Filelfo.
1482 Reuchlin at Rome.
1483 Hegius headmaster of Deventer.
1485 Accession of Henry VII. Agricola in Rome ; his death. Linacre goes to Italy.
1487 Erasmus enters the monastery at Stein.
1488 *Ed. Princ.* of Homer, printed at Florence.
1491 Grocyn teaches Greek at Oxford.
1492 Death of Lorenzo de' Medici. Discovery of America.
1494 Death of Poliziano : invasion of Italy by Charles VIII : the Aldine Press set up at Venice.
1495 Erasmus a student at Paris.
1496 Colet returns from Italy to lecture at Oxford.
1497 Birth of Melanchthon. C. Celtis teaches at Vienna. Wimpheling's *Isidoneus Germanicus* published.
1498 *Ed. Princ.* of Aristophanes (Aldus). Execution of Savonarola.
1499 Erasmus' first visit to England : his residence at Oxford.

1501 *Ed. Princ.* of Sophocles (Aldus).

1502 *Ed. Princ.* of Thucydides (Aldus). Foundation of University of Wittenberg.

1503 Death of Pope Alexander VI.

1505 Erasmus again in England.

1506 Erasmus leaves England for Italy. Reuchlin's *De Rudimentis Hebraicis* appears.

1508 Erasmus leaves Venice for Padua. Guicciardini completes his *Historia Florentina.*

1509 Accession of Henry VIII. The Reuchlin controversy begins. J. L. Vives goes to Paris. Melanchthon goes to Heidelberg. Erasmus returns (from Rome) to England.

1510 Colet's foundation of St Paul's.

1511 Erasmus at Cambridge—*De Ratione Studii* and *De Copia.*

1512 W. Lily made High Master of St Paul's. Melanchthon goes to Tübingen.

1513 Death of Julius II. Accession of Leo X. Machiavelli completes *Il Principe.*

1514 Erasmus leaves England.

1515 *Epistolae obscurorum virorum.* Accession of Francis I. Budé composes *L'Institution du Prince.*

1516 Erasmus : *Novum Instrumentum* and *Institutio Principis Christiani* ; More's *Utopia* ; Castiglione's *Il Cortegiano* finished. Christ's College, Cambridge, opened.

1517 Collegium Trilingue at Louvain opened. Corpus Christi College, Oxford, opened. Luther's *Theses* at Wittenberg.

1518 Melanchthon : *Institutiones Grammaticae Graecae* ; he teaches Greek at Wittenberg. Universities of Erfurt and Leipsic come under humanist control. Establishment of public Lectureships in Oxford by Wolsey.

1521 Death of Leo X.

1522 Erasmus settles at Basel.

1523 Vives appointed lecturer at Oxford : publishes *De Tradendis Disciplinis.*

1524 Foundation of the humanist school at Zürich through Zwingli's influence.

1525 School at Eisleben established. Luther's appeal to German States. Bembo : *Della Volgar Lingua.*

1526 The "Obere Schule" of Nuremberg established. Royal Press of France set up at Paris.

1527	Erasmus : *Ciceronianus*. Sack of Rome. Death of Froben.
1528	Vives settles at Bruges. *Schul-Ordnung* of Elector of Saxony. *Il Cortegiano* published.
1529	Erasmus quits Basel for Freiburg. *De Pueris instituendis*. Budaeus publishes his *Commentarii Linguae Graecae*.
1530	Beginnings of Collége de France. Coronation of Charles V at Bologna. Diet of Augsburg. End of the Florentine Republic.
1531	Sadoleto: *De Liberis recte instituendis*. Elyot's *Governour*. The First *Oration* of Julius Caesar Scaliger *Against Erasmus, in defence of M. T. Cicero*, circulated. Death of Zwingli.
1533	The *Pantagruel* of Rabelais published.
1534	Foundation of the Collége de Guyenne, and of the Society of Jesus.
1535	Reform of the University of Wittenberg. The *Gargantua* of Rabelais first (?) published. *De Ciceroniana imitatione* of Dolet.
1536	Cordier goes to Geneva. Death of Erasmus at Basel.
1538	Sturm's *De litterarum ludis* : foundation of the Gymnasium of Strassburg.
1540	Society of Jesus formally recognised by Paul III. Death of Vives.
1549	First Jesuit school in South Germany set up at Ingolstadt.
1551	Shrewsbury School founded.
1555	*Institucion of a Gentleman*.
1556	The Jesuit school opened at Cologne. Élie Vinet principal of the Collége de Guyenne.
1559	Amyot's translation of Plutarch's *Lives*.
1560	Death of Melanchthon. Westminster School founded.
1561	Hoby's translation of *The Courtyer*.
1564	Cordier's *Colloquia* published.
1567	Rugby School founded.
1570	Ascham's *Scholemaster*.
1572	Gilbert's *Queene Elizabethe's Achademy* composed.
1579	Montaigne writes the Essay *On the Education of Children*.
1580	First edition of Montaigne's *Essays*.
1598	Edict of Nantes. Bodley's Foundation at Oxford.
1599	The Jesuit *Ratio Studii* issued in its final form.

APPENDIX.

Certain Dialogues from the rare manual of Colloquies for beginners in Latin issued at Nuremberg in 1530 under the title *Formulae puerilium colloquiorum, pro primis tyronibus Sebaldinae scholae Norimbergae per Sebaldum Heyden eorundem praeceptorem conscriptae.*

Each Latin sentence has the German equivalent printed below, as in Dialogus I.

SALUTATIO MATUTINA.

DIALOGUS I.

Andreas. Balthasar.

A. Bonus dies.
   Ain güter tag.
B. Deo gratia.
   Gott sey danck.
A. Opto tibi bonum diem.
   Ich wünsch dir ainen güten tag.

B. Talem et tibi precor.
   Ich bit dir auch so vil.
A. Bene sit tibi hoc die.
   Dir sol an dem tag wol sein.
B. Nec tibi male sit.
   Es sol dir auch nit übel sein.

SALUTATIO MERIDIANA.

DIALOGUS II.

Blasius. Clemens.

B. Salve, Clemens.
C. Salve et tu.
B. Salve plurimum.
C. Et tu tantundem salve.
B. Salvus sis tu.
C. Tu quoque salve.

B. Salutem tibi precor.
C. Eandem et tibi opto.
B. Salute te impertior.
C. Et ego quoque te.
B. Jubeo te salvere.
C. Te quoque ego.

DUM ITUR AD SCHOLAM.

DIALOGUS VII.

Hanno. Joannes.

H. Heu quid facimus?
J. Cur sic vociferas?
H. Nimis diu dormivi.
J. Quid ita? Quid times?
H. Tempus praescriptum transiit.
J. Quod tempus dicis?
H. Horam primam.
J. Tu certe falleris.
H. Tamen audivi.

J. Non recte audisti.
H. Quotam tu audisti?
J. Audivi ultimam.
H. Quota ea est?
J. Duodecima.
H. Utinam verum sit!
J. Non est quod dubites.
H. Oppido laetor.

INTER DISCENDUM IN SCHOLA.

DIALOGUS IX.

Kilianus. Lampertus.

K. Heus, tu huc sede.
L. Quid istic facerem?
K. Discamus simul.
L. Rem gratam offers.
K. Alter alterum doceat.
L. Perlubens pareo.
K. Quidnam tu discis?
L. Disco legere.
K. Ubi nunc legis?
L. In hoc folio.
K. Scis lectionem?
L. Non admodum prompte.
K. Quoties recitasti?
L. Semel   I ⎫
     Bis   II ⎬ recitavi.
     Ter   III ⎪
     Quater IV ⎭

K. Cuinam recitasti?
L. Rectori Scholae.
K. Si quid nescis roga.
L. Qui hoc legam?
K. Collige literas.
L. Tu me observa.
K. Ut hesitas linguam?
L. Sic assuetus sum.
K. Desuesce rursus.
L. Pergam legere.
K. Jam verba praecipitas.
L. Tu melius doce.
K. Sic distincte legas.
L. Tam clare haud queo.
K. Usu addisce.
L. Tentabo quid possim

DE JENTACULO.

DIALOGUS XII.

Naevius. Osualdus.

N. Quo tu nunc abis?
O. Domum me confero.
N. Quid domi ages?
O. Sumam jentaculum.
N. Quanam iturus es?
O. Hac per forum.

N. Comitabor te.
O. Nihil opus est.
N. Aversaris me?
O. Non, sed parco.
N. Nihil est quod agam.
O. Lubens te accipio.

DE PARANDO CALAMO.

DIALOGUS XIIII.

Petrus. Quirinus.

P. Para mihi hanc pennam.
Q. Est tibi cultellus?
P. Est, sed valde hebes.
Q. Acutiorem adfer.
P. Ubi accipiam?
Q. Utendum expete.
P. Adfero, utere.
Q. Vis crassam an tenuem?
P. Mediam volo.
Q. Da atramentum.
P. En atramentarium.

Q. Da quoque papyrum.
P. Et haec in promptu est.
Q. Papyrus perfluit.
P. Non habeo aliam.
Q. Quid vis ut scribam?
P. Praescribe literas.
Q. Tu imitaberis?
P. Ita, in hoc peto.
Q. Saepe excribe.
P. Faciam ut jubes.

IN SCHOLA LUDENTIUM.

DIALOGUS XVIII.

Timotheus. Vitus.

T. Vae nobis, Vite.
V. Quid est? quid tremis?
T. Ego et tu perimus.
V. Quid ita? Qua de causa?
T. Praeceptor venit.
V. Quid ex te audio?
T. Vae nostris natibus.
V. Ubi is est obsecro?
T. Per gradus ascendit.
V. Quis id ait? quis vidit?

T. Egomet inquam vidi.
V. Viditne nos ludere?
T. Id est quod timeo.
V. Quid ergo agemus?
T. Amove orbiculos.
V. Recte admones.
T. Explicemus libros.
V. Certe astutus es.
T. Sic rebitur nos discere.

DE DIMISSIONE A LITERIS.

DIALOGUS XIX.

Ulysses. Xanthus.

U. Io gaudete sodales !

X. Quid est quod sic gestis?

U. Sunt nobis feriae.

X. Quas dicis ferias?

U. Ocium a literis.

X. Quando ociabimur?

U. Hodie a prandio.

X. Ergo ludemus.

U. Quidnam ludemus?

X. Ludemus globulis.

U. Ludus puerilis est.

X. Quem tu ludum malles?

U. Decertemus saltu.

X. Hunc ludum odi.

U. Quanam de causa?

X. Quia pedes lassat.

U. An non pudet te?

X. Cuius me puderet?

U. Quod tam piger es.

X. Certe piger non sum.

U. Quin ergo saltabis?

X. Cave ne provoces.

U. Imo te adiuro.

X. Videbis quid possim.

The little book contains in all twenty-seven dialogues, all of the same elementary type.

BIBLIOGRAPHICAL LIST.

The following list has been compiled to facilitate the identification of the works quoted and referred to in the present volume.

ADY (Mrs H.). *Isabella d'Este.* 2 voll. 8°. London 1903.

AGRICOLA (Rudolph). *De Inventione Dialectica.* Ed. Alardus. 4°. Colon. 1539.

AGRICOLA (Rudolph). *Lucubrationes, tomus posterior.* Ed. Alardus. 4°. Colon. [1539].

AGRICOLA (Rudolph). *Opuscula.* 8°. Louvain 1511.

AGRIPPA (Henricus Cornelius). *De Nobilitate et Praecellentia feminei sexus.* 8°. Antwerpiae 1529.

ALBERTI (Leon Battista). *Il Trattato della cura della Famiglia.* See BONUCCI (A.).

ALEXANDER DE VILLA DEI (Grammaticus). *Doctrinale.* Ed. Reichling. 8°. Berlin 1893.

ALLEN (P. S.). *The Letters of Rudolph Agricola.* In *Eng. Hist. Review,* April 1906. 8°. London 1906.

ALLEN (P. S.). *Opus Epistolarum Des. Erasmi Roterodami denuo recognitum et auctum.* Tom. I. (1484–1514). 8°. Oxford 1906.

ANON. *The Institucion of a Gentleman.* 2nd Ed. 4°. London 1568.

ANON. *Vocabularius Breviloquus.* f°. Argent. 1491.

ARNAUD (Car.). *Quid de pueris Instituendis senserit L. Vives.* 8°. Paris 1887.

ASCHAM (Roger). *The Scholemaster.* Ed. J. E. B. Mayor. 8°. Cambridge 1884.

BARBARO (F.). *De Re Uxoria.* 4°. Paris 1513.

BARLANDUS (Hadrianus). *Dialogi XLII, ad profligandam è scholis barbariem utilissimi.* 12°. Colon. 1530.

BASSI (Domenico). *Il primo libro della "Vita Civile" di Matteo Palmieri è l' "Institutio Oratoria" di Quintiliano.* In *Giornale Storico della Letteratura Italiana,* xxiii, p. 182 seqq. 8°. Torino 1894.

BENOIST (A.). *Quid de puerorum institutione senserit Erasmus.* 8°. Paris 1876.

BERCHER (William). *The Nobylytye of Women.* Roxburghe Club. 4°. London 1904.

BERTHAULT (E. A.). *De M. Corderio et creatis apud Protestantes litterarum studiis.* 8°. Paris 1875.

BEZOLD (F. von). *Rudolf Agricola.* 4°. München 1884.

BIAGI (G.). *La Vita privata dei Fiorentini:* in *La Vita Italiana nel Rinascimento.* 8°. Milano 1896.

BONUCCI (Anicio). *Opere Volgare di L. B. Alberti.* 5 voll. 8°. Firenze 1843 &c.

BOSSERT (A.). *De Rud. Agricola Frisio, Litterarum in Germania restitutore.* 8°. Paris 1865.

BRETSCHNEIDER (C. G.). *Corpus Reformatorum.* 4°. and 8°. Halis Sax. 1834.

BRUNI (Domenico). *Opera intitolata, Difese delle Donne, nella quale si contengono le difese loro delle calumnie dategli per gli Scrittori.* 8°. Firenze 1552.

BRUNI (Lionardo). *De Studiis et Literis.* 8°. [1477].

BUDE (Guillaume). *De l'Institution du Prince.* 8°. Paris 1547.

BURCKHARDT (Jacob). *The civilisation of the Renaissance in Italy.* Translated by S. G. C. Middlemore. 8°. London 1892.

CAPELLA (Galeazzo). *Della Eccellenza et Dignità delle Donne.* 8°. Vinegia 1526.

CASTIGLIONE (B.). *Il Cortegiano.* f°. Venezia 1528.
    The same. *The Book of the Courtier...done into English by Sir Thomas Hoby,* with introduction by Walter Raleigh. 4°. London 1900.

CATO (Dionysius). *Disticha Moralia, cum Scholiis Erasmi.* 4°. Argent. 1521.

CHARPENNE (Pierre). *Traité d'Education du Cardinal Sadoleto...traduit avec Notes.* 8°. Paris 1855.

CHRISTIE (R. C.). *Étienne Dolet.* New ed. 8°. London 1899.

CITTADELLA (L. Napoleone). *I Guarini.* 8°. Bologna 1870.

CLELAND (James). ΗΡΩ-ΠΑΙΔΕΙΑ or *The Institution of a Young Nobleman.* 4°. Oxford 1607.

COLLURAFFI DA LIBRIZZI (A.). *Il Nobile Veneto.* 4°. Venetia 1623.

CORDERIUS (Maturinus). *De Corrupti Sermonis Emendatione Libellus.* 8°. Paris 1530.

CORDERIUS (Maturinus). *School-Colloquies, English and Latine,* by Charles Hoole, M.A. 8°. London 1657.

CREIGHTON (Mandell). *Historical Essays and Reviews.* 3rd ed. 8°. London 1903.

DESPAUTERIUS (Joannes). *Rudimenta J. D. in tres partes divisa.* 4°. Paris 1512.

DOLCE (Lodovico). *Dialogo della Institution delle Donne.* 8°. Vinegia 1557.

DOMENICHI (Lodovico). *La Nobiltà delle Donne.* 8°. Ven. 1549.

DOMENICHI (L.). *La Donna di Corte.* 4°. Lucca 1564.

DOMINICI (Giovanni). *Regola del Governo di Cura Familiare.* Ed. Salvi. 8°. Fir. 1860.

EINSTEIN (Lewis). *The Italian Renaissance in England.* 8°. New York 1902.

ELYOT (Sir Thomas). *The Boke named the Governour.* Ed. H. H. S. Croft. 2 voll. 4°. London 1883.

ELYOT (Sir Thomas). *Of the Knowledeg* (sic) *whiche maketh a Wise Man.* 8°. Lond. 1533.

ERASMUS (Desiderius). *Opera omnia...cura J. Clerici.* 10 voll. f°. Lugd. Bat. 1703.

FAIRBAIRN (A. M.). *Tendencies of European Thought in the age of the Reformation* (ch. xix. in the *Cambridge Modern History*, vol. ii.). 8°. Cambridge 1904.

GALATEO (Antonio). *De Educatione.* In Casotti (Francesco), *Scritti inediti o rari di diversi autori trovati nella provincia d'Otranto e pubblicati con prefazioni ed altre memorie originali da F. C.* 8°. Napoli 1865.

GASPARY (A.). *Storia della Letteratura Italiana : trad. da Zingarelli.* 3 voll. 8°. Torino 1887.

GAULLIEUR (E.). *Histoire du Collége de Guyenne.* 8°. Paris 1874.

GAZA (Theodore). *Grammaticae Institutionis Liber primus, translatus per Erasmum Roterodamum.* 4°. Basileae 1516.

GEIGER (L.). *Johann Reuchlin, sein Leben und seine Werke.* 8°. Leipzig 1871.

GEIGER (L.). *Renaissance und Humanismus in Deutschland und Italien.* 8°. Berlin 1882.

GERINI (G. B.). *Gli Scrittori Pedagogici Italiani.* 8°. Torino 1896.

GILBERT (Sir Humphrey). *Queene Elizabethes Achademy.* In *Early English Text Society.* (Extra Series) 8°. 1859.

GUARINO DA VERONA. *Regulae Grammaticales.* 4°. Ven. 1475.

GUARINO (Battista). *De ordine docendi et studendi.* 8°. Heidel. 1489.

GUENTHER (S.). *Geschichte des mathematischen Unterrichts im deutschen Mittelalter.* 8°. Berlin 1887.

HARTFELDER (Dr Karl). *Melanchthoniana Paedagogica.* 8°. Leipzig 1892.

HARTFELDER (Dr Karl). *Philipp Melanchthon als Praeceptor Germaniae.* 8°. Berlin 1889.

HARTFELDER (Dr Karl). *Unedierte Briefe von Rudolf Agricola.* (Festschrift zum Heidelb. Jubil.) 4°. Karls. 1886.

HEYDEN (Sebaldus). *Formulae puerilium colloquiorum pro primis Tyronibus Sebaldinae scholae Norimbergae.* 12°. Aug. Vindel. 1530.

HUARTE (Juan). *Essamina degl' ingegni degli Huomini.* (From the Spanish.) 8°. Venet. 1603.

HUMFREY (Dr Laurence). *The Nobles, or Of Nobility...lately Englished.* 8°. London 1563.

JEBB (R. C.). *The Classical Renaissance* (ch. xvi. in the *Cambridge Modern History*, vol. i.). 8°. Cambridge 1902.

JEBB (R. C.). *Erasmus* (Rede Lecture, 1890), 2nd edition. 8°. Camb. 1897.

JOLY (A.). *Étude sur J. Sadolet.* 8°. Caen 1856.

KAN (Dr I. B.). *Erasmiani Gymnasii Programma*, 1894. 4°. Roter. 1894.

LA CASA (G. de). *Il Galateo.* In *Rime e Prose.* 4° Ven. 1588.

LUTHER (M.). *An den Christlichen Adel deutscher Nation.* Ed. Benrath. 8°. Halle 1884.

LUZIO (A.) and RENIER (R.). *I Filelfo e l'Umanismo alla Corte dei Gonzaga.* In *Giornale Storico della Letteratura Italiana*, vol. xvi. (1890), p. 119.

LUZIO (A.) and RENIER (R.). *Il Platina e i Gonzaga.* In *Giornale Storico della Letteratura Italiana*, vol. xiii. 1889.

MANCINI (Girolamo Maria). *Vita di L. Battista Alberti.* 8°. Firenze 1882.

MANCINI (G. M.). *Vita di Lorenzo Valla.* 8°. Firenze 1891.

MASSEBIEAU (Louis). *Schola Aquitanica, programme d'Études du Collége de Guyenne au xvie Siècle.* 8°. Paris 1886.

MASSEBIEAU (Louis). *Les Colloques Scolaires.* 8°. Paris 1878.

MELANCHTHON (P.). See BRETSCHNEIDER and HARTFELDER.

MESSERI (Antonio). *Matteo Palmieri.* In *Archivio Storico Italiano.* 8°. Torino 1894.

MONROE (Paul). *Thomas Platter and the Educational Renaissance of the xvi century.* 8°. New York 1904.

MORNEWEG (Karl). *Johann von Dalberg.* 8°. Heidelberg 1887.

MUELLER (Joh.). *Vor- und frühreformatorische Schulordnungen und Schulverträge in Deutscher und Niederländischer Sprache.* 8°. Zschopau 1885.

NAMÈCHE (A. J.). *Mémoire sur la vie et les ouvrages de L. Vivès.* 4°. Bruxelles 1842.

NOLHAC (P. de). *Pétrarque et l'humanisme.* 8°. Paris 1892.

NICHOLS (F. M.). *The Epistles of Erasmus, from his earliest letters to his fifty-first year.* Voll. i. and ii. 8°. London 1901—4.

PALMIERI (Matteo). *Libro della Vita Civile.* 8°. Firenze 1529.

PATRIZI (Francesco), Bp. of Gaeta. *De Regno et Regis Institutione.* 8°. Paris 1567.

PATRIZI (Francesco), Bp. of Gaeta. *Discorsi...sopra alle cose appartenenti ad una città libera trad. da G. Fabrini* [from the *De Inst. Reipublicae*]. 8°. Vinegia 1545.

PAULSEN (Dr F.). *Geschichte des gelehrten Unterrichts auf den deutschen Schulen* etc., Zweite Auf. 2 voll. Leipzig 1896.

PAULSEN (F.). *The German Universities and University Study.* Eng. trans., with preface by M. E. Sadler. 8°. London 1906.

PEROTTUS (Nicolaus). *Rudimenta Grammatices.* 4°. s. l. s. a.; 1471.

PFEIFFER (Dr Franz). *Rudolf Agricola.* In *Serapeum* x. 97. 113. 8°. Leipzig 1849.

PICCOLOMINI (Alessandro). *De la Institutione di tutta la Vita de l' Huomo nato nobile e in Città libera, libri X.* 12°. (no place) 1543.

PRIMAUDAYE (P. de la). *The French Academie, wherein is discoursed the Institution of Maners.* Translated by T. Beard. 3rd ed. 4°. London 1594.

PUECH (E.). *Maturin Cordier.* 8°. Montauban 1896.

REBITTÉ (D.). *Budé restaurateur des études Grecques.* 8°. Paris 1846.

REICHLING (D.). *Johannes Murmellius.* 8°. Freib. im Breisgau 1880.

ROMEI (Il Conte Annibale, gentil' huomo Ferrarese). *Discorsi...divisi in Sette Giornate.* 4°. Verona 1586.

[Englished as " The Courtier's Academie," by J. K. London 1598.]

RÖSLER (A.). *Kard. Joh. Dominicis Erziehungslehre.* 8°. Freib. 1894.

SABBADINI (R.). *La Scuola e gli Studi di Guarino Guarini Veronese.* 8°. Catania 1896.

SABBADINI (R.). *La Vita di Guarino Veronese.* 8°. Genova 1891.

SADOLETUS (J.). *Opera quae exstant omnia.* 4 voll. 4°. Veronae 1738.

SANDYS (John Edwin). *Harvard Lectures on the Revival of Learning.* 8°. Cambridge 1905.

SANDYS (J. E.). *A History of Classical Scholarship.* 2 voll. 8°. Camb. 1903, etc.

SCHMID (Dr Karl A.). *Geschichte der Erziehung vom Anfang an bis auf unsere Zeit.* 5 voll. Stuttgart 1884–1892.

SCHMIDT (Charles). *La vie et les travaux de Jean Sturm.* 8°. Strasbourg 1855.

Serapeum. Zeitschrift für Bibliothekswissenschaft ; herausgegeben von Dr Robert Naumann. 31 voll. 8°. Leipzig 1840–1870.

THIBAUT (F.). *Quid de Puellis instituendis senserit Vives.* 8°. Paris 1888.

TILLEY (Arthur). *Literature of the French Renaissance.* 2 voll. 8°. Cambridge 1904.

TRESLING (T. P.).   *Vita et Merita Rudolphi Agricolae.*   8°. Groningae 1830.

TRIWUNATZ (Dr Milosch).   *Guillaume Budé's " De l'Institution du Prince."*   8°. Leipzig 1903.

VEGIUS (Mapheus).   *De Educatione puerorum et eorum Claris Moribus libri sex.*   4°. Mediol. 1491.

VEIL (Dr Heinrich).   *Zum Gedächtnis Johannes Sturms.*   In *Festschrift des Protest. Gymnasiums zu Strassburg.*   8°. Strassb. 1888.

VERGERIUS (P. P.).   *De Ingenuis Moribus.*   4°. Ven. (?) 1470.

VOIGT (G.).   *Die Wiederbelebung des Classischen Alterthums.*   2te Ausg. 2 voll.   8°. Berlin 1893.

WATSON (Foster).   *Cordier.*   In *School Review* (of Chicago), vol. xii.   8°. Chicago 1904.

WOODWARD (W. H.).   *Desiderius Erasmus concerning the aim and method of Education.*   8°. Camb. 1904.

WOODWARD (W. H.).   *Vittorino da Feltre and other Humanist Educators.*   8°. Camb. 1905.

WOTTON (Sir Henry).   *A Philosophicall Surveigh of Education, or Moral Architecture,* by Henry Wotton, Kt., Provost of Eton College. [First published in *Reliquiae Wottonianae.*]   12°. Lond. 1651.

INDEX.

337

LAWRENCE STONE, Dodge Professor of History at Princeton University, was born in Surrey, England, in 1919. He studied at the Sorbonne in Paris and at Christ Church, Oxford. From 1946 to 1950 he was a Lecturer at University College; and from 1950 to 1963, when he joined the Faculty of Princeton University, was a Fellow of Wadham College, Oxford. Professor Stone's published works include *Sculpture in Britain: The Middle Ages* (1955), *An Elizabethan: Sir Horatio Palavicino* (1956), and more recently, *The Crisis of the Aristocracy, 1558-1641* (1964). He is a member of the Editorial Board of the journal, *Past and Present,* and is a Fellow of the Royal Historical Society and the Royal Archaeological Society.

F